IMAGES
of America

WATERFORD

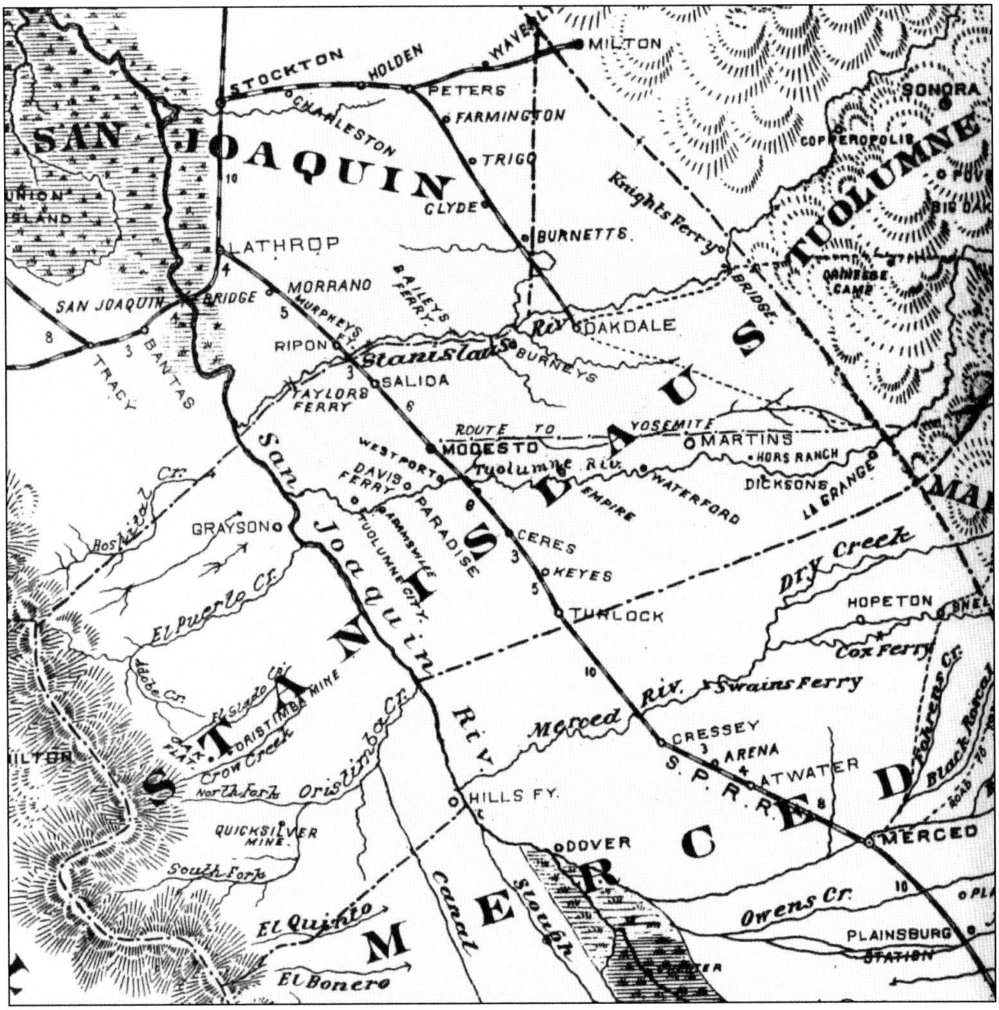

This map of Stanislaus County, drawn in the early 1890s, shows the tiny settlement of Waterford on the Tuolumne River. East of Waterford is Horr's Ranch, the settlement that was to become Roberts Ferry. Adamsville, Davis Ferry, and Tuolumne City no longer exist. (Author's collection.)

On the Cover: The Summers Hotel was constructed in 1868 by Waterford pioneer William K. Summers. His two-story hotel had 10 guest rooms, a kitchen, a dining room, and a bar. Pictured at left here around 1915 are Fred Gatzman (left) and an unidentified man. In Henry Turpen's two-cylinder Maxwell are, from left to right, Manila Walther Gatzman, Verna Knowles, and Julius Johnson, with Charles "Bo" Walther on the fender. Albert Roen is at far right, but the man to his immediate left is unidentified. At the time, the Waterford Hotel's owner was Charles A. Walther, who lived here until 1918. A period advertisement for the hotel promises, "When supper is o'er, 'Tis a good place to snore." (Betty Roen.)

IMAGES
of America

WATERFORD

Jeff Benziger

ARCADIA
PUBLISHING

ISBN 978-0-7385-7452-3

Published by Arcadia Publishing
Charleston, South Carolina

Printed in the United States of America

Library of Congress Control Number: 2010939495

For all general information, please contact Arcadia Publishing:
Telephone 843-853-2070
Fax 843-853-0044
E-mail sales@arcadiapublishing.com
For customer service and orders:
Toll-Free 1-888-313-2665

Visit us on the Internet at www.arcadiapublishing.com

Waterford is simply home; the place where my wife, Karen, and I raised our children—Bret, Brandon, Jennifer, and Jeremy—in one house. I lovingly dedicate this work to them—and to my fellow brothers and sisters in Christ at Community Baptist Church, who helped in our spiritual upbringing.

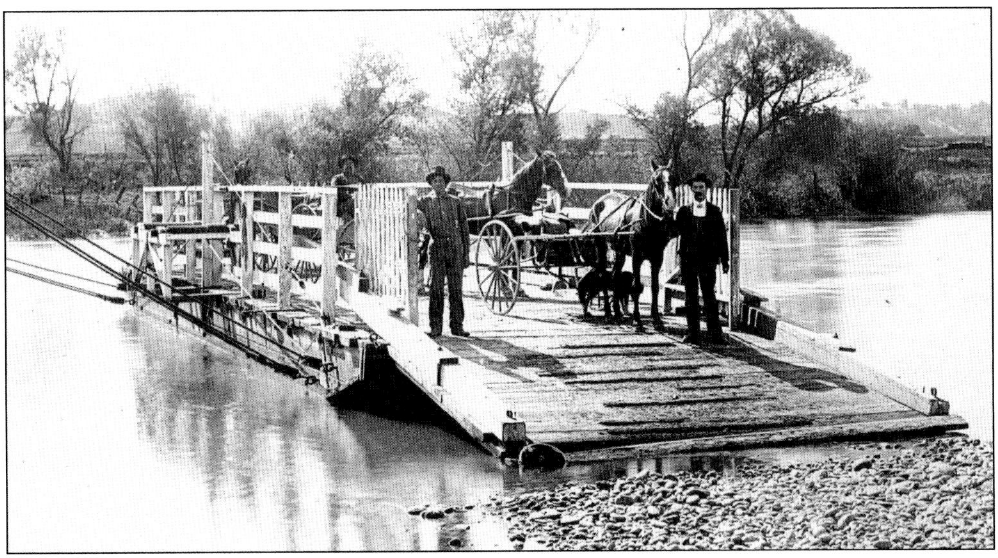

Ferries were plentiful along the Tuolumne River near Waterford. While no known pictures exist of Waterford ferries, this of the Basso Ferry near La Grange is representative of their design. Italian immigrant Angelo Basso operated this ferry west of La Grange from 1902 to 1912. The ferry was made obsolete when the county opened its $27,000 steel Basso Bridge in March 1912. Basso came to Stanislaus County in 1870 to mine for gold. (Leo Overstreet.)

Contents

Acknowledgments

No effort to accurately revisit the history of a city as old as Waterford, California, is possible without great people who embrace the preservation of history. I offer my sincere thanks to a number of people for helping make this book a reality.

Donna Dugo was the first to share photographs accumulated by longtime resident Alison Bodes, including the earliest photographs of Community Baptist Church.

The Waterford Historical Society wholeheartedly embraced this project and eagerly opened their archives to supply many of the photographs in this book. Especially helpful were Maryan Brush and Ellie Cupit.

Betty Roen was a champion in loaning some of the rarest glimpses into Waterford's past. Her husband, John Roen, was helpful in supplying information.

Lori Martin of Waterford City Hall assisted in providing photographs of Waterford mayors. Sid Long deserves thanks for providing rare photographs of the construction of the first Don Pedro Dam in 1922. It was the dam—located in the foothills above Waterford on the Tuolumne River—that truly transformed the Waterford area into the prosperous farming area that it is today.

Brothers Bob and Bill Crabtree and Jeanne Richards Kampen shared glimpses from family archives to provide a fascinating look at life in Roberts Ferry. Linda and Rowe Barney opened the Ketcham family photograph archive to show early life in Roberts Ferry.

Valerie Turpen, Mildred Dennis, Leo Overstreet, Kim Petroni, Lucille and Roland Whitehead, Meredith Gatzman, and Sharlyn and Joe Casey all shared images of Waterford.

Shirley Schultz, town librarian from 1956 to 1982, was of great help in supplying images and information on the Waterford Library, which also assisted. The cooperation of Terry Appling and sister Sandra Burley allows this work to include images of the Appling family.

I also owe a debt of gratitude to previous history publications, including L.C. Branch's 1881 *History of Stanislaus County* and a special publication produced in 1957 for the town's 100-year anniversary, *Waterford Centennial: 1857–1957.*

If you would like to experience more Waterford history, be sure to stop by the Waterford Museum inside the former Grange Hall at the corner of Bentley Street and Yosemite Boulevard.

INTRODUCTION

Central California was a magnet for persons throughout the world in 1849. Word of gold being discovered in the Sierra Nevada by James W. Marshall in 1848 prompted a mass exodus of easterners to the west for their own fortunes. They came by ship—sailing around South America—or across land by wagon, a most daring and dangerous endeavor.

Families often traveled together—such as when the Baker and Summers families sojourned out west—for support and safety as they headed to California to carve out a new life in this untamed land. The dusty roads spoking out from the delta port of Stockton to the southern mines in Mariposa county cut through the land that would later become Stanislaus County. Each time the road crossed the Tuolumne River, an enterprising soul set up a ferry.

Gold may have got them to California, but it proved a most disappointing lure. Placer mining was backbreaking work, and few found wealth. Many gold-seekers stayed but resorted to other means of making a living. Many took up freighting, others farming.

Digger Indians populated the Waterford area. They would often catch salmon and dry them in smokehouses set up along the Tuolumne River. For the most part, the Indians and settlers got along, but some Indians were accused of stealing horses. By 1854, about 1,000 people lived in the county, mostly in river villages at the ferries. Towns also sprang up for the purpose of shipping grain aboard barges pulled by steamboat. Depending on water levels, a steamboat was able to make it up the Tuolumne River as far as the Davis Ranch (near what is now Hazeldean Road).

Many villages sprang up in a short time. On the west side of the future county there were Ward's Ferry, Westport Landing, Adamsville, Hill's Ferry, and Carpenter's Ferry. In central Stanislaus County were Whitmore Ferry, Empire City, Tuolumne City (near future Ceres), and Burneyville Ferry (Riverbank). On the east side were the hamlets of Horr's Ferry (later renamed Dickinson's Ferry and then Roberts Ferry), La Grange, Knight's Ferry, and Thompson's Ferry. The largest were La Grange and Empire City.

Settled in the 1850s, Waterford developed slowly at first. It would be decades before irrigation water would be channeled from the nearby Sierra Nevada, so farmers mostly concentrated on wheat.

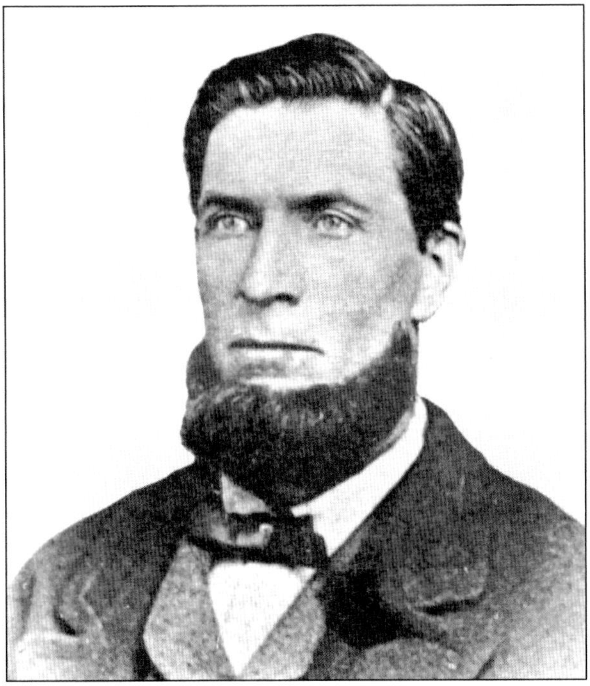

In 1856, William Wilkerson Baker homesteaded 160 acres on the south side of the Tuolumne River, and in 1857, he traveled back to Berryville, Arkansas, to marry his fiancée, Caroline Pinkston. Returning to the Tuolumne with his bride, Baker set up a ferry across the river and charged travelers for passage. In 1862, Baker built a general merchandise store at the northeast corner of Yosemite Boulevard and Tim Bell Road. The store burned down in 1873, but the Bakers rebuilt. Elected county treasurer in 1885, William W. Baker died on October 2, 1885, before he could assume office. He was 51 years old. (*Waterford Centennial: 1857–1957.*)

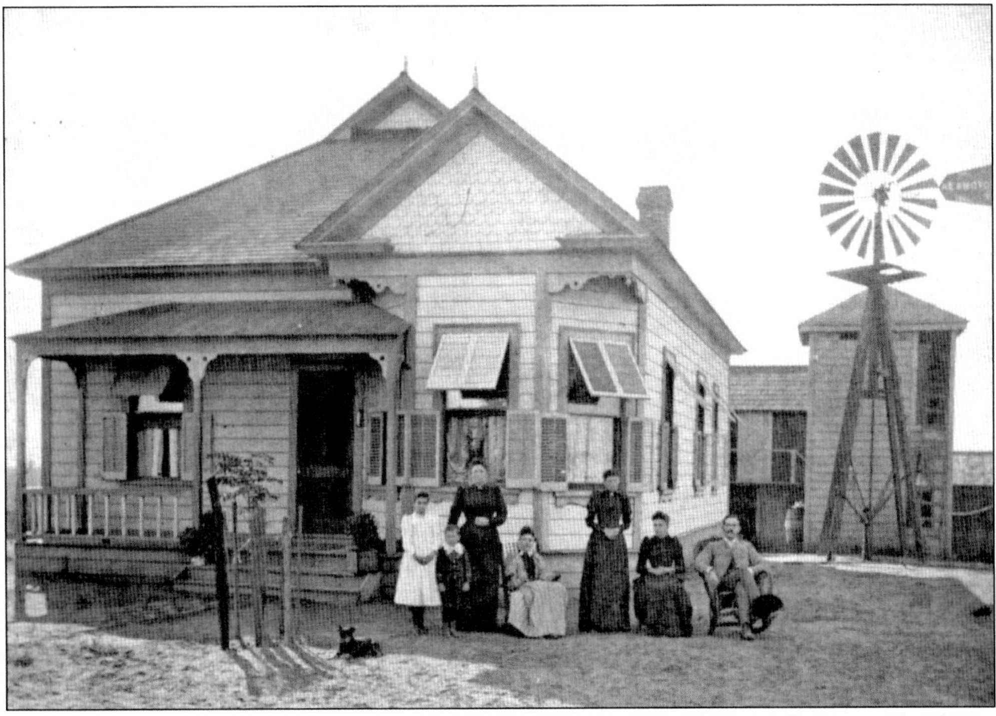

One of Waterford's first homes, built in 1869 by William W. Baker for one of his twin daughters, is still standing at 12952 Covey Street. Its perch high on the bluff overlooks the old Bakersville town site. The woman standing at right may be Caroline Baker, widow of William W. Baker, dating this picture before her death in 1889. The two women who are seated are probably the Baker twins, Alice and Belle. (Betty Roen.)

One

Waterford's Beginnings
A River Town Springs Forth

Benjamin Horr, Josiah Covey, and Elihu Beard were first to set up residence in the Waterford area. But the man who was to establish the town of Bakersville (later Waterford) was William Wilkerson Baker. The Berryville, Arkansas, native took a look at dry-farming opportunities in the Waterford area in the late 1850s and acquired 160 acres south of the river on a gentle slope near Lampley Road. Around 1859, Baker sold his land to John and Rachel Search to move downriver and across to the north bank. Baker established a business around 1866 charging miners and other travelers to ferry them across the river, which could swell with winter flooding. Men named ? James, William Sturtevant, and W.P. Crow operated a different ferry at Sturgeon Island from 1878 to 1879.

Baker's ferry was run by J.A. Hayter after April 12, 1880; it operated until October 1889, when the county opened the wooden bridge it had built for $20,000. Stores, homes, saloons, and other businesses quickly sprang forth. One of the first buildings was a small cement structure dubbed the "Old Adobe," built by Adrian Faure, an enterprising French man. The building served also as a store and home at the southeast corner of Yosemite Boulevard and Tim Bell Road.

For mail, Bakersville residents had to travel to Horr's Ranch Post Office, eight miles to the east. Postal officials granted permission in 1871 for a new post office under the name of Waterford. The new town name was ordered because mail for the 40 to 60 residents was often misdirected to other California towns of similar names, including Bakersfield. The name Waterford was logical, due to the practice of fording the slow river in summer, made possible by low-cut banks on which the old town was anchored.

As Waterford's civic and social ties began to grow, Grange No. 57 was one of first organizations to be established. The Grange operated from 1873 to 1881 (later resurrected in 1934), first meeting in a hall adjacent to the Baker and Summers Hotel, with S.M. Gallup as the first Grange master.

When the Stockton-Visalia Railroad came to Waterford in 1891, the entire town location shifted closer to the tracks. The old part of Waterford became known as "Old Town."

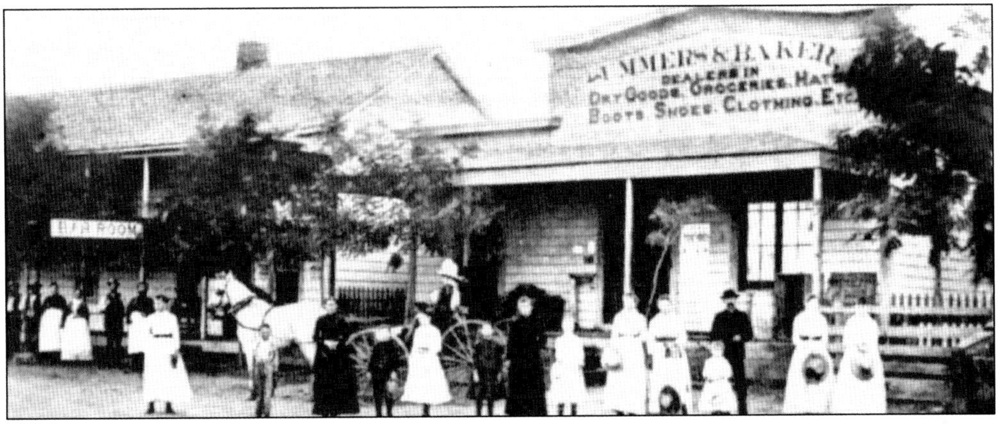

The Summers and Baker General Mercantile, located on Yosemite Boulevard just east of Tim Bell Road, sold dry goods, groceries, hats, boots, shoes, and clothing. Established in 1862, the store and its stock burned in 1873. In 1868, along came the Summers Hotel (at left). Baker died in 1885; this picture was probably taken in the 1870s or early 1880s. Summers died in 1897. (*Waterford Centennial: 1857–1957.*)

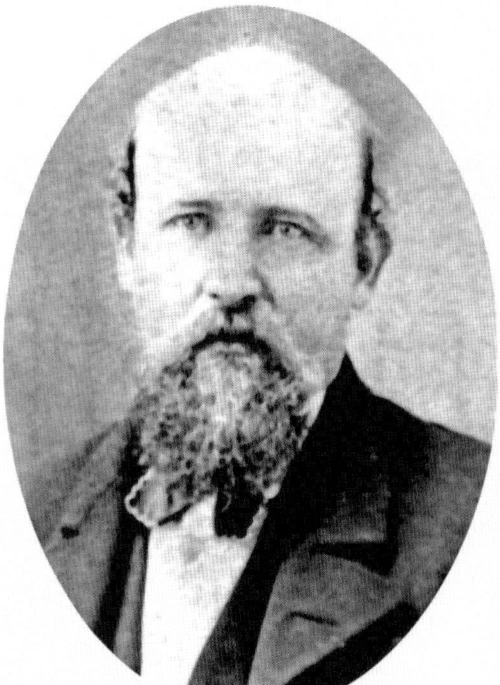
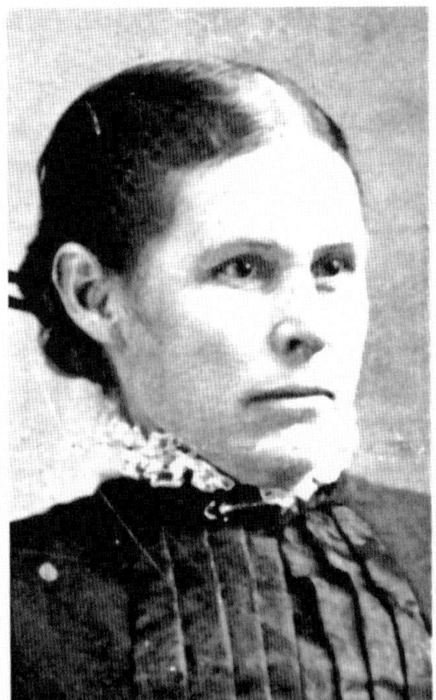

William and Joanne Summers came to Waterford in 1857 with the Baker party. William was a native of Kentucky, while Joanne, sister of Caroline Baker, was born in Tennessee. She was known to all in Bakersville as "Aunt Babe." Together, they ran the store and hotel at Yosemite Boulevard and Tim Bell Road while raising a large family. He died on November 10, 1897, and Joanne died on September 10, 1923. Both outlived their children, Frances and Nancy. (*Waterford Centennial: 1857–1957.*)

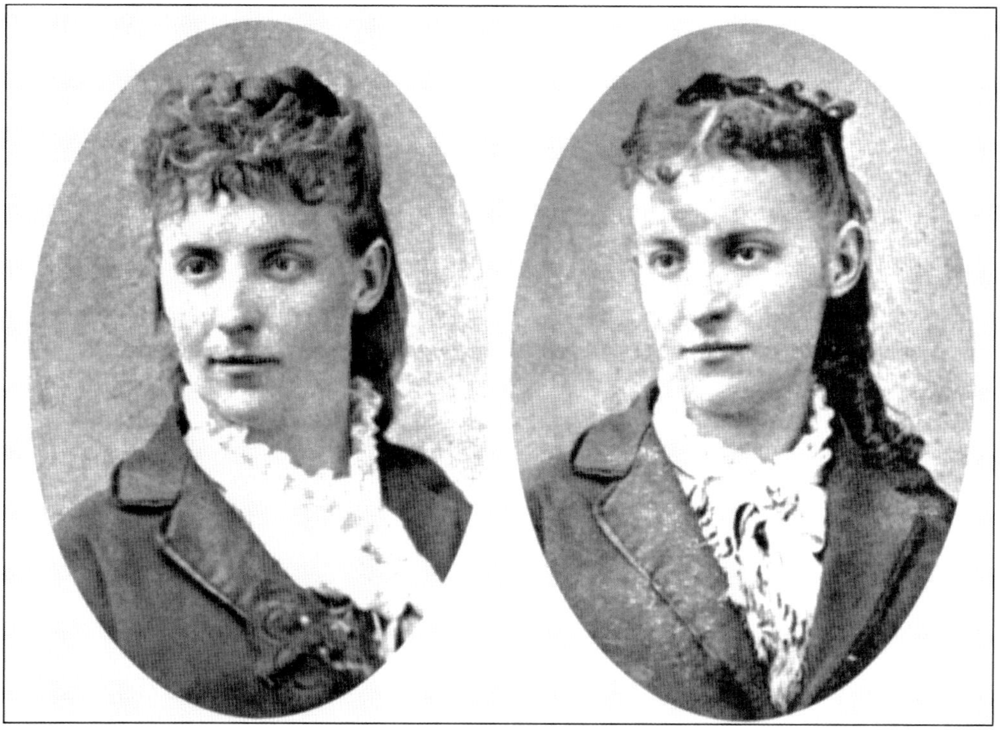

Belle (left) and Alice Baker were twin daughters of Waterford founder William W. Baker. They were born on December 5, 1857, in Nevada during the Bakers' covered wagon trek from Arkansas to California. The girls lived in neighboring houses at the southwest corner of Covey Street and Tim Bell Road. Belle married in 1876, and Alice married in 1881. Both were honored as "Covered Wagon Babies" during the 1937 Stanislaus County Fair. Alice G. Baker Hayter died in 1942, Belle Elder in 1944. (*Waterford Centennial: 1857–1957.*)

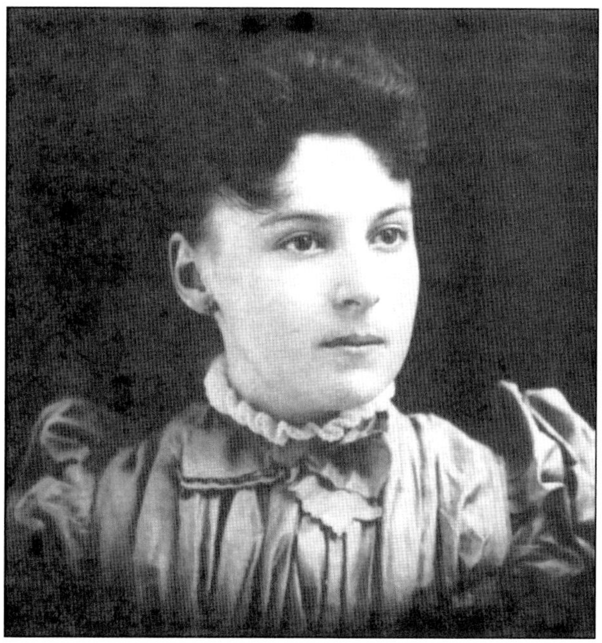

Disease and accidents, abetted by the ineffectiveness of medicine, cut many lives tragically short in the 19th century. Ida Mae Baker, the third child of William and Caroline Baker, died at age 17 from an unrecorded cause on April 24, 1891. She is buried in the Roberts Ferry Cemetery next to her parents. (*Waterford Centennial: 1857–1957.*)

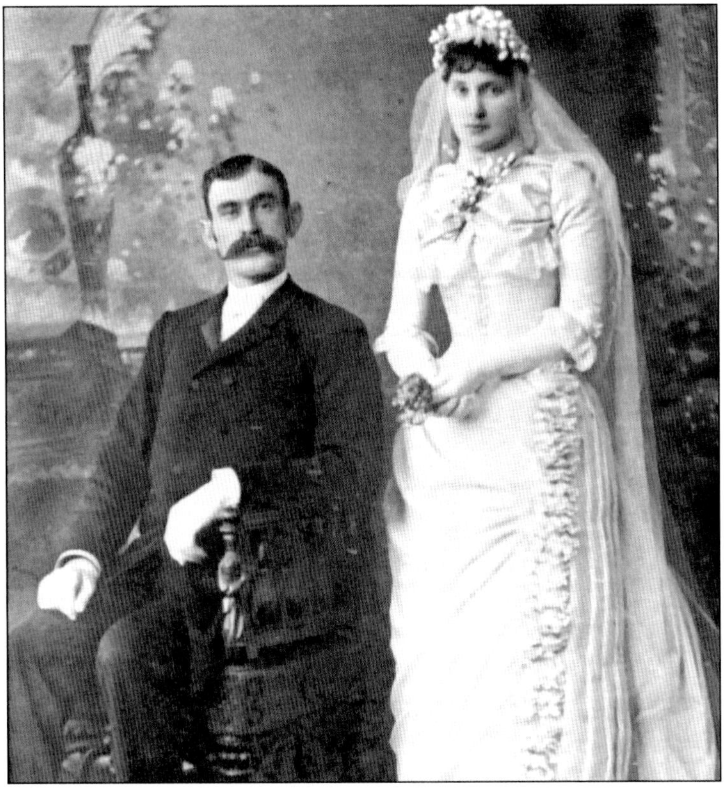

Born March 3, 1870, Nettie Baker, daughter of William and Caroline Baker, was married on January 14, 1891, to James Dolan, a local woodworker and shop owner who lived in a house at the southwest corner of F Street and Welch Street. Just over three years later, on April 7, 1894, Nettie passed away at age 24. (*Waterford Centennial: 1857–1957.*)

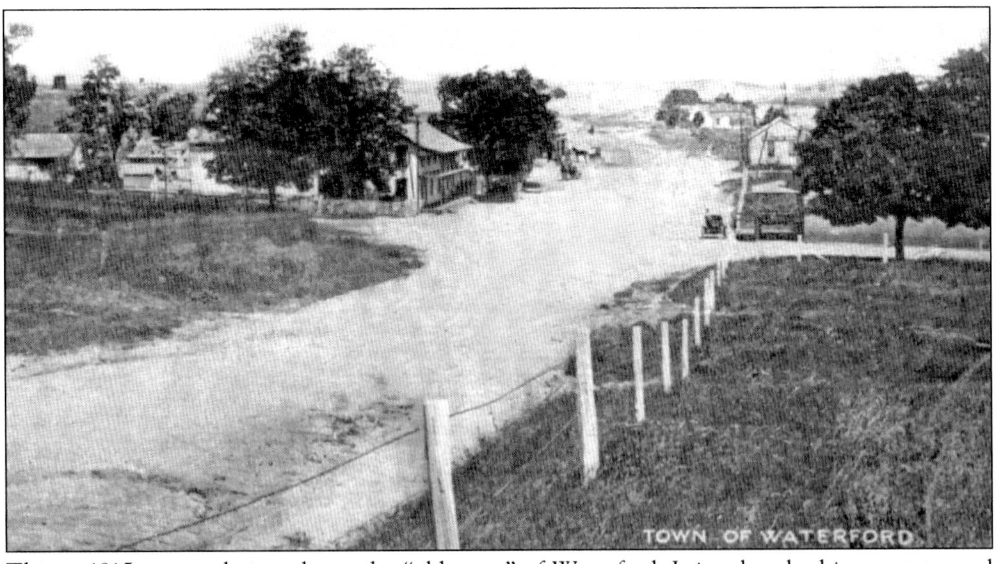

This c. 1915 postcard vista shows the "old town" of Waterford. It is taken looking east toward the intersection of Yosemite Boulevard and Tim Bell Road and Baker Street (at right). The old two-story Summers Hotel is the large prominent building at center. The trees on what was then called the La Grange Highway obscure what appear to be other buildings. (Sandra Burley.)

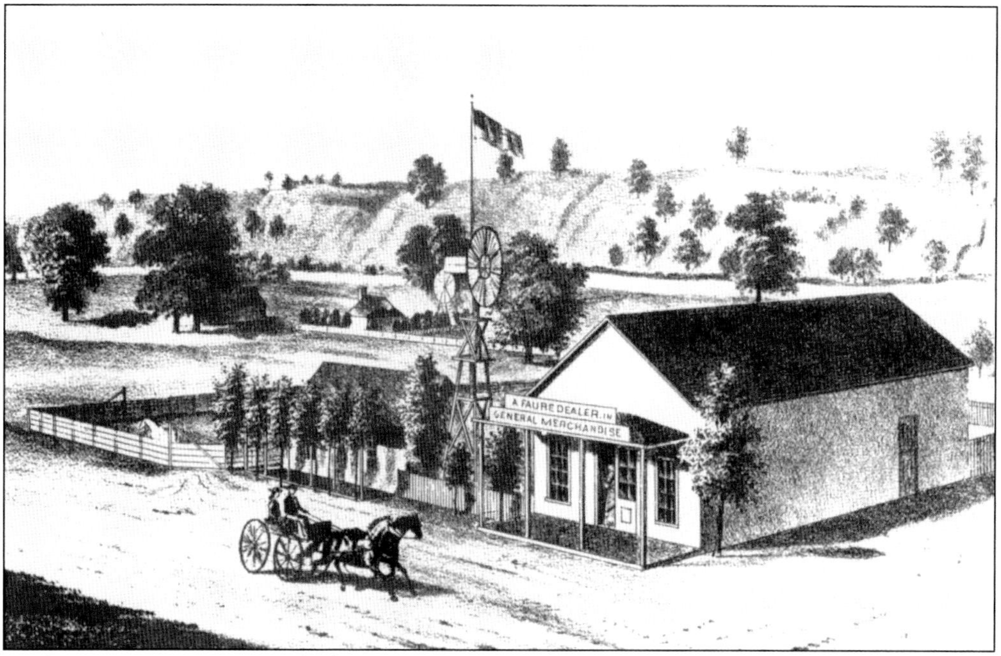

Andre Faure came to Waterford in 1869 and set up the area's first crude irrigation system. He constructed this store in 1877 of brick and concrete at the southeast corner of Yosemite Boulevard and Baker Street. Faure was born in 1830 and fled France during its political turmoil. He set sail for California in 1849. Faure eventually bought up 106 of the 192 original town lots and sold half of them in 1883 for $2,600. (L.C. Branch's *History of Stanislaus County*, published in 1881.)

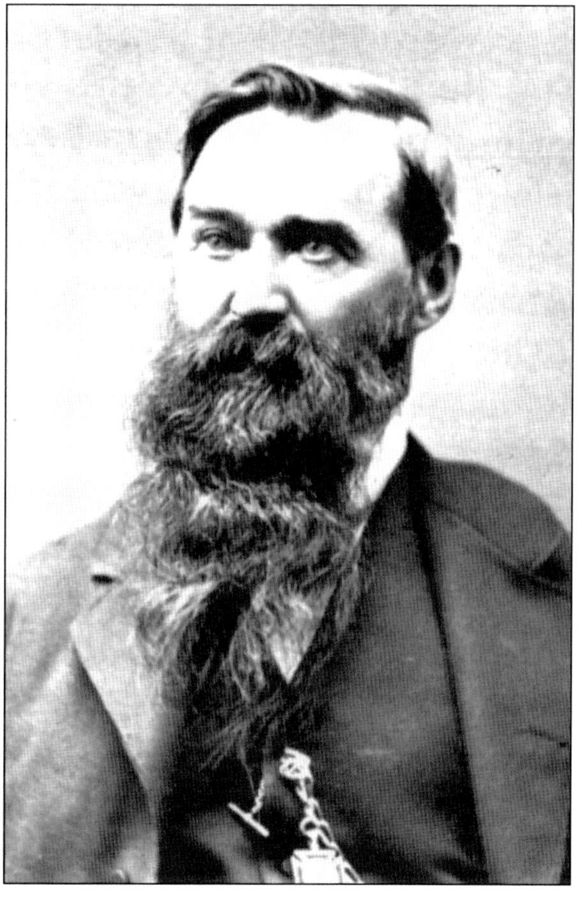

With a massive landholding near Dry Creek, Elihu Burritt Beard was one of the earliest Waterford settlers. Beard came to California by wagon train in 1849, arriving near Waterford in 1852. He farmed, raised cattle, and became wealthy. Elihu married Anne Kennan Beard on October 7, 1865. He retired from ranching in 1873 and moved to Modesto. Beard served as the first county assessor from 1854 to 1862 and the first superintendent of schools. He also served in the California State Assembly. Beard died in 1901. (Waterford Historical Society.)

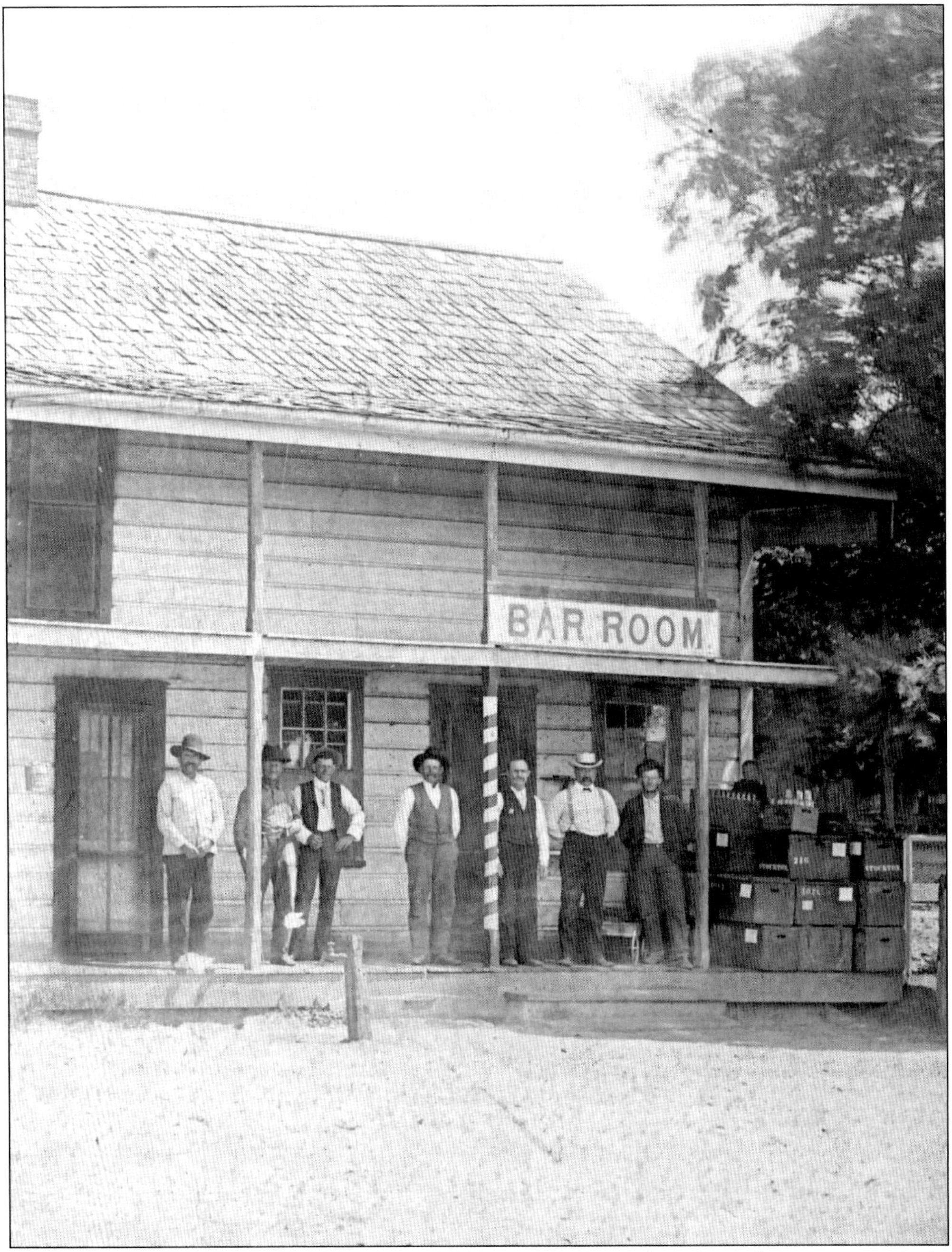

A group of men stand outside the portion of the Summers Hotel used as a bar room, no doubt excited by the delivery of bottles of liquor. Note the small child scampering on top of the stack. This photograph was probably taken in the late 1880s or early 1890s. This building, the same as the one on the cover, stood just east of Tim Bell Road on the north side of La Grange Road—today's Yosemite Boulevard. (Betty Roen.)

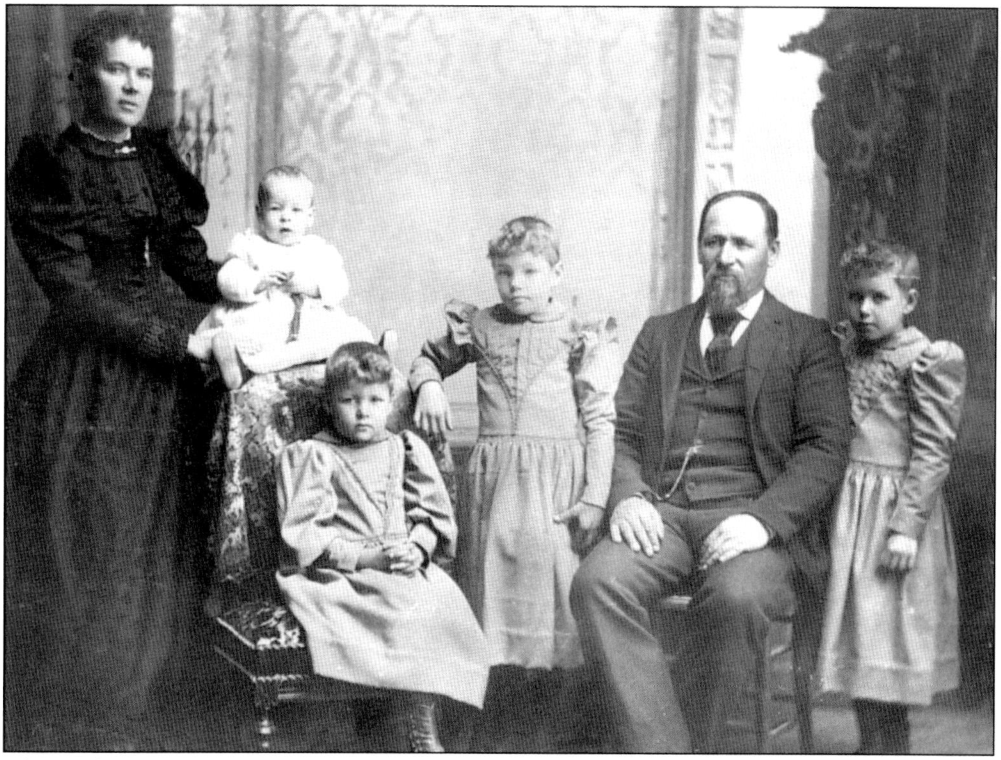

John and Oline Roen (above and below) were a well-known Waterford couple. Born in 1850 in Norway, John came to Crows Landing in 1867 and worked for Louis Hickman driving a harvester. John Roen returned to Norway to marry Oline in December 1883 and raised a large family in Waterford. He farmed the area of Yosemite Boulevard and Hazeldean Road. Pictured from left to right in May 1893 are Oline Roen, Louie Roen, Olga (seated), Clara Roen, John Roen, and Emma Roen. When this portrait was taken, the Roens were preparing for a four-year stay in Norway. The Roens lived at 219 D Street in 1888, later moving to the house at the corner of Yosemite Boulevard and Church Street. The couple had eight children—Clara, Emma, Olga, Thora, Louie, a second Thora, Ottar, and Albert. John died on September 1, 1936, and Oline died on August 23, 1941, both in the house at the corner of Yosemite Boulevard and Church Street. (Both, LaVerne Johnson.)

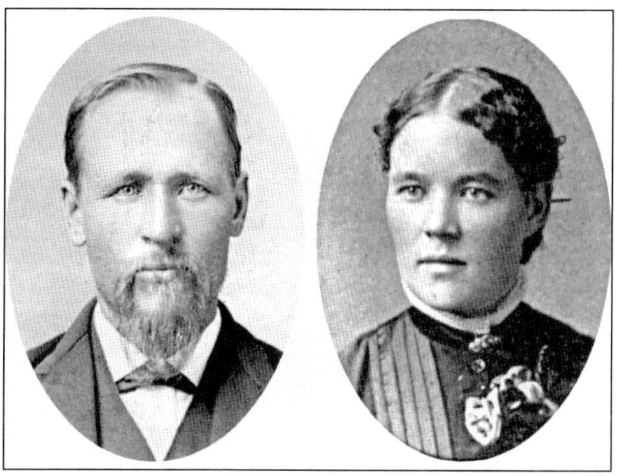

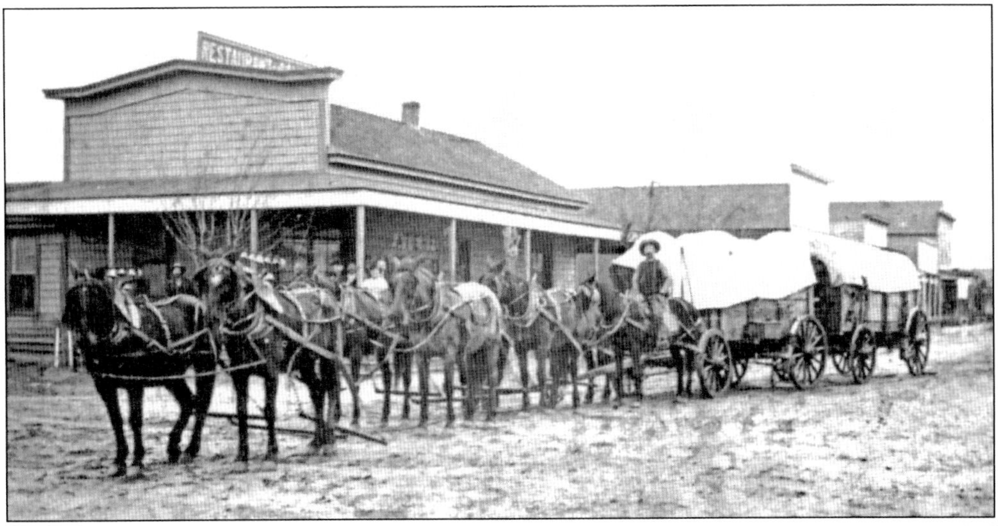

Freight wagons head north to Oakdale on Front Street (later F Street) around 1895. (*Waterford Centennial: 1857–1957.*)

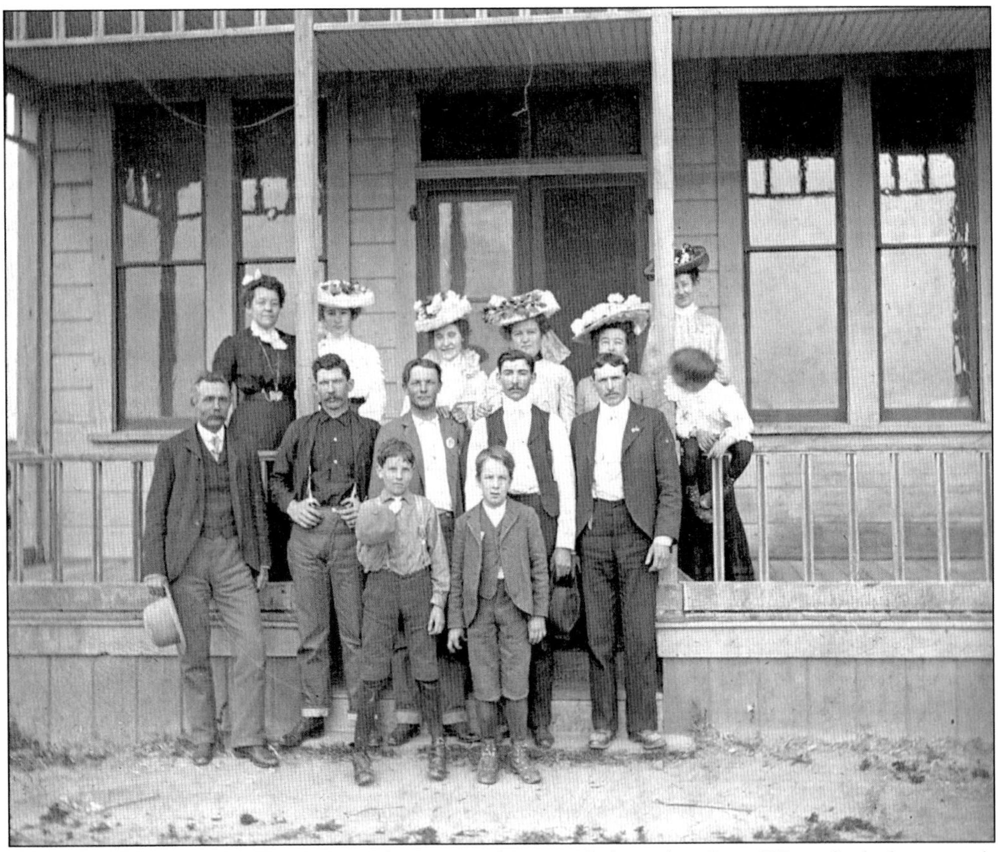

There is no history accompanying this image, but it is believed to be a Waterford photograph since it was in the collection of Johanna Johnson, who passed it onto her daughter Alma Johnson Prouty. The building may be a home in either Waterford or La Grange. (Betty Roen.)

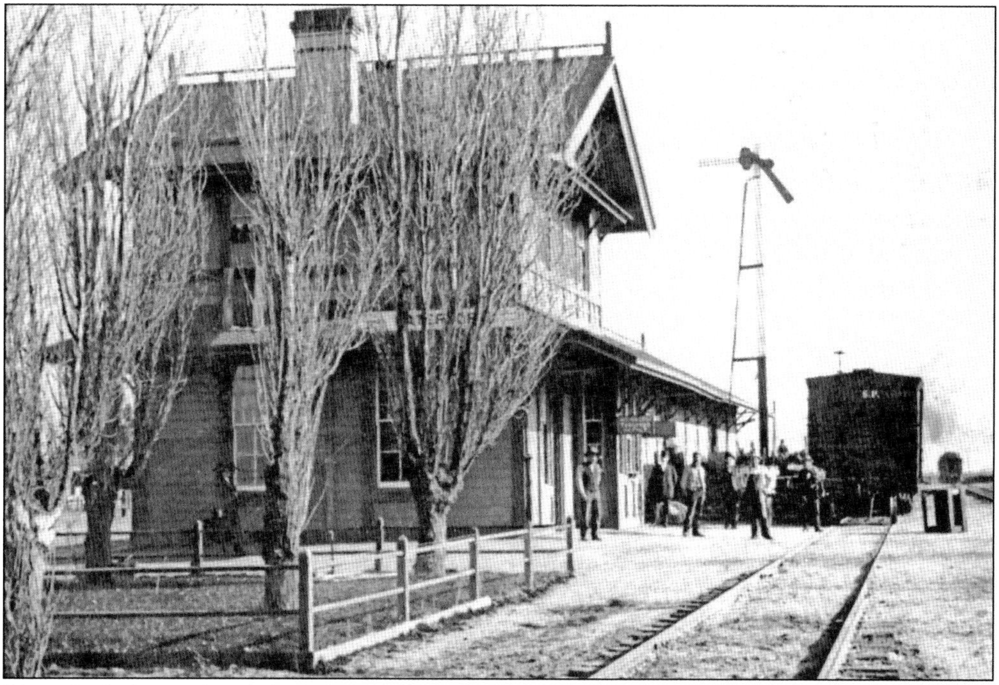

Waterford's first railroad depot is seen here, looking north toward Oakdale. Southbound trains departed here for Hickman and Montpelier. Northbound passengers could ride to Oakdale and then to San Francisco. (Betty Roen.)

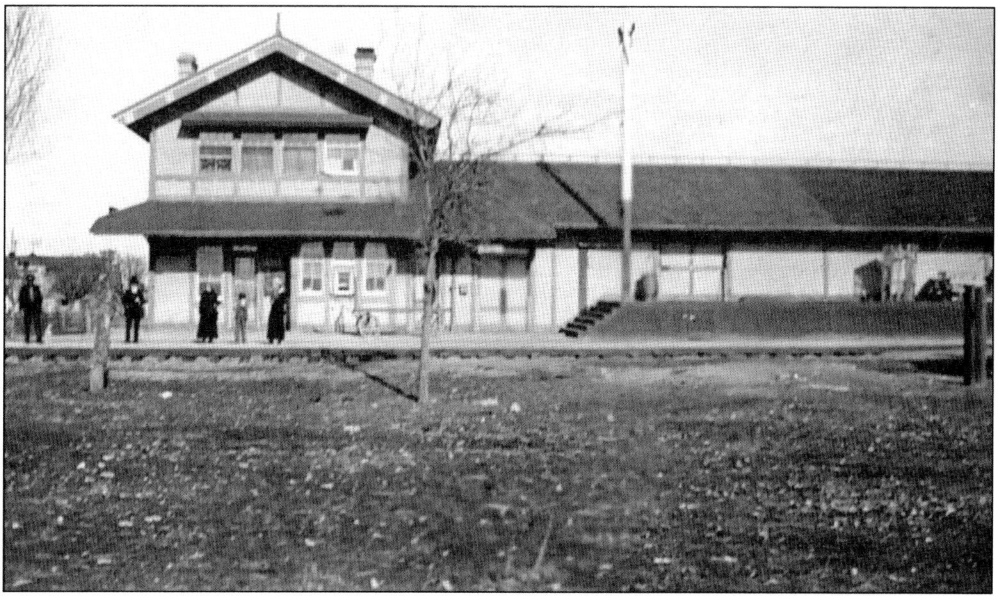

The first Southern Pacific Railroad depot in Waterford faced the east toward the tracks. This depot was constructed in 1896, after the tracks reached Waterford in 1890. The depot's existence was short-lived; it burned down in 1921 and was replaced by a second, smaller depot. An August 31, 1921, Modesto newspaper article stated that the "county library suffered an $80 loss in the recent depot fire," indicating that the library operated from the depot building. (Betty Roen.)

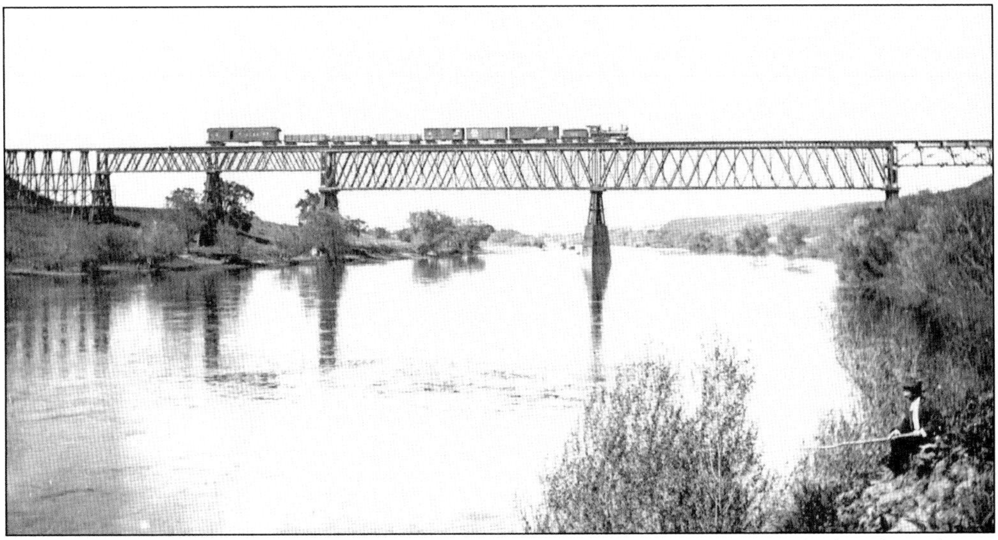

This wooden railroad trestle spanned the Tuolumne River between Waterford and Hickman around 1901 at a location west of the present-day concrete road bridge. This first trestle, erected by the Southern Pacific Railroad in 1890, served until an iron trestle was built between 1906 and 1907. During construction, railroad worker Harry Theinon, 24, was struck and killed by a train on February 13, 1906, on the first trestle. Note the man fishing on the bank at right as steam locomotive No. 1190 enters Waterford from Hickman. (*Waterford Centennial: 1857–1957.*)

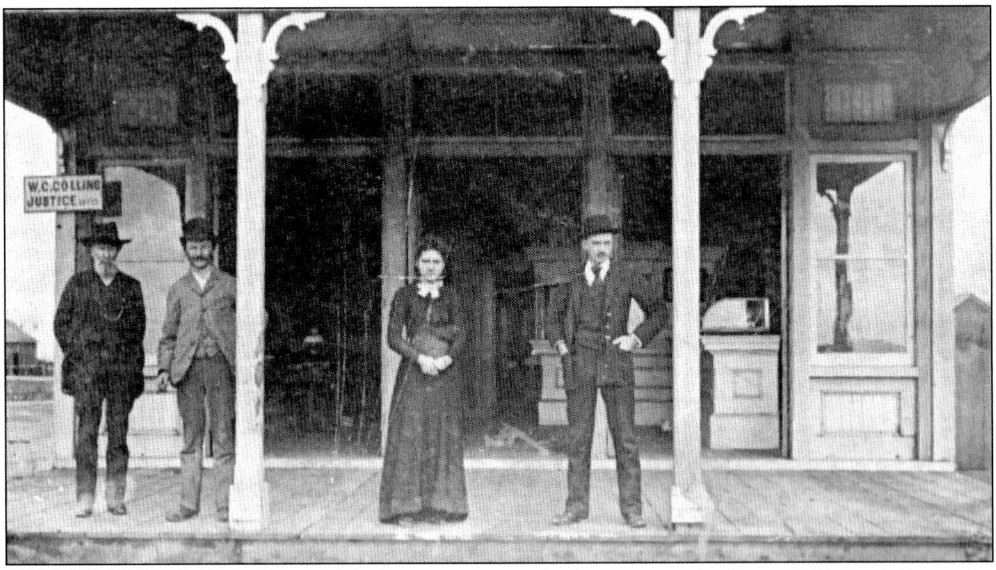

Pictured around 1895 are several persons in front of a business and office of W.C. Collins, the Waterford justice of the peace. The man at right is believed to be Dr. J. Hennemeth. The woman is possibly his wife. (*Waterford Centennial: 1857–1957.*)

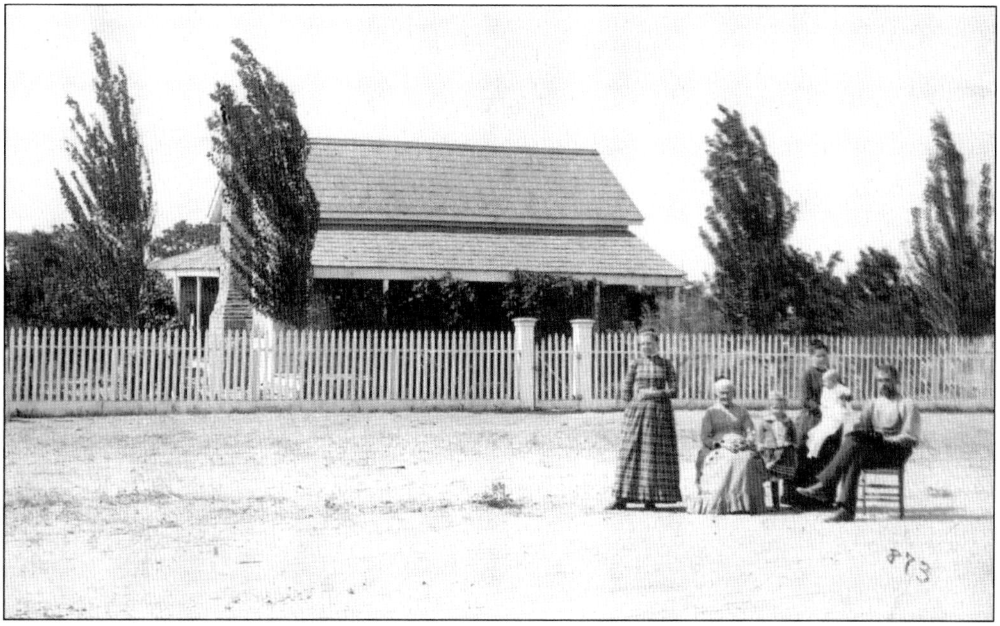

Town blacksmith Joseph Prouty and his family were photographed in front of the family house around 1895. Prouty came to Waterford in 1880. He married Katie Davis in July 1882, and they had two children, Lee and Ella. Lee later married Alma Johnson, who possessed this c. 1895 photograph. This lot was in the 12 square blocks that were surveyed in 1868 and 1869 by George Schell, with the first lot sale coming in 1873. Owning the town site were L.H. Pinkston, Charles Dallas, and Sarah E. Browder. (Betty Roen.)

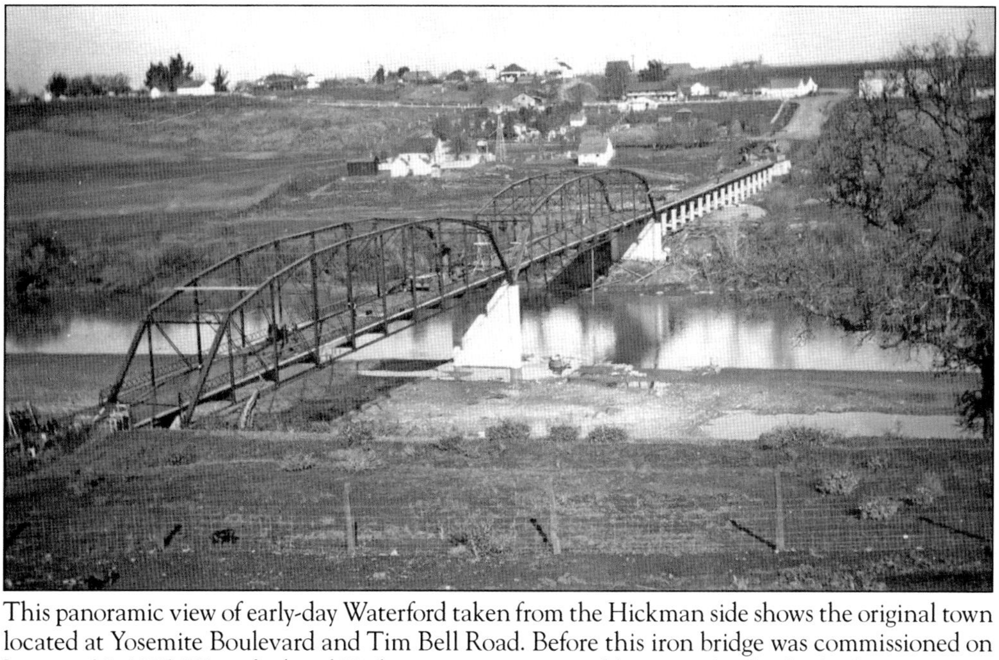

This panoramic view of early-day Waterford taken from the Hickman side shows the original town located at Yosemite Boulevard and Tim Bell Road. Before this iron bridge was commissioned on January 30, 1915, Waterford and Hickman were connected by a wooden bridge built in 1889 at a cost of $21,000. This iron bridge, consisting of two 200-foot spans and a 340-foot approach, was removed in 1964. Visible are the White Oak School and the Summers Hotel. (Betty Roen.)

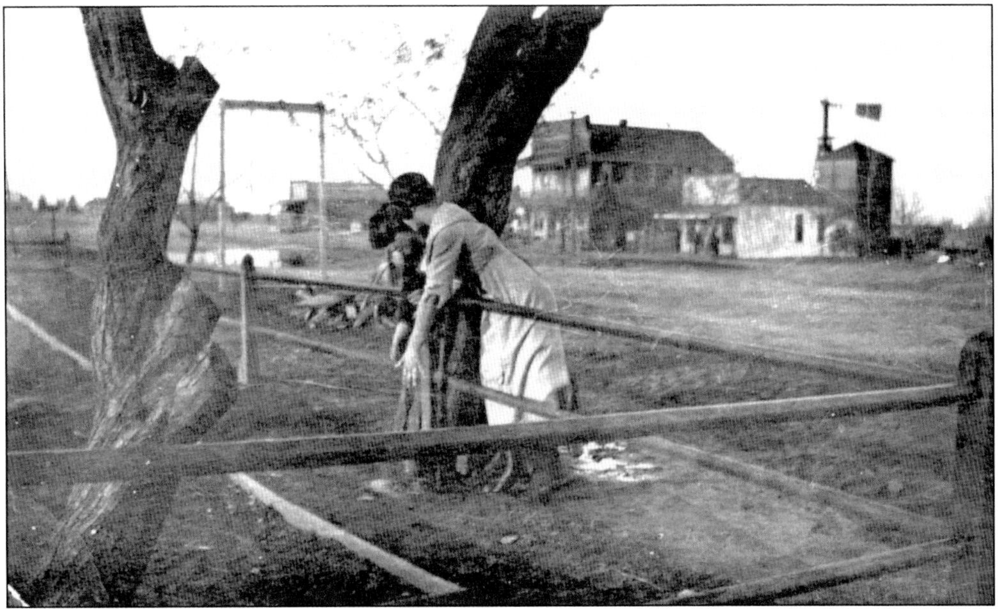

These young women were visiting over a fence on Front Street—known today as F Street. The spot on which they are standing is likely today's post office property at F and Bentley Streets. In the background are the Knights of Pythius Hall and Armentrout's store. (Betty Roen.)

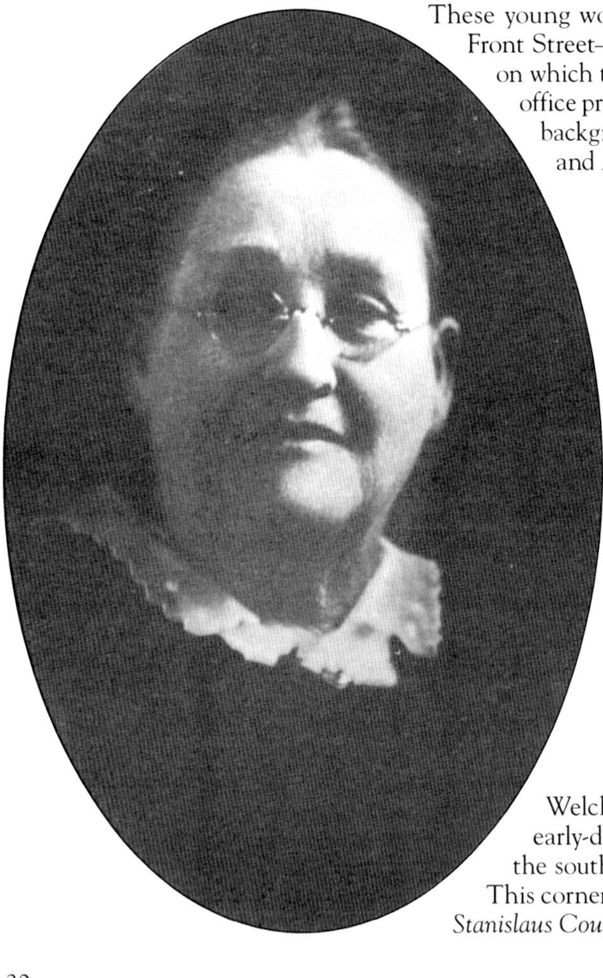

Welch Street in Waterford is named after early-day resident Sarah Welch. She lived at the southwest corner of F and Welch Streets. This corner later housed a post office. (*History of Stanislaus County*.)

Many Waterford residents worked with the La Grange Dredge Company miles upstream from Roberts Ferry. The La Grange Dredge was put into operation in 1908, after a powerhouse was built in 1907 near the dam to power it. The dredge chewed up much of the La Grange area in its search for gold. The dredge was rebuilt in 1922 and again in 1934. Today, it sits as a partially dismantled state. In 1946, Stanislaus County ranked the fourth-largest gold-producing county in California, mostly on account of gold mined at La Grange. (Author's collection.)

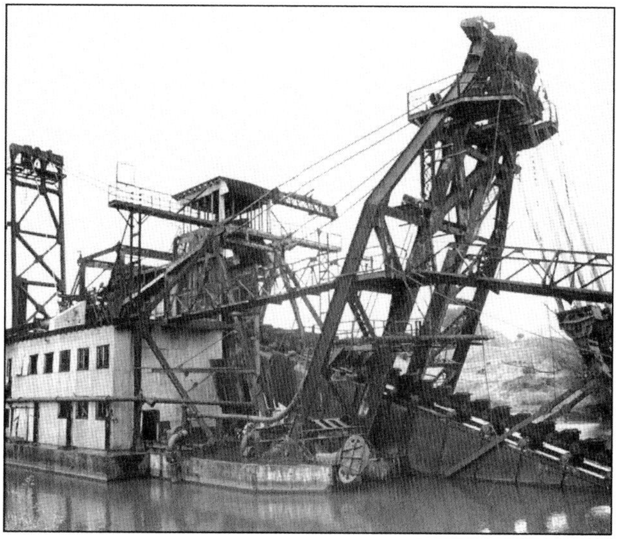

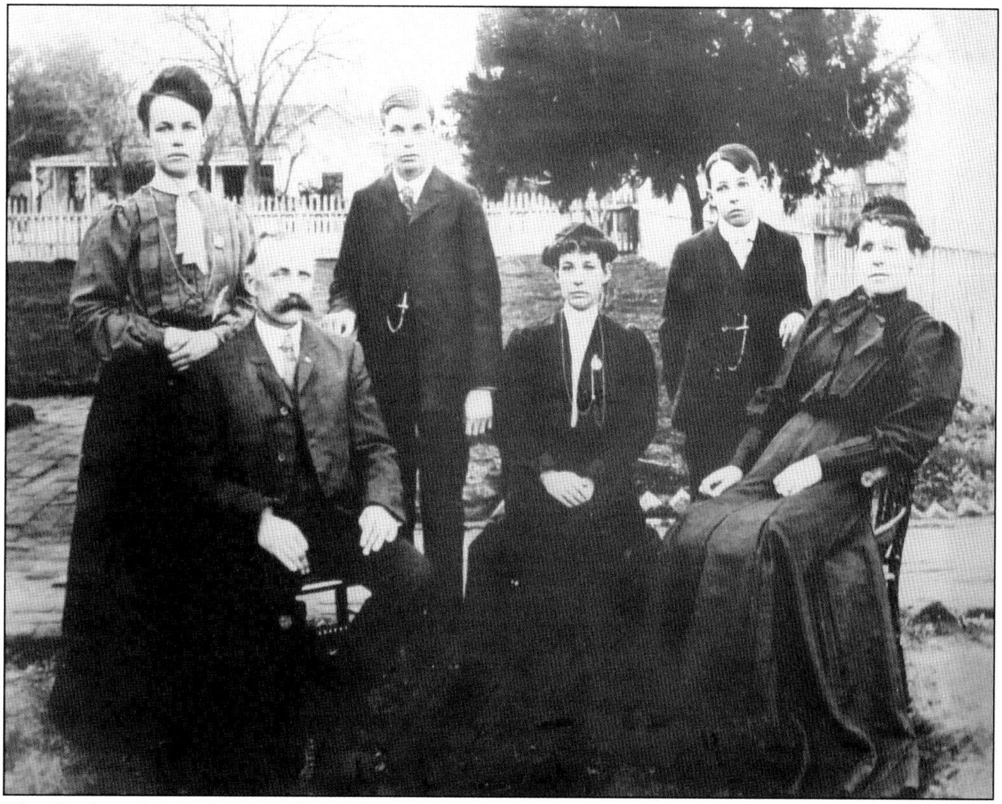

The Andrew P. Monk family farmed oat and barley north of what is now the Waterford Sportsman's Club. Pictured from left to right in this c. 1900 photograph are (seated) Andrew P. Monk, Carrie Monk, and Inga Larsen Monk; (standing) Eva Monk Nielsen, Alfred Monk, and Hardy Monk. Inga Monk had her eye surgically removed by a doctor on the kitchen table, offering her only whiskey to help her through the ordeal. A.P. Monk immigrated from Denmark in the 1890s and arrived in Waterford. The farm was originally the farm of Elihu Beard. Monk's son-in-law, Charlie Nielson, took the farm over in 1910. He sold it in 1924. (Carl Nielsen.)

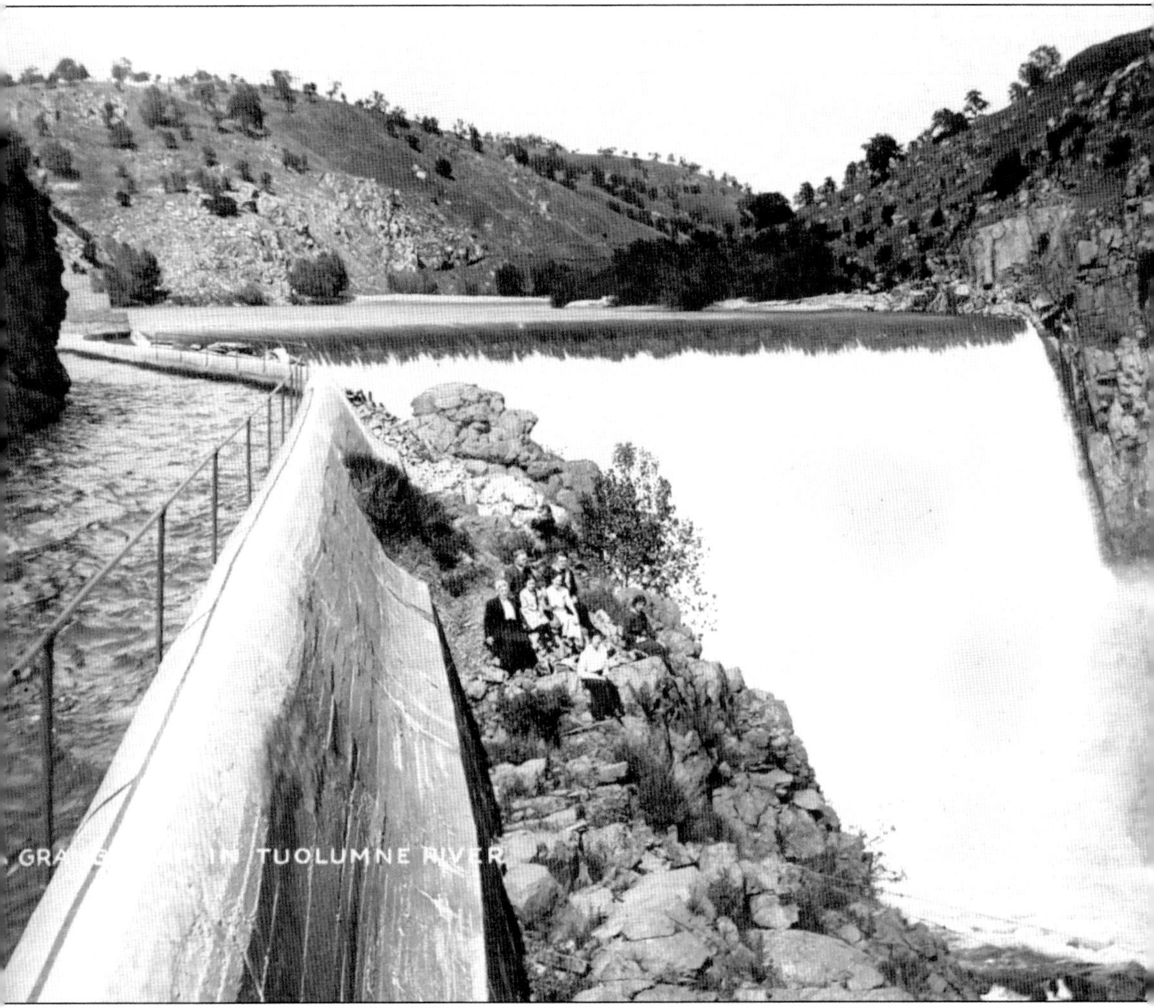

The La Grange Dam, completed in 1893 on the Tuolumne River, brought irrigation water to the area. Located above La Grange, the diversion dam was built 336 feet long and 127 feet high. As a result of the dam, Turlock Irrigation District formed June 6, 1897. The dam was inadequate for the expanding farming region. By early July each year, the river's flow began decreasing, and by August, irrigation officials were unable to divert water down the canals—at a time when farmers needed to irrigate crops. Thus, plans were made for a much larger storage capacity, hence the construction of Davis Reservoir (Turlock Lake). The reservoir, completed in 1913, covered 3,000 acres. The Stanislaus County Board of Trade issued this promotional photograph to lure others to come to the flourishing agricultural region around Waterford, Hickman, and the county. The dam was a destination vista for local picnickers, as evidenced by the visitors seen here catching the breathtaking view as they rest on the boulders. (Turlock Irrigation District.)

Two

Farming and Irrigation
The Land of Milk and Honey

Irrigation water revolutionized Waterford farming after 1903. Before dams and canals, farmers' reliance on rainwater limited farmers to dry crops such as wheat and barley. Channeling water from the foothills to the Central Valley was ambitious.

The first dam on the Tuolumne River was built in 1852 above La Grange by M.A. Wheaton for hydraulic mining. He sold his water rights in 1891 to the Modesto Irrigation District (MID), formed in 1887 after passage of the Wright Act. Modesto and Turlock Irrigation Districts teamed up to dismantle the second Wheaton Dam to build the La Grange Dam of cut boulders cemented into place. Cement for the project was brought to Waterford on rails and hauled by wagon. Finished in 1893 at a cost of $543,154—and three human lives—the dam was touted by one newspaper as "the Pacific Coast's answer to Niagara Falls" and attracted many curiosity seekers.

Politics delayed a connecting gravity flow canal system to channel water to the Central Valley for a decade. Some opposed irrigation, fearful of higher taxes while forecasting failure in transitioning from dry crops to new crops made possible by irrigation. Anti-irrigationists claimed seats on the MID board but were later politically trumped by Thomas K. Beard, a visionary who equated irrigation with prosperity. Water first flowed down canals in 1903.

Because more water was needed for farms from July through November, work began in 1911 to build a reservoir out of Warner Lake east of Waterford. Work was laborious, with horse and mule teams digging with Fresno scrapers. Work on the Dallas-Warner Reservoir (renamed the Modesto Reservoir) was completed in 1912 to add 28,000 acre-feet of storage.

Meanwhile, Waterford-area farmers also desired irrigation water. Roberts Ferry farmer Alf Ketchum led formation of the Waterford Irrigation District (WID) on September 15, 1913, chiefly to convert large land holdings into small farm operations. A reluctant MID agreed to sell water to WID, and in 1916, Waterford voters approved a $465,000 bond to enlarge MID's canals and to build WID's canal system. By 1920, WID was irrigating 2,400 acres. In 1970, the old Don Pedro Dam was covered when the lake was expanded with the new earthen Don Pedro Dam. WID and MID merged in 1978.

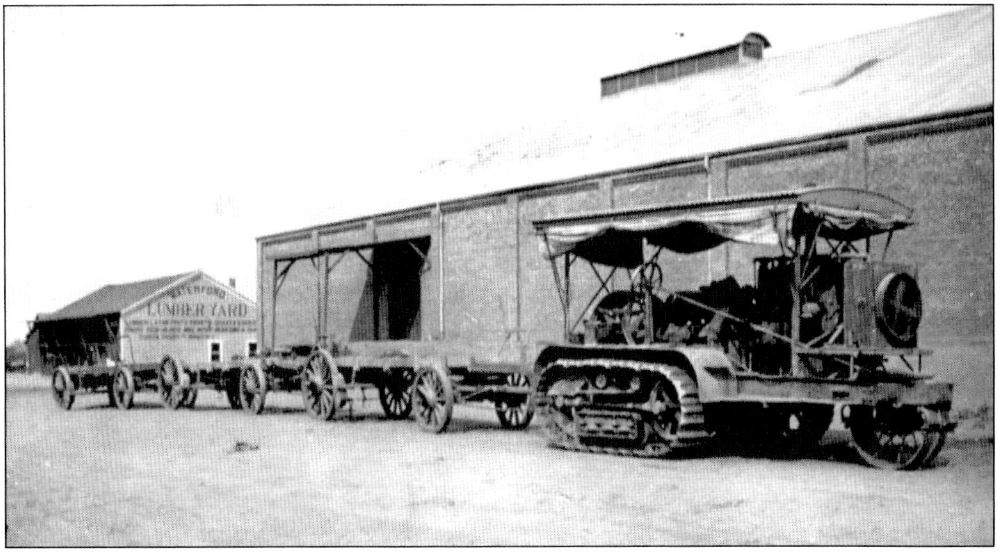

This antique gas tractor was pulling three wagons from the brick warehouses to the west of the Stockton and Visalia Railroad tracks used to store grain. It is said that the bricks used in this warehouse were made from clay taken from land at the northeast corner of Lake Road and Hickman Road. Visible in the background is the Waterford Lumber Yard on Bentley Street. (Betty Roen.)

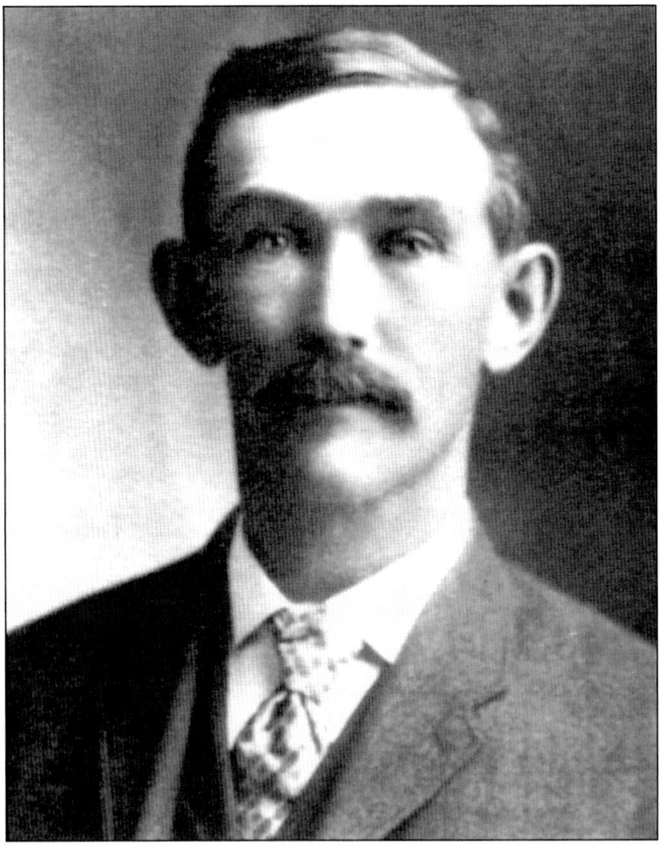

Thomas Kennan Beard (1857–1925) was perhaps the biggest promoter of Waterford since its infancy. The son of Elihu Beard was given 1,000 acres to farm at age 20. He promoted irrigation and eventually owned approximately 6,000 acres around Waterford that he subdivided into farming parcels of generally 20 to 30 acres. In 1917, Beard's Waterford Development Company subdivided thousands of acres just west and north of Waterford, stretching from Dry Creek to the Tuolumne River. Beard later moved to Modesto. (Author's collection.)

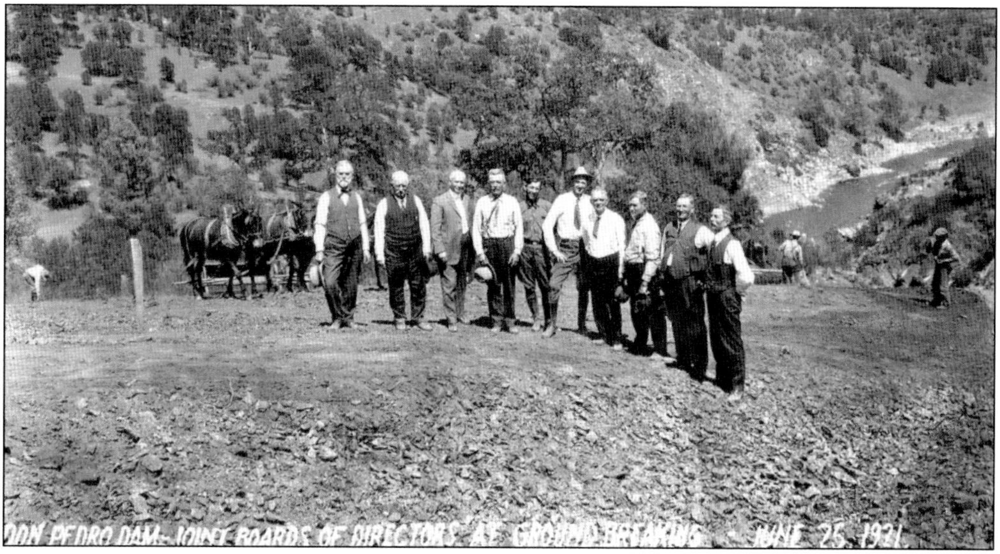

Irrigation district officials gathered on June 25, 1921, in the hills above La Grange to break ground on a tremendously ambitious project to dam the Tuolumne River to supply water and power for the Central Valley. The river is visible at right. At 284 feet, Don Pedro Dam would be one of the tallest manmade structure of its time. Water from this 289,000-acre-foot storage facility was used by Waterford farmers to grow a variety of crops. (Sid Long.)

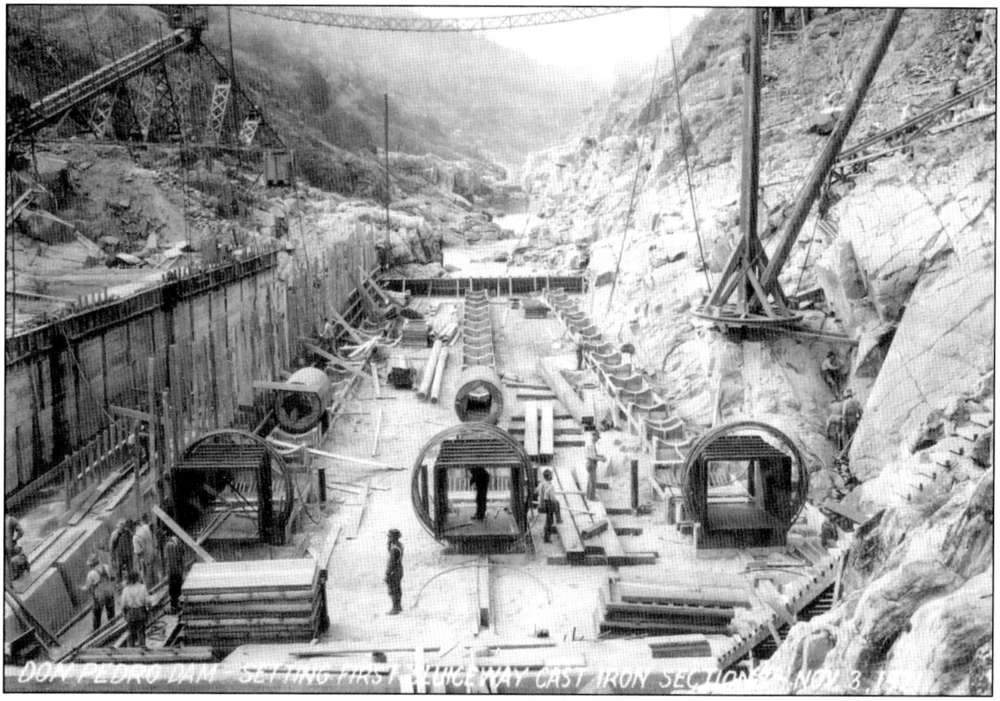

The giant tubes that would channel water through the base of the first Don Pedro Dam were constructed here on November 3, 1921. The reservoir held barely enough water to accommodate growers' irrigation needs for a single growing season. After numerous dry winters, Turlock and Modesto Irrigation Districts decided to replace the 1922 dam with a larger one in order to store more water. (Sid Long.)

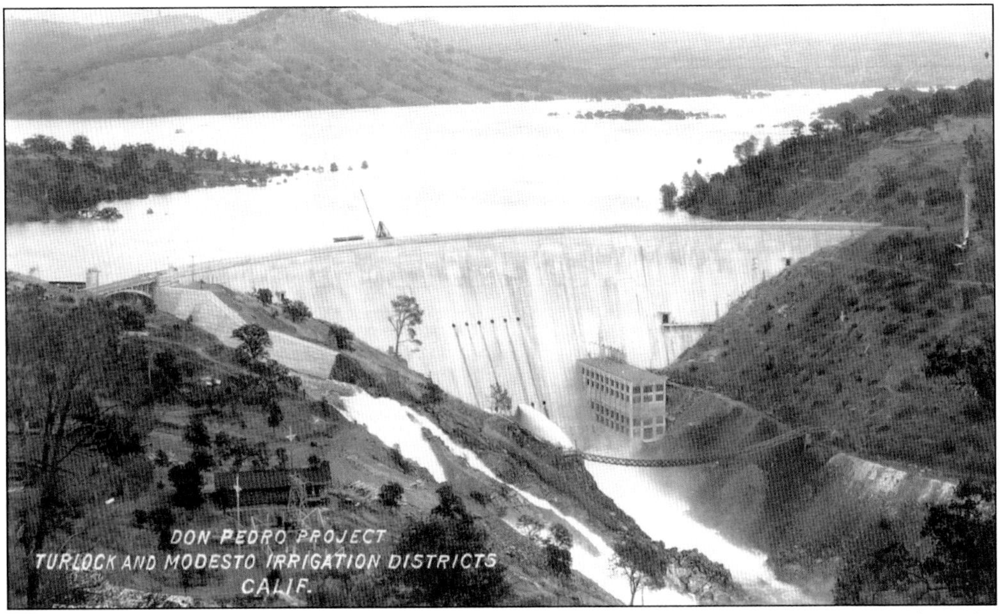

The first Don Pedro Dam of 1922, as seen here in a 1930s postcard, was covered up when the second Don Pedro Dam lifted the elevation of the reservoir in 1971. When the water filled up to the new earth-filled dam, Roy V. Meikle, the man who engineered the first dam in the 1920s, said, "Let it rest in peace." In drought years, the old dam has appeared as a white ghost in the murky waters. (Author's collection.)

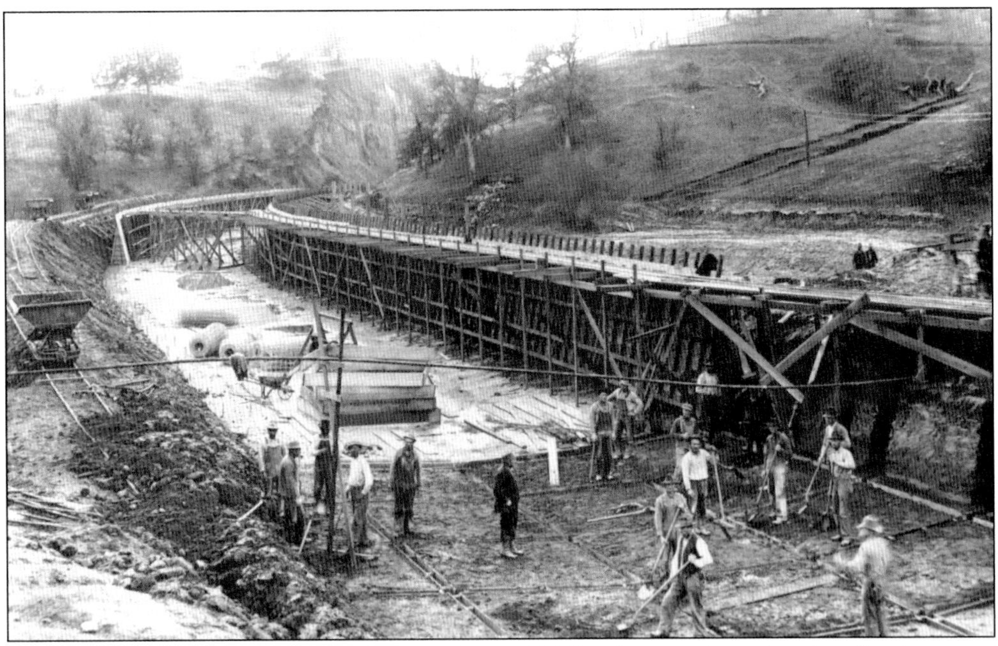

Water flowed from the La Grange Dam to Central Valley farmers through a free-flowing canal system that snaked through the hills. Workers built a canal of concrete with wood frames, wire mesh, and cement. Ground was cut by horse-drawn Fresno Scrapers. (Sid Long.)

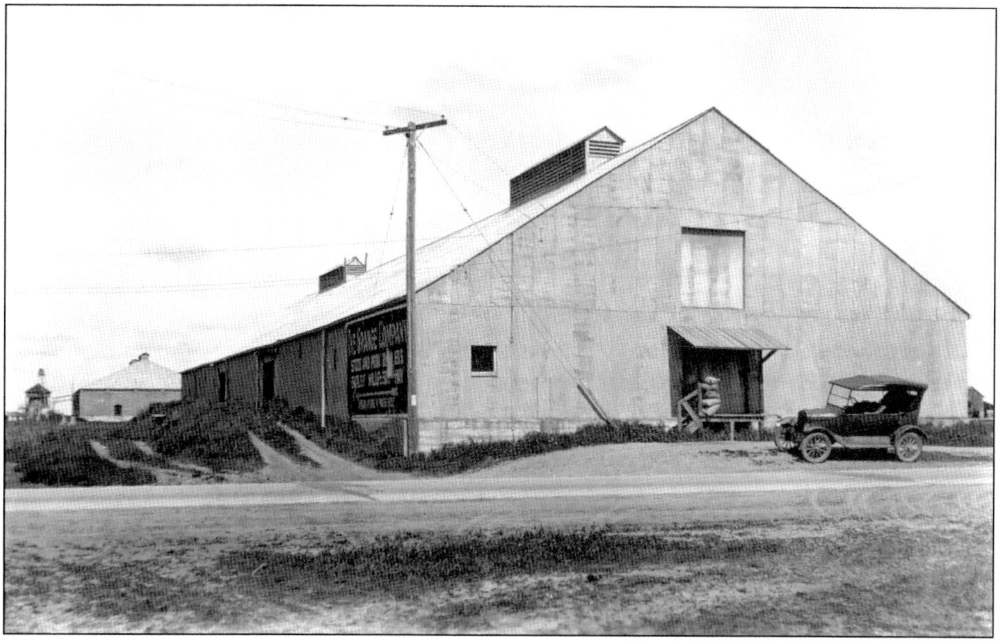

The Old Grange Warehouse is seen as it appeared in 1927. Leland Hayter, grandson of Waterford founder William W. Baker, was the manager of the business, which sold barley mill feeds and hay. Hayter was also postmaster from 1915 to 1918. He died in 1953. Today, the building sits just to the west of the Waterford Post Office on Bentley Street. (Waterford Historical Society.)

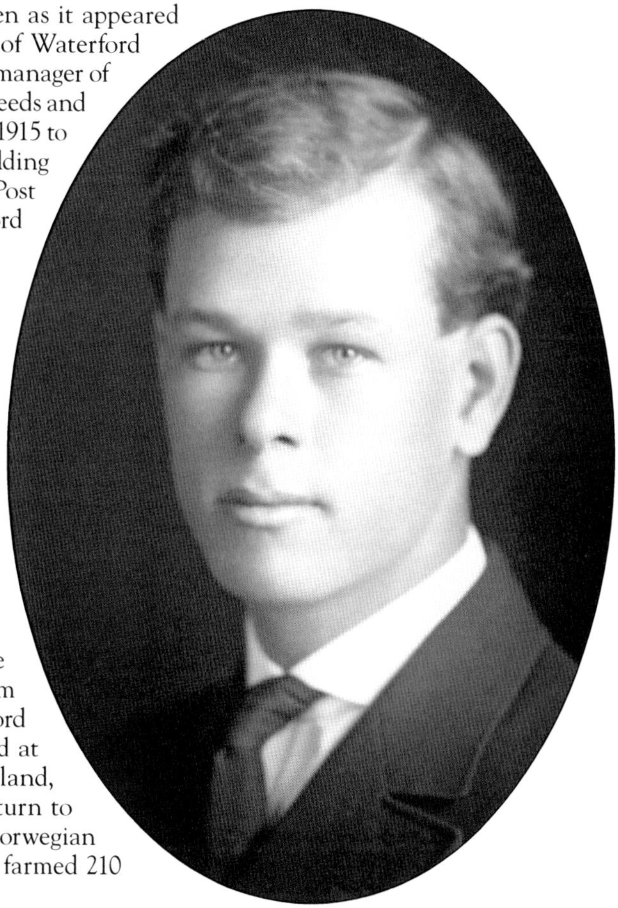

Louie Roen (1892–1959) traded business with the Grange Warehouse (above), as he operated a grain farm and dairy a few miles east of Waterford between 1929 and 1956. He studied at Pacific Lutheran Academy in Parkland, Washington, before he chose to return to his farming roots. After marrying Norwegian native Norma Moen in 1929, Roen farmed 210 acres of grain. (LaVerne Johnson.)

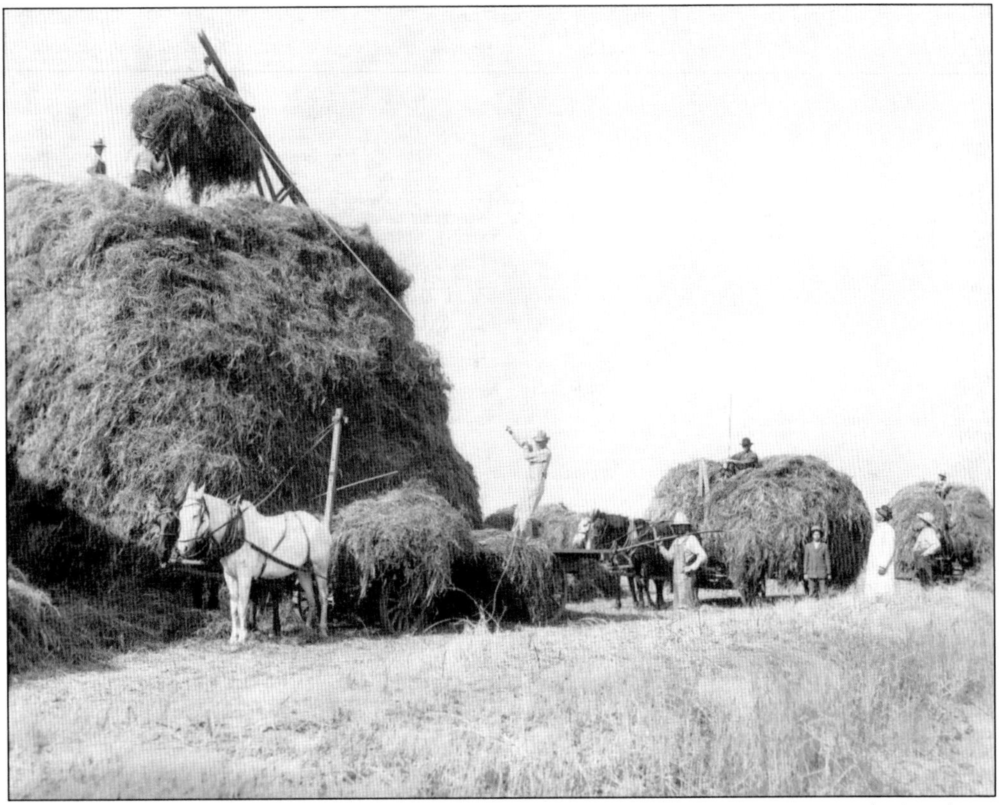

The Waterford and Hickman area was a major hay-growing region. Hay was stacked in large piles by use of a Jackson fork and stand-by balers. It was dusty and dirty work to be done by those without allergies. (Waterford Historical Society.)

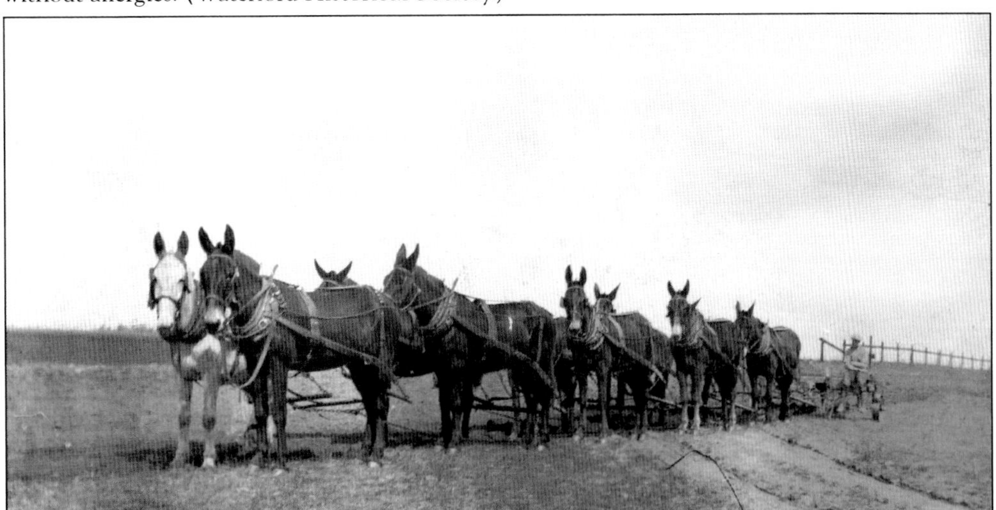

The use of mules to do farm work was commonplace in the Waterford area. This photograph of Earl Bowman and his team was featured on an April 1913 postcard sent to D. Howard Rinehart of Cambridge, Indiana, but who later came to Waterford. Bowman wrote: "I didn't get my pension. If I ever do, I will surely leave here." (Waterford Historical Society.)

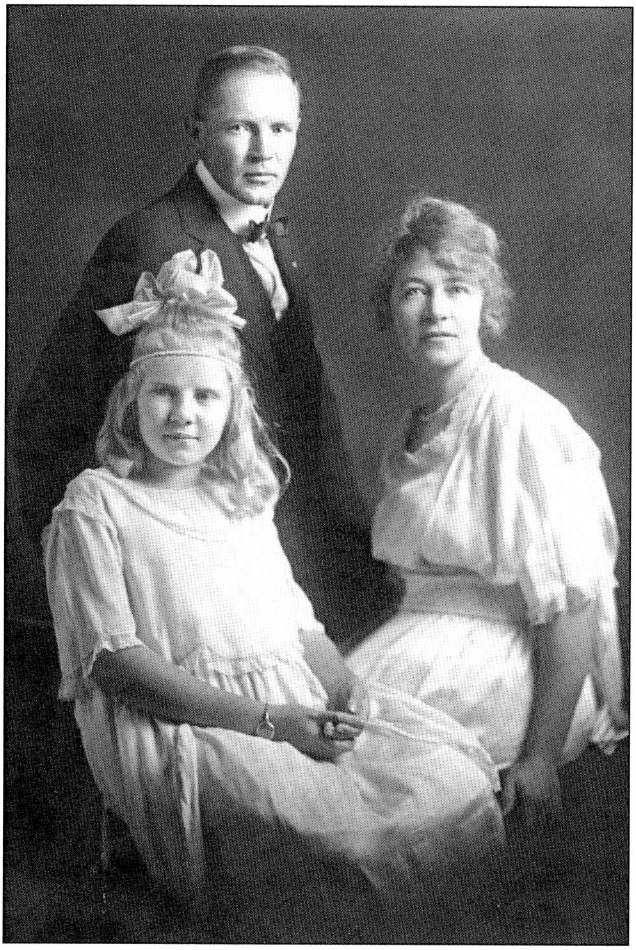

The Erb family was well known for its enterprising candied figs produced on a ranch just north of the Modesto Irrigation District canal north of Waterford. George, wife Elizabeth "Betty" Steffan Erb, and daughter Elizabeth (at right) came to Southern California in 1917 from Jefferson, Colorado. They moved to Waterford the next year and started growing Kadota figs. The Erbs ran the fig operation from 1923 to 1940 and lived in the house (below) built in 1925. Although remodeled, it stands today west of the Oakdale-Waterford Highway. In the 1930s, their figs were shipped by air from the Modesto Airport. (Both, Maryan Brush.)

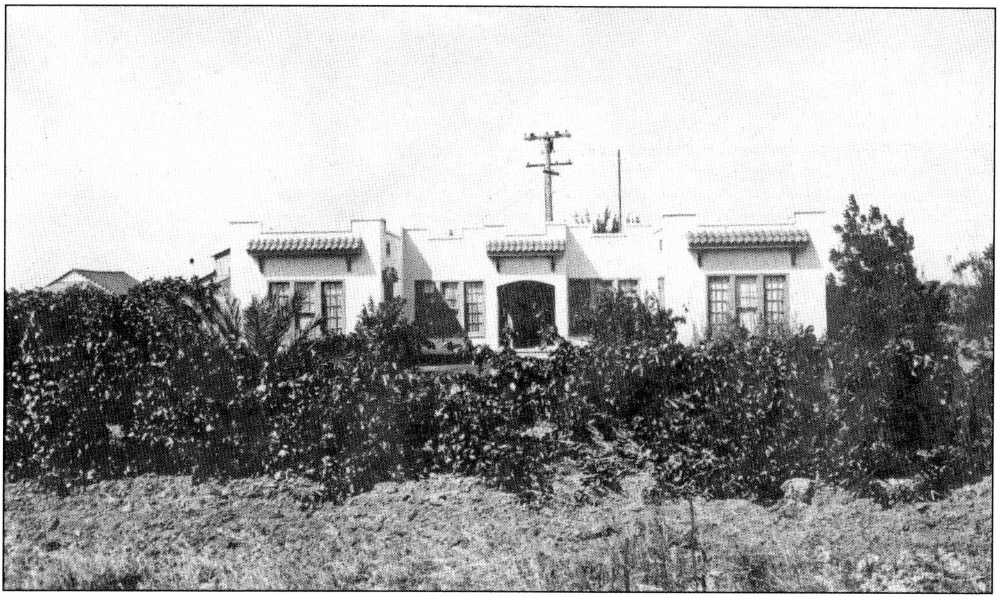

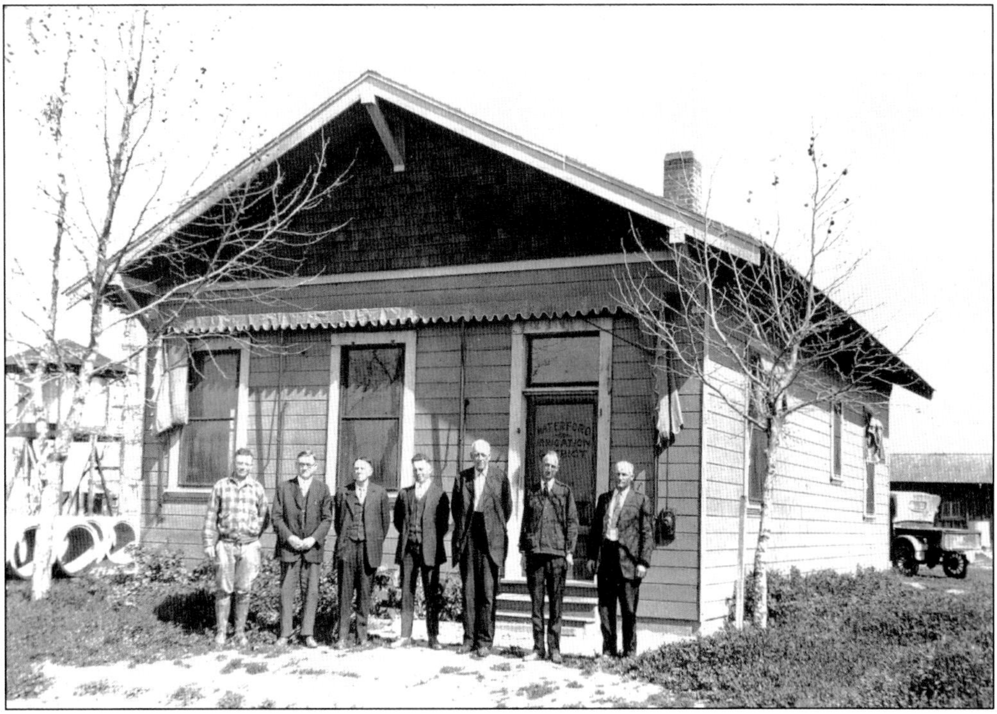

The Waterford Irrigation District office was located in today's police department on E Street north of Bentley Street. Gathered in front are, from left to right, engineer William Lehmkuhl, secretary Jim R. Browder, and directors Al Perry, C.W. Quinley, Joe Prouty, Tom Cooper, and Alf Ketcham. (Waterford Historical Society.)

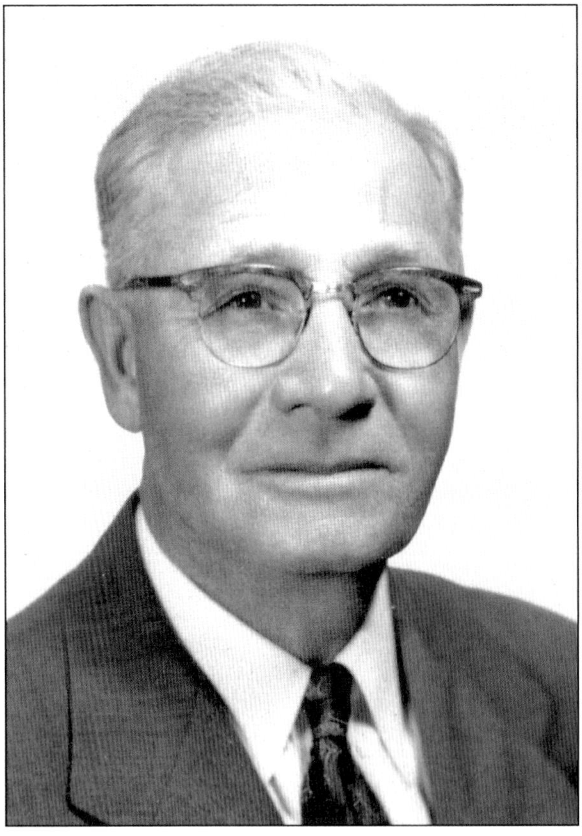

William "Bill" Lehmkuhl (1886–1977) was instrumental in the birth of the Waterford Irrigation District. He came to Waterford in 1919 after being hired by Thomas K. Beard in 1913. In 1920, Lehmkuhl accepted a "temporary" job as WID engineer, but he remained in that capacity for 45 years. Also Waterford's first fire chief, this is a 1957 portrait of him at age 70. (Meredith Gatzman.)

Clarence Winston "C.W." Quinley served as the secretary of the Waterford Irrigation District Board of Directors. He was born in 1897 east of Hickman, near Tilden School, which he attended. After marrying in 1920, he farmed in Montpelier, but he was broke during the Depression. He moved to North Blossom Avenue; in 1929, he moved to Charley Horsley's house on E Street. Quinley was the town's second fire chief. (Waterford Historical Society.)

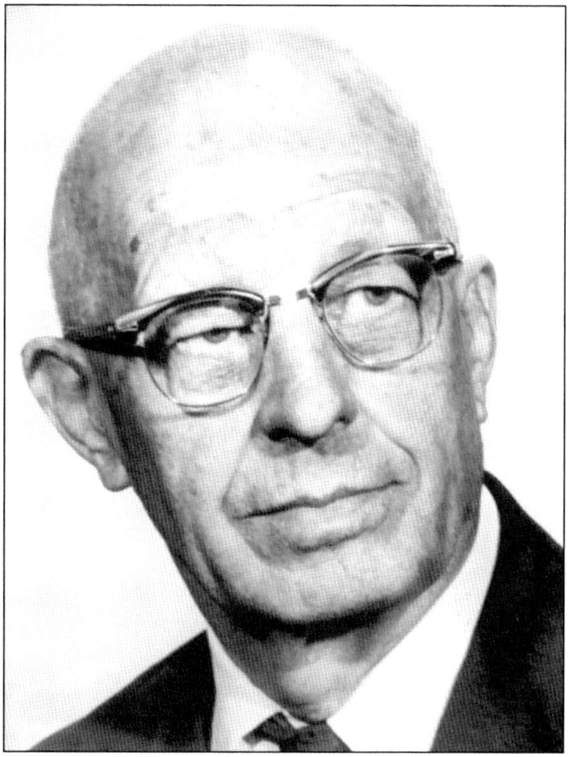

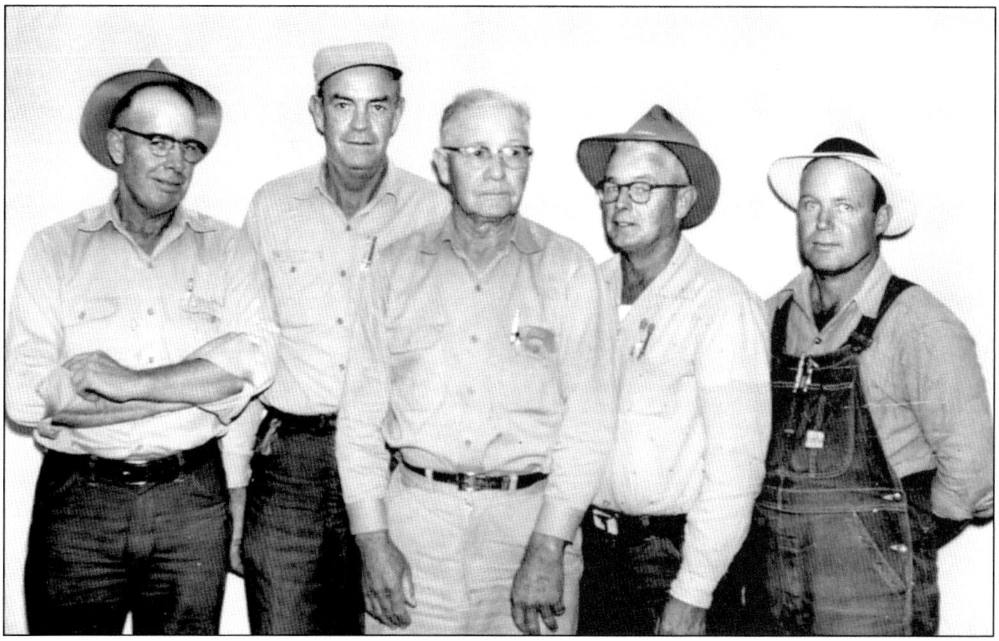

This crew of Waterford Irrigation District employees made sure that water was delivered to farmers in the area in the 1950s. Pictured from left to right are Supervisor Floyd Gold, ditch-tender Frank Dickinson, engineer William Lehmkuhl, and ditch-tenders George Zimmerman and Troy Ward. Ward was the father of Ben Ward, Waterford real estate agent and former school board trustee. (Meredith Gatzman.)

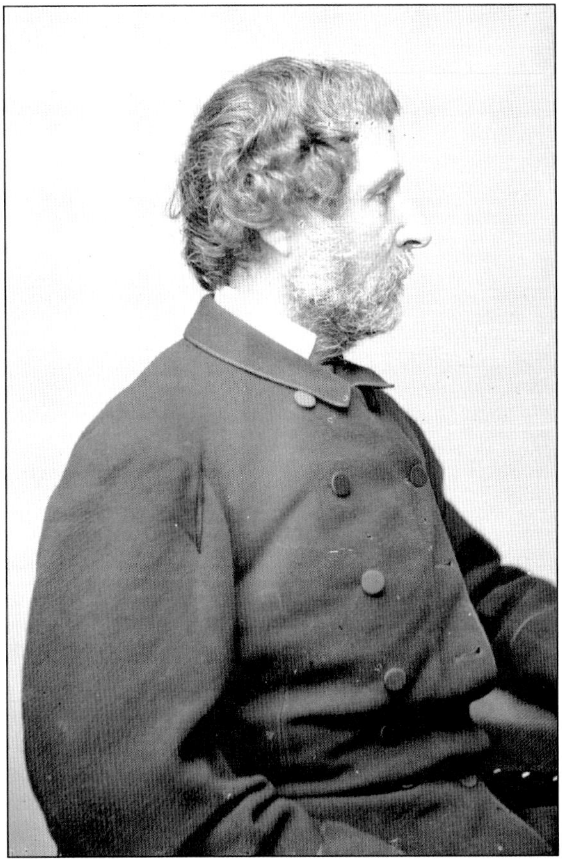

John Charles Frémont, the "Great Pathfinder," explored the Roberts Ferry area and helped create the Stockton-Mariposa Road through Indian Ranch, later Horr's Ranch, Dickinson's Ferry, and finally Roberts Ferry. One of Frémont's men died in the area and was buried here. Frémont, later the Republican Party's first-ever presidential nominee in 1856 and the Radical Republican faction's 1864 rival to President Lincoln for the Republican nomination, built his home at Bear Valley, the center of his 44,000-acre grant near Mariposa. Spanish army officer Gabriel Moraga had also led an expedition here in 1806 and 1808. (Both, Author's collection.)

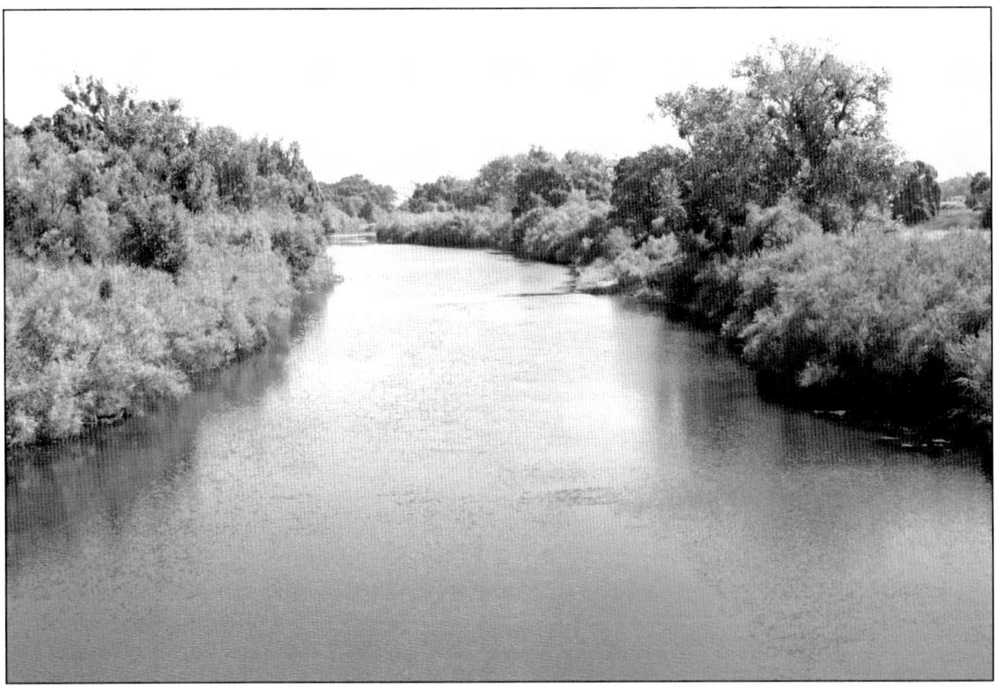

Three

Roberts Ferry
Neighbor to the East

Roberts Ferry (originally Horr's Ranch), eight miles east of Waterford, came about because of the Gold Rush stampede from Stockton to the southern placer mines of Mariposa, Hornitos, Mount Bullion, and Merced Falls. The Stockton-Mariposa Road was carved as a military road through eastern Stanislaus County and reached a crossing at the Tuolumne River known originally as Indian Ranch.

Alden Jackson and Benjamin D. Horr established a ferry there in 1850, less than a mile downstream from Roberts Ferry. Gallant Duncan Dickinson bought it and charged 50¢ for a large wagon and 22¢ for a saddle horse to cross the river. The route through Horr's Ferry was advertised as "the nearest road to Sonora, Mariposa, and the Southern mines." The ferry boasted that it could "cross eight mules and wagons with safety and dispatch."

Horr's Ferry boasted a hotel, store, saloon, post office, stables, corrals, and even a justice of the peace. The post office was established prior to July 28, 1851, and was discontinued in December 1896, when operations moved to Waterford.

The first action taken by Stanislaus County Board of Commissioners occurred at Horr's Ferry on May 29, 1854; commissioners set up election precincts and an election for a county seat selection (Adamsville).

In 1859, John Talbot and Company erected a flour mill on the south side three miles upstream, but it washed away in the flood of 1862.

Dickinson sold his ferry to Cornelius O. Osburn in March 1857. The ferry and a hotel and stables were sold to John Wesley Roberts and G.W. Gibbs in May 1862, but within a year, Gibbs sold his interest. Roberts's wooden hotel burned on February 22, 1865, but he rebuilt in brick about a mile upstream. His ferry was replace by a toll bridge in 1887.

Nothing remains of the original settlement. Roberts Ferry now consists of scattered homes and ranches, an elementary school, and the Roberts Ferry Nut Company, established by Bill and Phyllis Mallory. The Diamond S Dairy has been operating since 1907 and made news when it hosted Indonesian president Suharto in 1970.

Today, many enjoy strolling the wide covered bridge constructed in 1999 after the 1997 flood weakened the old 1916 steel bridge.

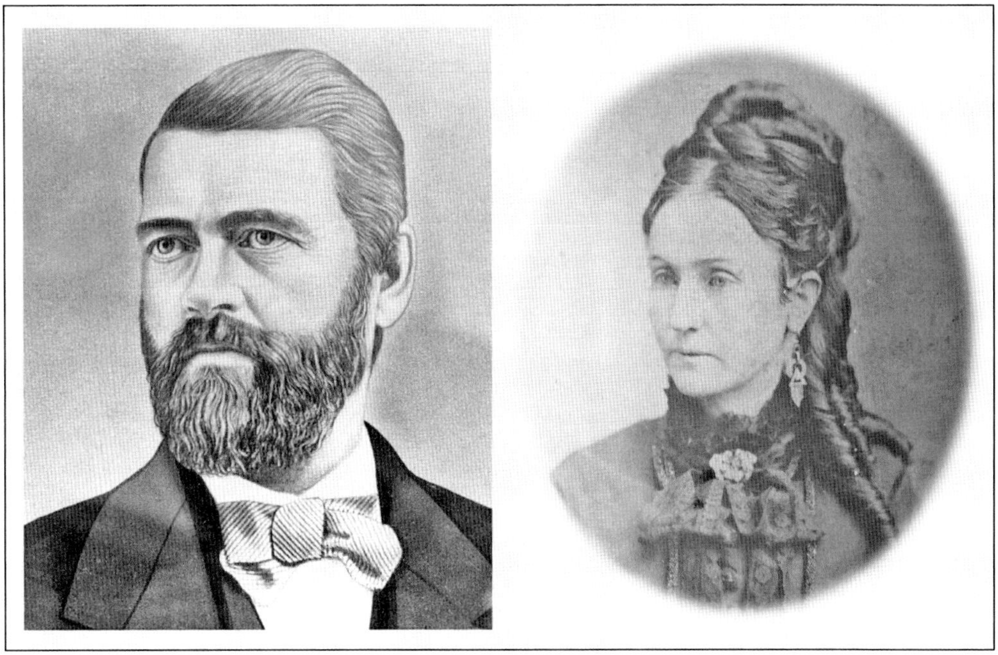

Roberts Ferry was named after John Wesley Roberts and wife Ann Ketcham Roberts. Born in Boston, Massachusetts, in 1828, John Roberts came to California in 1849 on a 207-day ocean voyage aboard the brig *Tryumph*. After arriving in San Francisco in April 1849, he set up a Tuolumne County butcher shop, which was wiped away in an 1850 fire, then tried his luck at mining in Jamestown. Six years later, Roberts came to the future Waterford town site (1856), where he operated a slaughterhouse. Roberts bought Dickinson's ferry in 1862. He also sold supplies to miners, ranchers, and farmers. His wooden hotel was charred to rubble in 1865. (Linda Barney.)

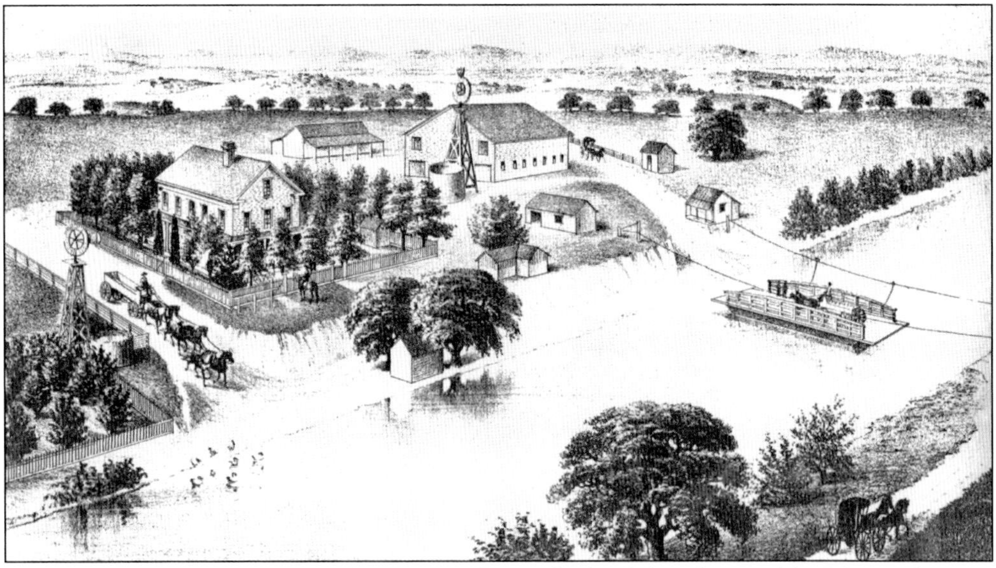

This 1881 artist rendering of Roberts Ferry shows the brick hotel owned by John Roberts at left and the ferry a few hundred yards up the Tuolumne River. The short road where the team is illustrated is now the northern approach to the present-day Roberts Ferry Bridge. (*History of Stanislaus County*.)

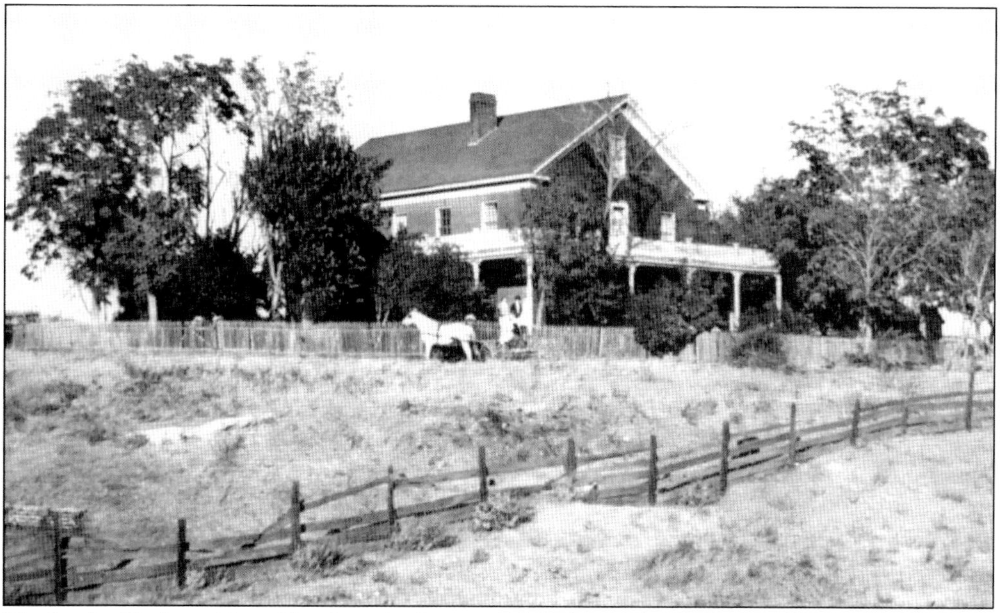

The bricked Roberts Ferry Hotel was built in 1865 by John and Ann Roberts. A grand Christmas ball attended by state legislators helped christen the use of the two-story structure, seen here probably in the 1890s. Its second floor was removed after damage from a 1950s earthquake. The hotel stood just northeast of the Roberts Ferry bridge until it was razed into a pile of brick in 2009. It's said that Ann Roberts is sitting in the buggy here, as the white horses are hers. (Linda Barney.)

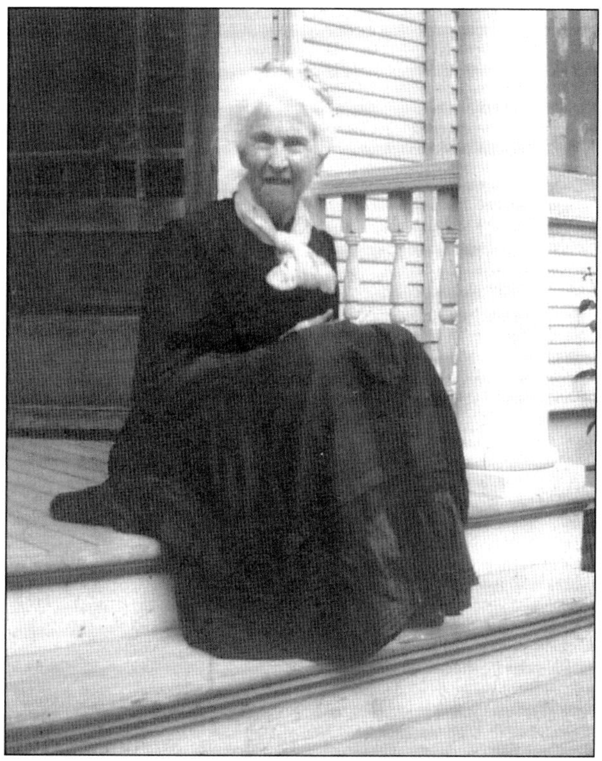

Ann Ketcham Roberts, pictured around 1910, lived alone after her husband, John W. Roberts, died in 1894. Ann turned the ranch over to her nephews and moved to Fourteenth and K Streets in Modesto, where she died in 1911. Ann married 29-year-old John W. Roberts on March 13, 1856. Born in Illinois, Ann was eight when she and her sister Sarah Ann came to California, led by uncle Will Shoemake. They trekked across the Isthmus of Panama to arrive in Columbia in 1852. Her only child, Andrew Ambrose Roberts, was born March 30, 1857, but was killed at age 17 in a wagon accident. (Linda Barney.)

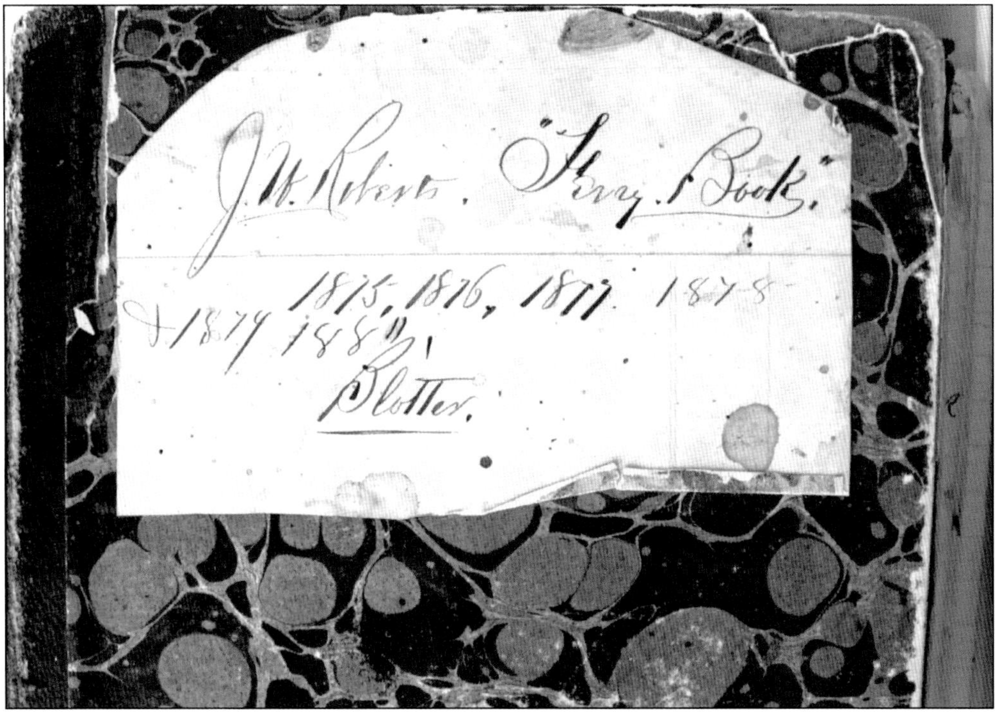

John W. Roberts recorded all charges for services offered at his ferry and hotel in this worn ledger book. The blotter records operations for 1875 through 1880. The book was handed down from his widow, Ann Roberts, to nephew Alf Ketcham, then his son, Donald Ketcham. The rare item is now in possession of Don's granddaughter, Linda Ketcham Barney. (Linda Ketcham Barney.)

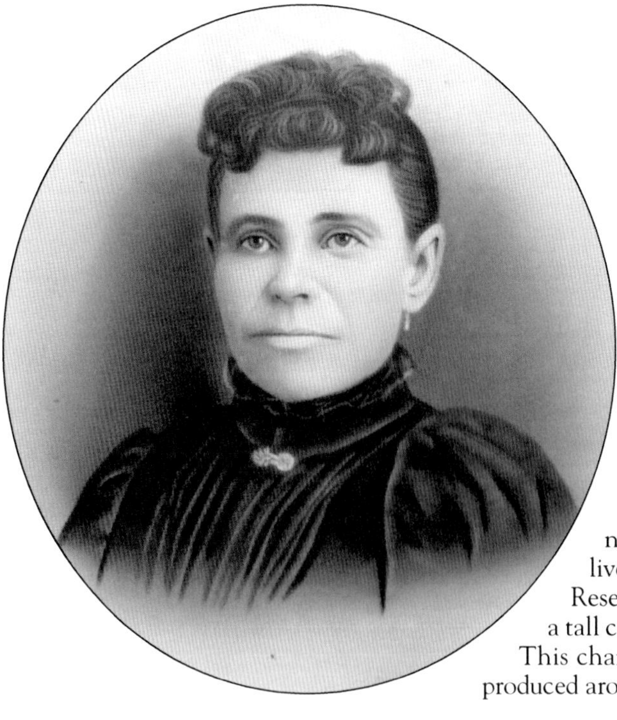

Karen Andrine Nielsen Larsen lived near the old road to Roberts Ferry and the Mariposa mines beyond and did business at Horr's Ferry. Born on November 22, 1840, Karen married Iver Larsen—brother of John Larsen, who later changed his name to John Roen. Karen and Iver lived north of what is now the Modesto Reservoir. Their homestead is marked by a tall concrete water tank that exists today. This charcoal drawing of Karen Larsen was produced around 1879. (Carl Nielsen.)

Richard A. Webb and bride Elizabeth F. Amer Webb were the parents of Edith Vera Crabtree. Richard Webb was born in 1847 in Wisconsin to English immigrants. His mother, Mary Ann Warner Webb, cared for nine children while raising her younger brothers—William, James, John, and Joseph Warner—after their parents died in 1846. When Richard was old enough, he followed his uncles to the Roberts Ferry area, where he met and married Elizabeth on January 15, 1884. Elizabeth was born in 1856 in Utah and came to Stockton and then Horr's Ranch. Her funeral at Warner's Ranch in 1893 was well attended. Richard died in 1903. (Bob Crabtree.)

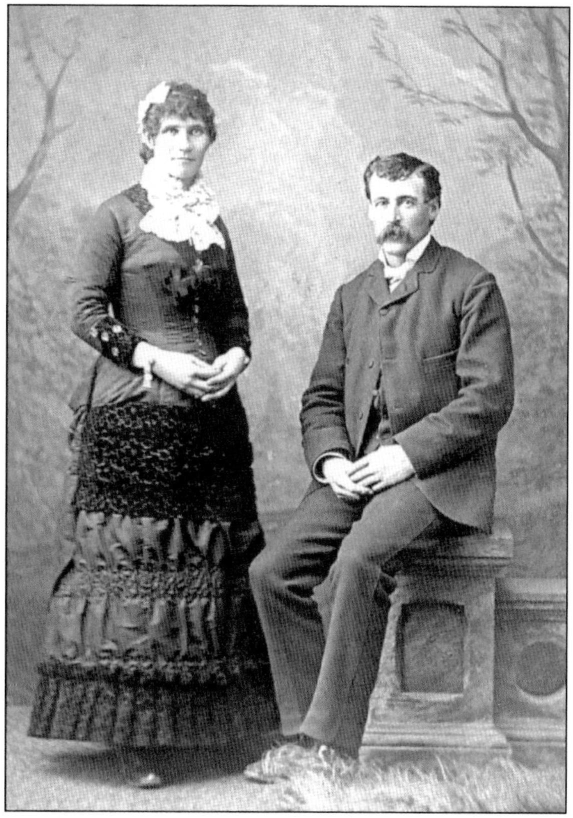

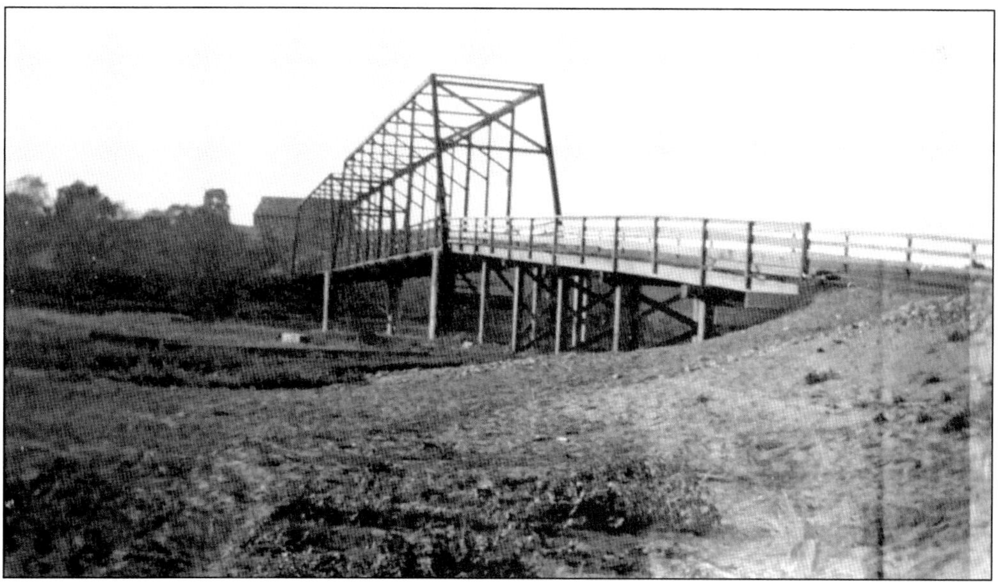

This iron toll bridge over the Tuolumne River at Roberts Ferry was built by John Roberts in 1887 to replace his ferry. Users hated paying the toll, so they petitioned the county to take it over as a free bridge. In 1892, the county leased it from Roberts. It was replaced in 1915. Steel from the first bridge was used to build bridges to the construction site of the Hetch Hetchy Dam in Yosemite National Park. (Linda Barney.)

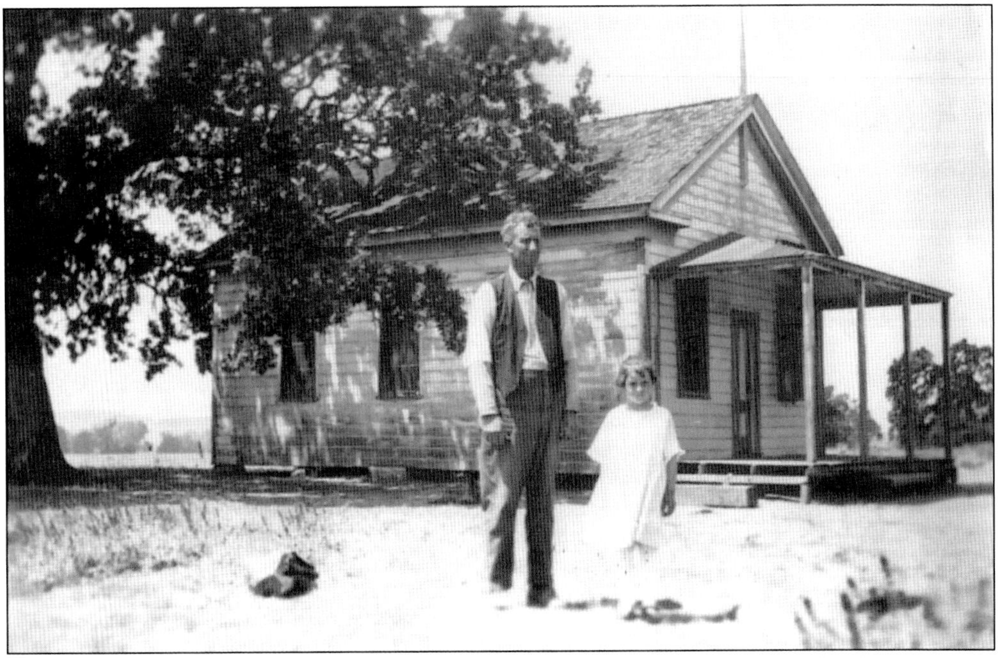

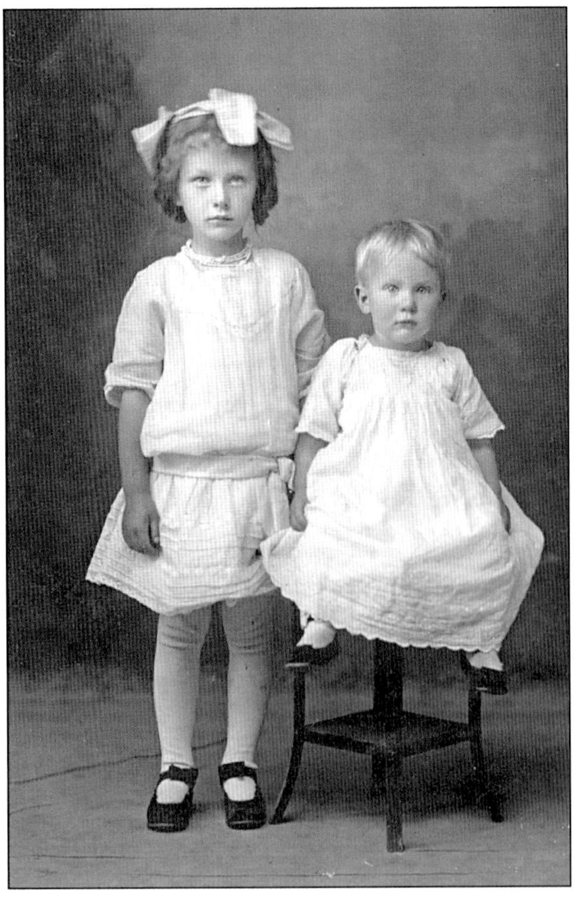

Fred McMillan and daughter Mabel McMillan (Cree) stand outside the Hermitage School in 1923. The school was established in 1867 and was located on the south side of Yosemite Boulevard between Crabtree Road and Rushing Road on the McMillan property. Fred McMillan was born in 1876 southwest of La Grange and died in 1978. Tilden School closed in 1924 to merge with a new Roberts Ferry School. (Valerie Turpen.)

Mabel is pictured here with an unidentified family member. After her marriage, Mabel Cree was a prominent member of the community between Roberts Ferry and La Grange. This photograph postcard was sent to Alma Johnson (later Alma Prouty). (Waterford Historical Society.)

Luther Crabtree (at right and below) and Edith Vera Webb are pictured on their wedding day, October 21, 1908. Luther was born in Missouri on December 3, 1888, and moved to the Ceres area with his parents (Albert Watson Crabtree and Rebecca Ingram) and his sister Susie in the early 1890s. His mother died on August 4, 1896, and Luther stayed with his grandparents in Benton County, Missouri, until about 16, when he returned to California. Edith was born on February 27, 1888, to Richard A. Webb and Elizabeth F. Amer at the Warner Ranch. (Bob Crabtree.)

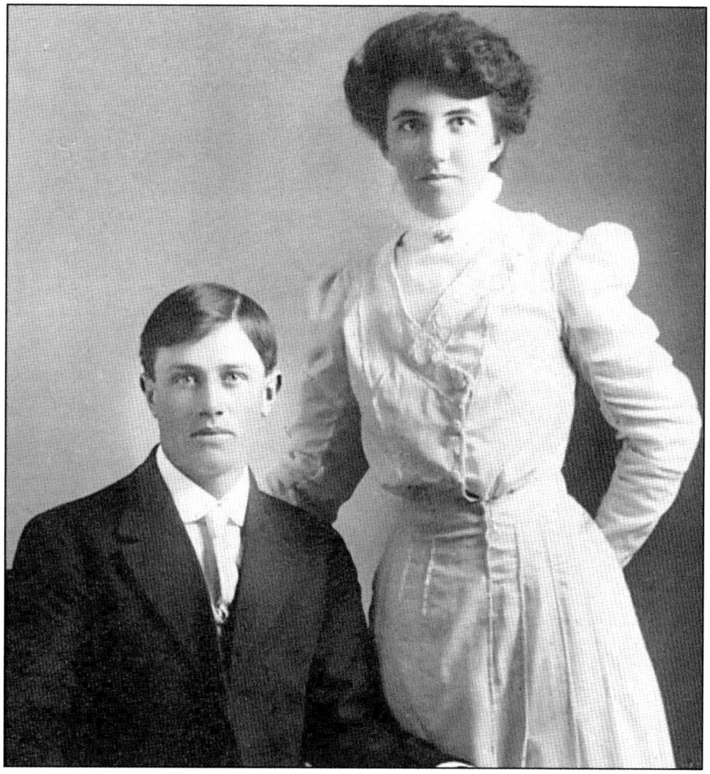

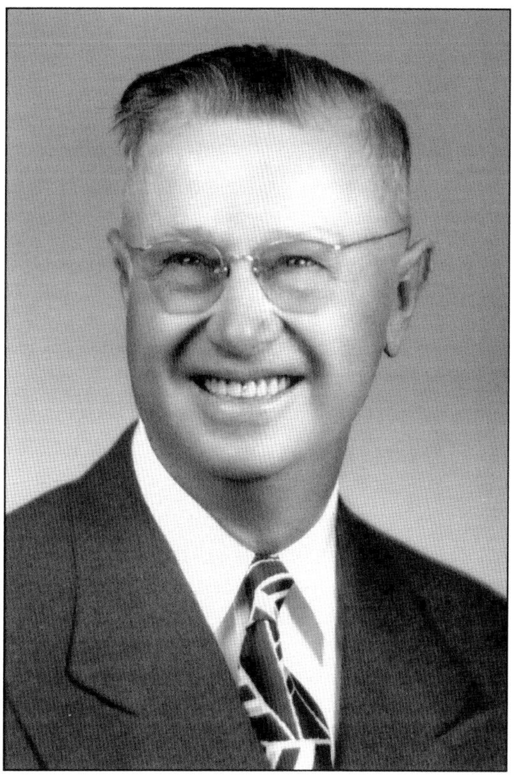

Luther Crabtree, who maintained a large cattle ranch in Roberts Ferry, was the third president of the Waterford Grange organization. The first Waterford Grange No. 7 was organized on August 25, 1873, with 31 charter members but fell by the wayside. It was revived as Waterford Grange No. 53 on April 10, 1934. The Grange first met in the Waterford School auditorium, then moved to Community Baptist Church in February 1938. The present Grange Hall was opened on April 12, 1938. (Bob Crabtree.)

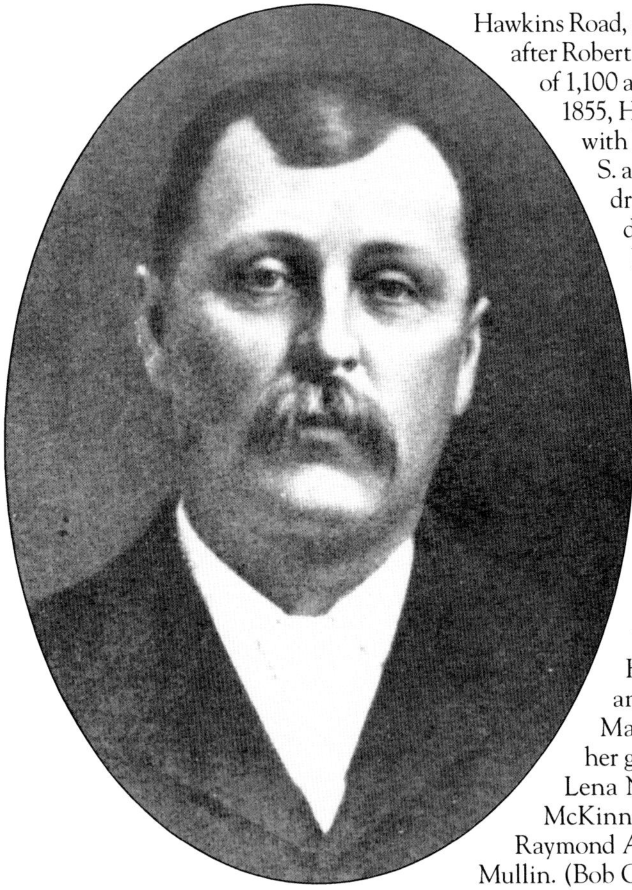

Hawkins Road, southeast of Roberts Ferry, is named after Robert Timothy Hawkins, a pioneer farmer of 1,100 acres in the area. Born in Georgia in 1855, Hawkins came to the Central Valley with his wife, Mary, and children Robert S. and Mamie Hawkins. R.T. found work driving a group of laborers in a horse-drawn wagon to La Grange for the building of the La Grange Dam. In 1903, Hawkins bought a 320-acre farm east of Hickman. (*History of Stanislaus County.*)

Tilden School, southwest of Roberts Ferry, doubled as a church on Easter Sunday in 1911. The building was built in 1877 on the Hooker Ranch south of Lake Road and east of Hawkins Road. In 1897, Maggie E. Church taught here, and her graduating pupils that year included Lena Nelson, George C. Nelson, Willie McKinney, Ira Perkins, Emergy Hudelson, Raymond Appling, Hugh Appling, and Willie Mullin. (Bob Crabtree.)

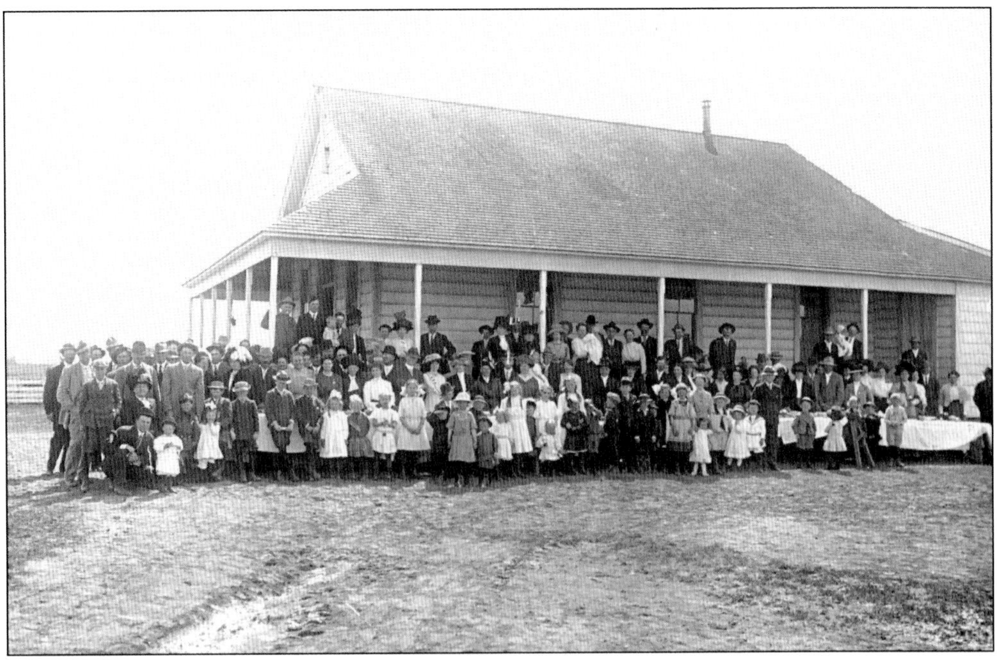

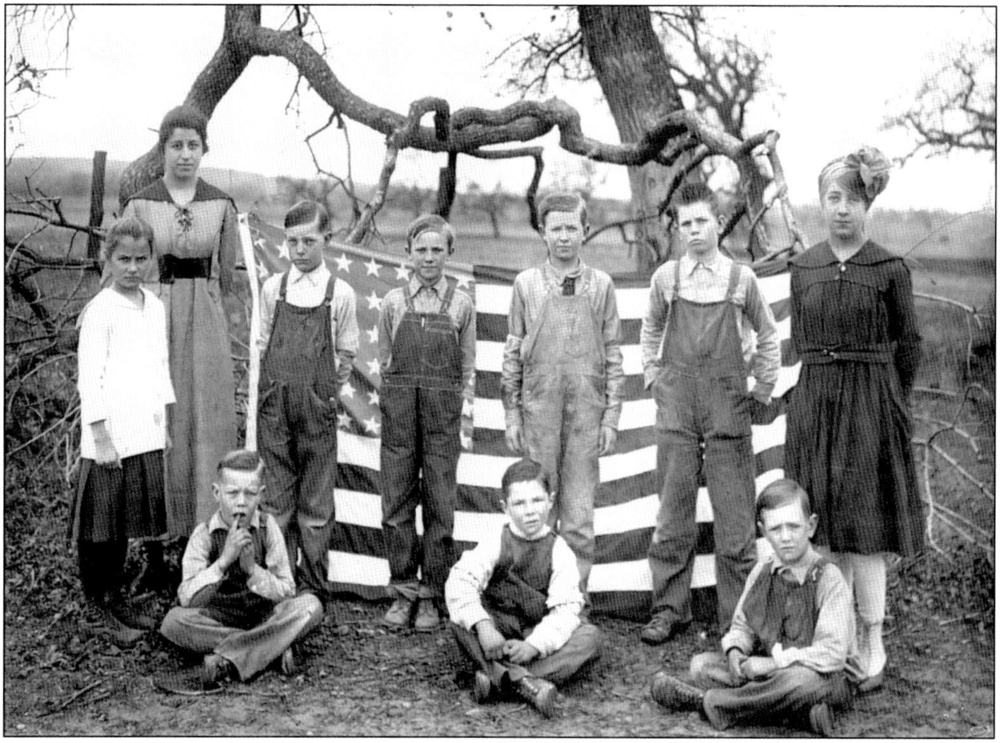

Established in 1867, Hermitage School operated as a one-room schoolhouse on Yosemite Boulevard (then called La Grange Road) near the McMillan farm east of Roberts Ferry. Pictured in 1918 are the teacher and her students. Seen from left to right are (first row) Iver "Ole" Funk, Frank Bolchini, and Albin Crabtree; (second row) Rachel Bolchini, teacher Edith Gallo, and students Anver Funk, Donald Ketcham, Jim Hammett, Louie Erickson, and Lila Funk. (Bob Crabtree.)

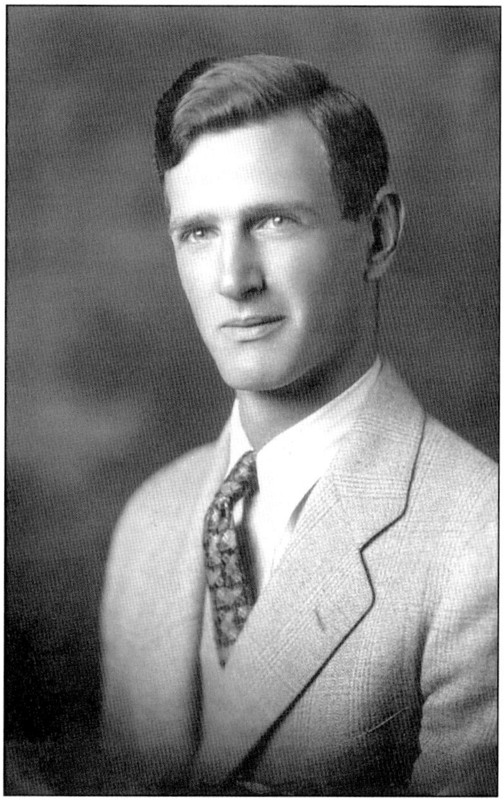

Albin Crabtree, pictured here in a 1928 senior portrait, lived his entire life in Roberts Ferry and operated a ranch there with wife, Berniece. He served on the Roberts Ferry School Board in the 1950s. (Bob Crabtree.)

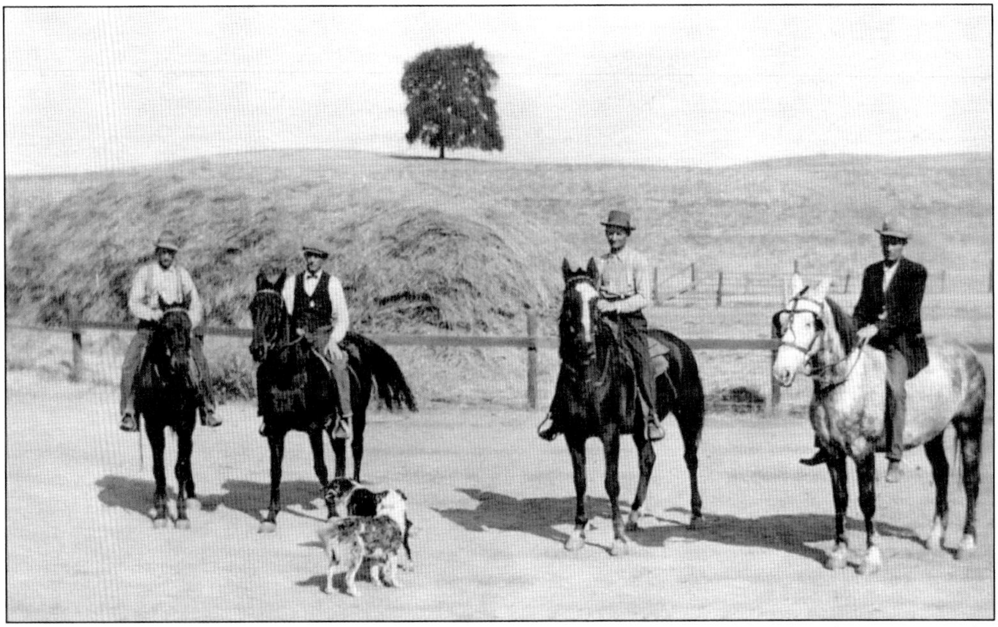

Cattle ranching was a primary occupation in Roberts Ferry. The Ketcham brothers stop in the middle of their cattle roundup for this photograph around 1912. From left to right are an unidentified ranch hand, Burns Ketcham, Alf Ketcham, and Ollie Ketcham. All three inherited sections of aunt Ann Ketcham Roberts's land holdings when she passed in 1910. (Linda Barney.)

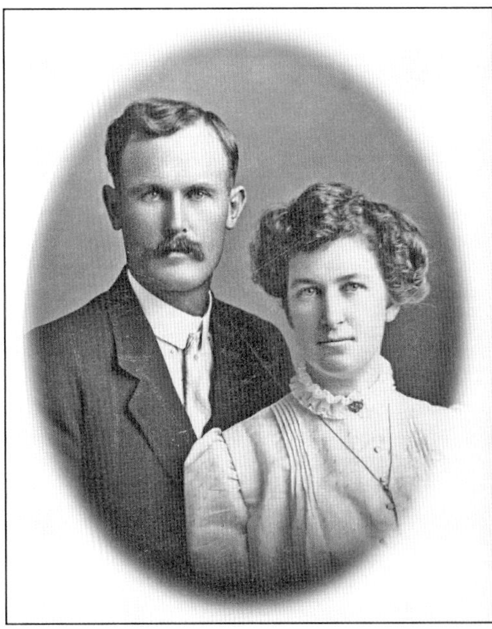

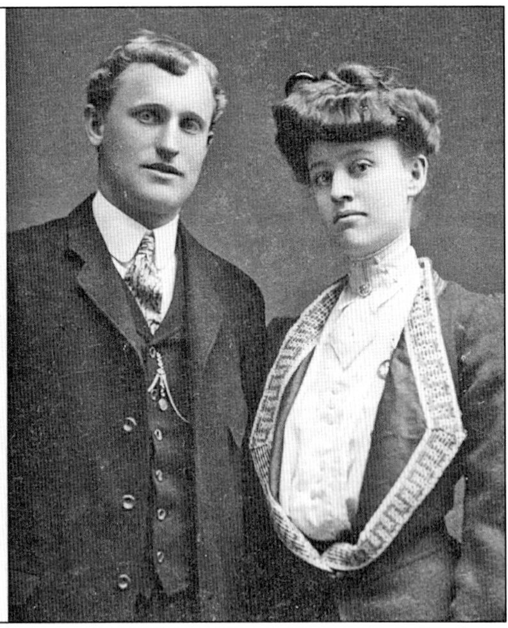

The Ketcham brothers—Alf, Oliver, and Burns—came to Roberts Ferry to manage and inherit aunt Ann Ketcham Roberts's land holdings. Oliver and Pearl Ketcham (left) came to Roberts Ferry in 1905. Oliver, a no-nonsense overseer, lived in what is now the Zanker home on Lake Road. Alf and bride Iva Ketcham (right) were photographed on their wedding day in San Francisco. Alf played a key role in starting the Waterford Irrigation District. (Linda Barney.)

Burns Ketcham left Alameda in 1912 to go into a farming partnership with brother Alf Ketcham at Roberts Ferry. Pictured here in uniform, Burns enlisted in the US Cavalry to serve in the Spanish-American War. His company fought in the Philippines against Gen. Emilio Aguinaldo. During the war, Burns sustained a bad case of sunstroke that affected him for the rest of his life. (Linda Barney.)

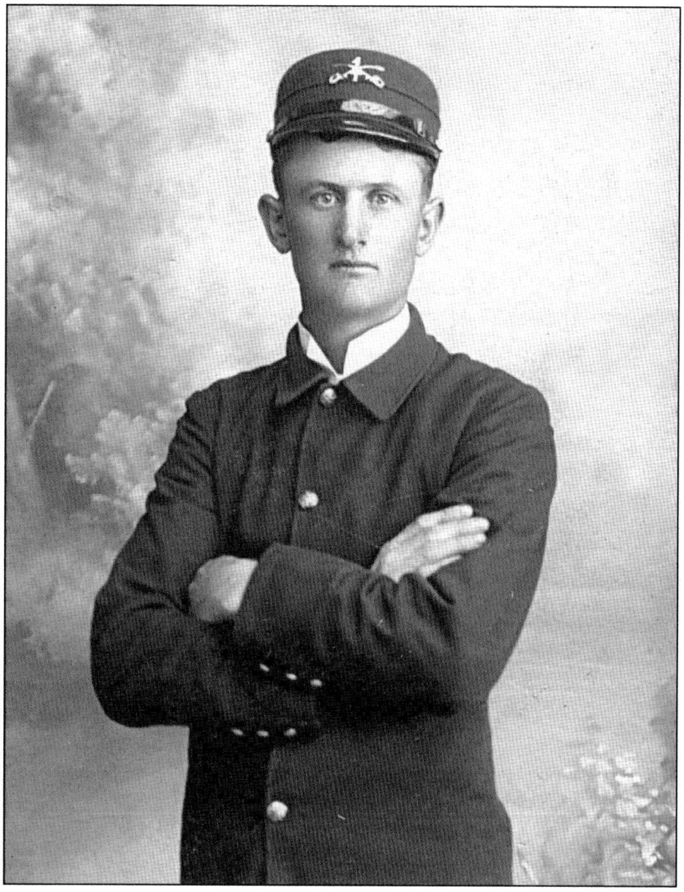

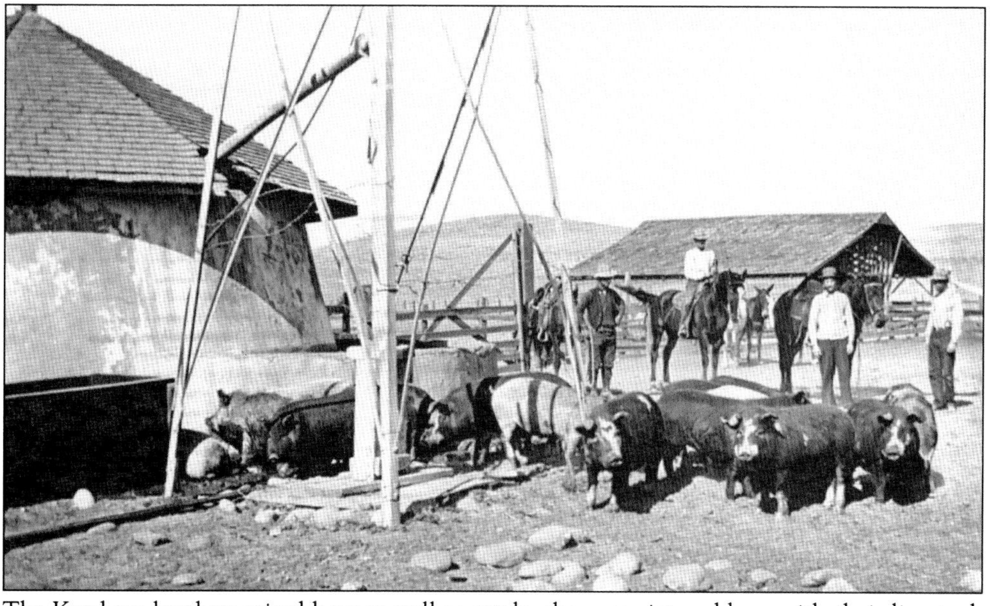

The Ketcham brothers raised hogs as well as cattle; they are pictured here with their livestock near Roberts Ferry's historic 17-foot-diameter cistern, which still stands today. (Linda Barney.)

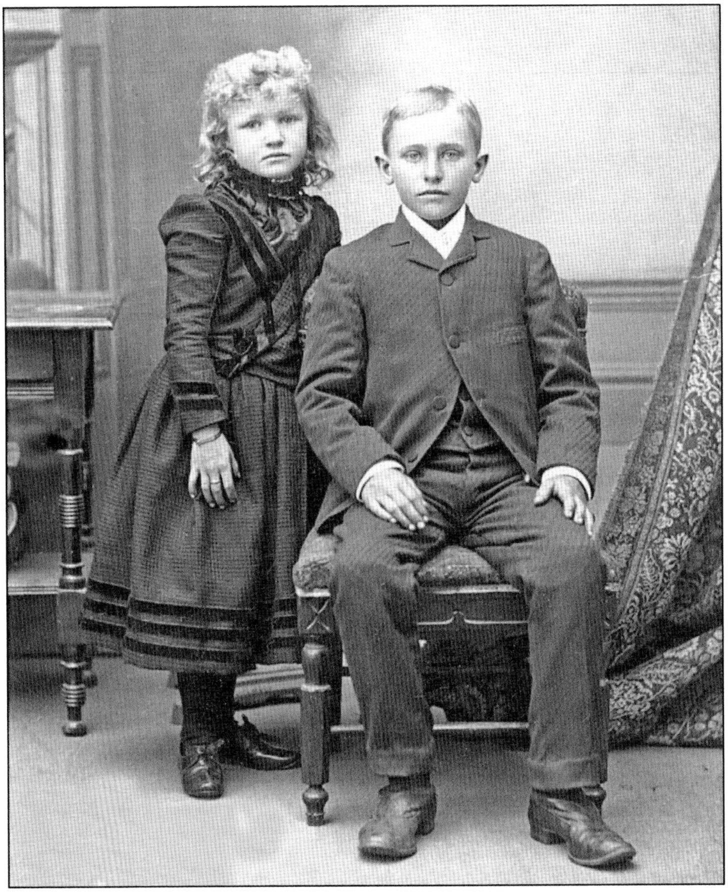

Alf and sister Jessie Ketcham Hurlbut strike a heartwarming childhood pose. (Linda Barney.)

Tilden School and Hermitage School merged to become Roberts Ferry Elementary School, which opened on February 10, 1924. From left to right, the first eighth-grade graduates are seen here: Evelyn Sawyer, Albin Crabtree, Zelda Ketcham, Ole Funk, and Mabel Gilbertson. (Albin's flowers are wilted because he tossed them in the trash the day before, not realizing that they were intended for this photograph. He later fetched them out.) (Bob Crabtree.)

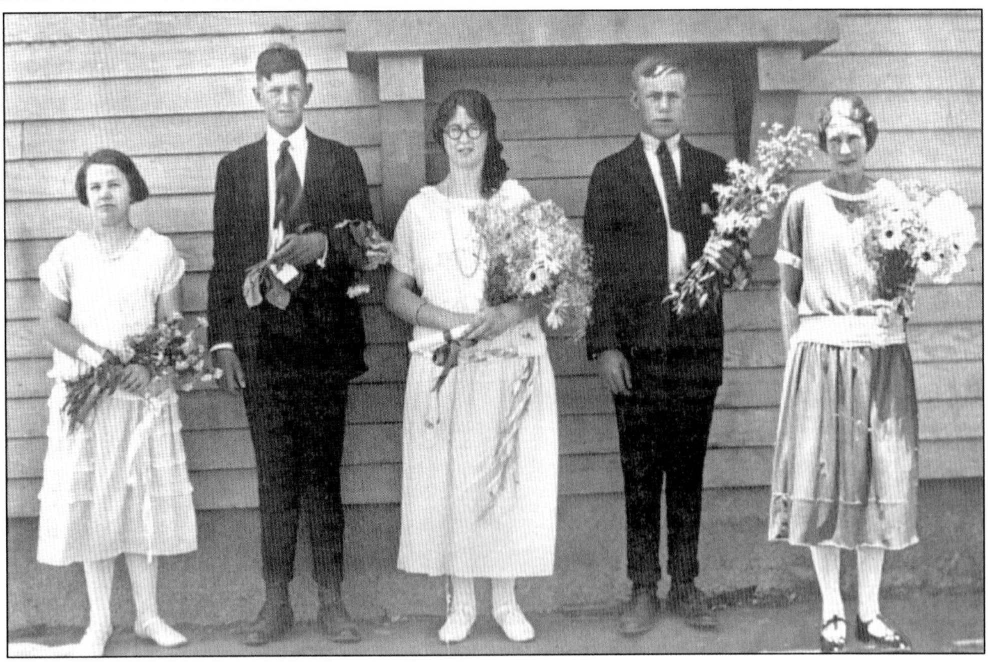

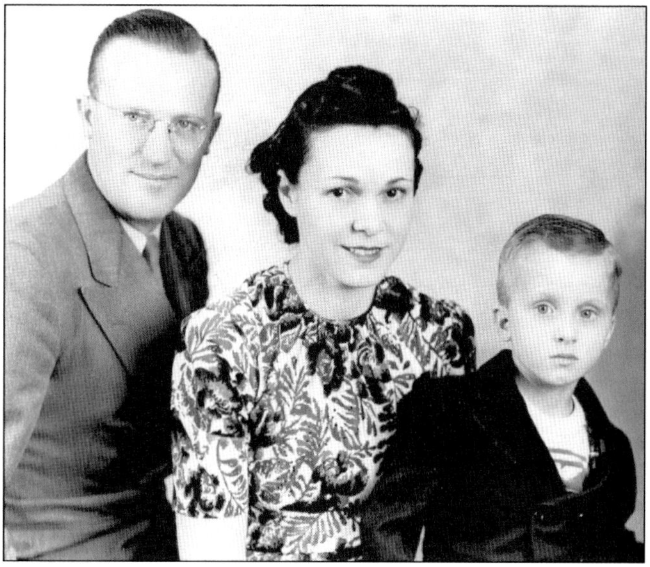

Donald Ketcham (seen here with wife Edith and son Larry) was the great-nephew of Ann Ketcham Roberts. Don was part of the Roberts Ferry scene for 101 years. Born in 1907, he attended Hermitage School from 1914 to 1922, graduated from Oakdale High School in 1926, and left for college. He returned to farm the family property while teaching high school. He served as president of the Roberts Ferry School Board from 1948 to 1958. Edith came to Roberts Ferry in 1935 and operated a clothing store in Waterford. (Linda Barney.)

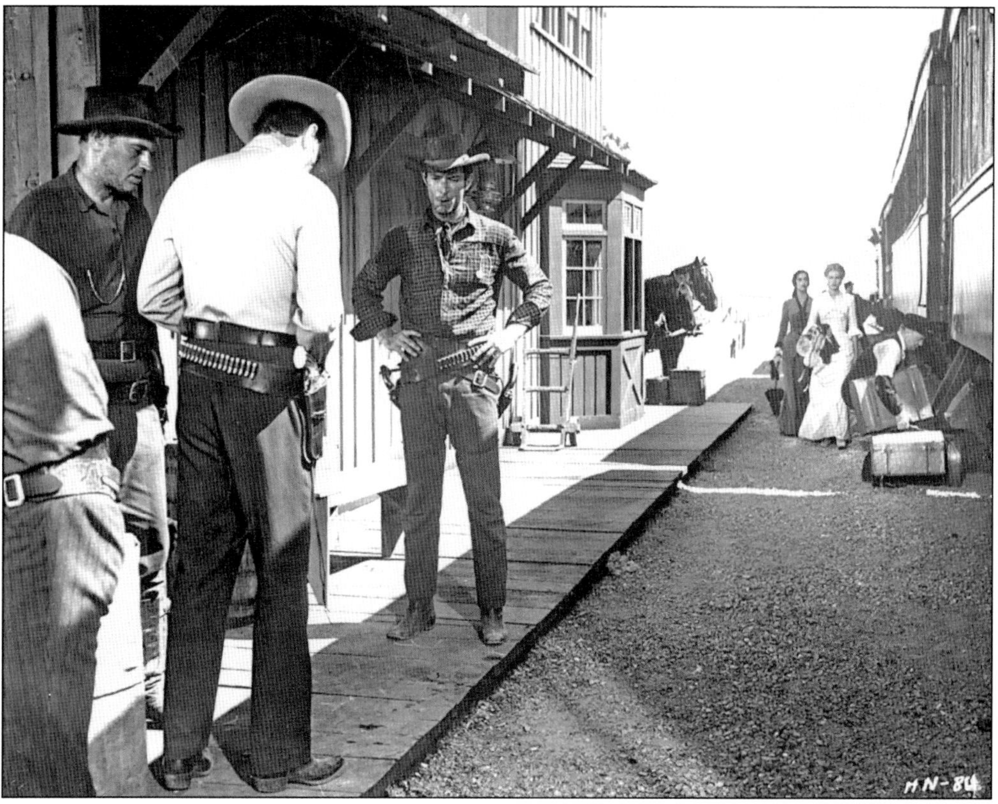

In 1952, Gary Cooper and Grace Kelly visited the intersection of Crabtee and Warnerville Roads north of Roberts Ferry to film *High Noon*. At the depot, Hollywood bad men Sheb Wooley (partially obscured), Robert J. Wilke (left), Ian MacDonald (back to camera), and Lee Van Cleef plan to attack Cooper (playing Will Kane). Actresses Katy Jurado and Grace Kelly (at right) prepare to board the train aided by the stationmaster, played by Ted Stanhope. (Author's collection.)

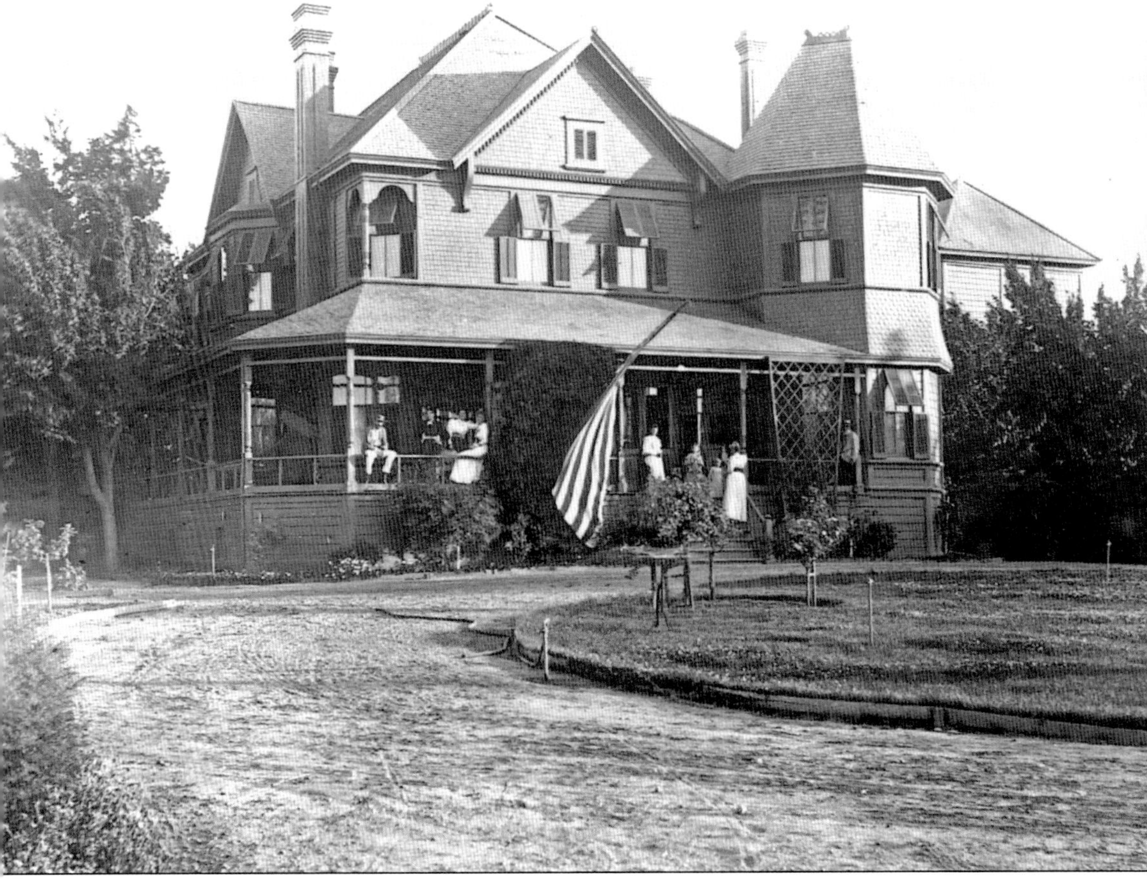

Charles Dallas lived in this grand home at Hickman Road at Whitmore Avenue. The house was later lived in by his daughter, Mary, and son-in-law, Louis Hickman. Dallas was a major landowner and one of the first to settle in the Hickman and Waterford area. Early maps show the area named for Dallas until his daughter married Louis Hickman, and the town took his name. Dallas also owned a major portion of the Waterford town site. The home burned to the ground in June 1930. (Waterford Historical Society.)

Four

Hickman
Waterford's Cozy Southern Neighbor

The history of Waterford and its neighbor to the south, Hickman, are inextricably linked together.

William W. Baker, the first settler in the Waterford region, first settled miles upstream on the Hickman side in the area south of the Tuolumne River near Lampley Road. He later moved to the flat area on the river's north side for excellent ferrying opportunities. It was north, not south, where Baker established his town.

The first major settler of the area that would become Hickman was Charles Dallas, who arrived in 1849 or 1850. In fact, early maps designate the area as Dallas. The town, however, would be named for Louis McLean Hickman, who married Dallas's daughter, Mary. Louis Hickman arrived in Stockton in the 1850s.

In the latter part of the decade, Hickman came to the eastern Stanislaus County area, where he met the Dallas family. Smitten by Mary Dallas, Hickman took his bride on February 1, 1860.

Hickman served as mayor of Stockton in neighboring San Joaquin County in 1869. He was a hardware store owner in the 1860s as he settled on the Dallas Ranch. On his 11,000-acre ranch, Hickman grew grain, hay, olives, figs, oranges, grapes, and other fruits.

Introduction of the Stockton-Visalia Railroad in 1891 precipitated the development of Hickman as a town. Large brick buildings were constructed to store grain adjacent to the tracks that extended southward to Montpelier. Hickman became official with the establishment of a post office on June 8, 1891, and Robert Davis became its first postmaster.

The Hickmans later moved to Sausalito in Marin County. In 1909, Louis Hickman formed a corporation for agriculture and land development, but he passed away the following year at age 77. Mary Hickman lived another 20 years, dying in 1930. Their grand former home at Whitmore Avenue on Hickman Road burned to the ground in June 1930.

The Hickman children first attended Grant School on the south side of the Tuolumne River. It burned and was rebuilt and later renamed Rowe School. The school relocated to the corner of Whitmore Avenue and Hickman Road. Some Hickman children also attended Tilden School near Roberts Ferry. In 1911, a new brick elementary school was constructed in Hickman.

Rowe School District merged with the Hickman district in 1932. Hickman's brick schoolhouse was razed in 1956 because it didn't meet state safety standards.

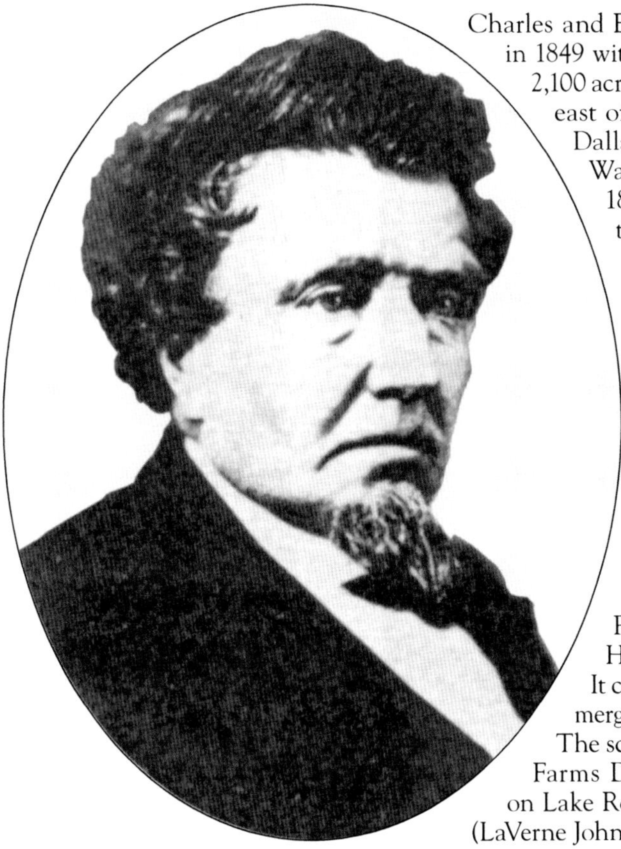

Charles and Elizabeth Dallas came to the area in 1849 with their six children. He purchased 2,100 acres south of the river about four miles east of Hickman where he operated the Dallas Ferry. After 12 square blocks of Waterford were surveyed in 1868 and 1869 by George Schell, owning the town site were Dallas, L.H. Pinkston, and Sarah E. Browder. In 1879, Dallas sold two lots of Adrian Faure for $50. (Waterford Historical Society.)

Rowe School was established at Hickman Road and Whitmore Avenue. It closed when the Rowe School District merged with the Hickman district in 1932. The schoolhouse was moved onto a Foster Farms Dairy, two miles east of Hickman on Lake Road, and was converted to a home. (LaVerne Johnson.)

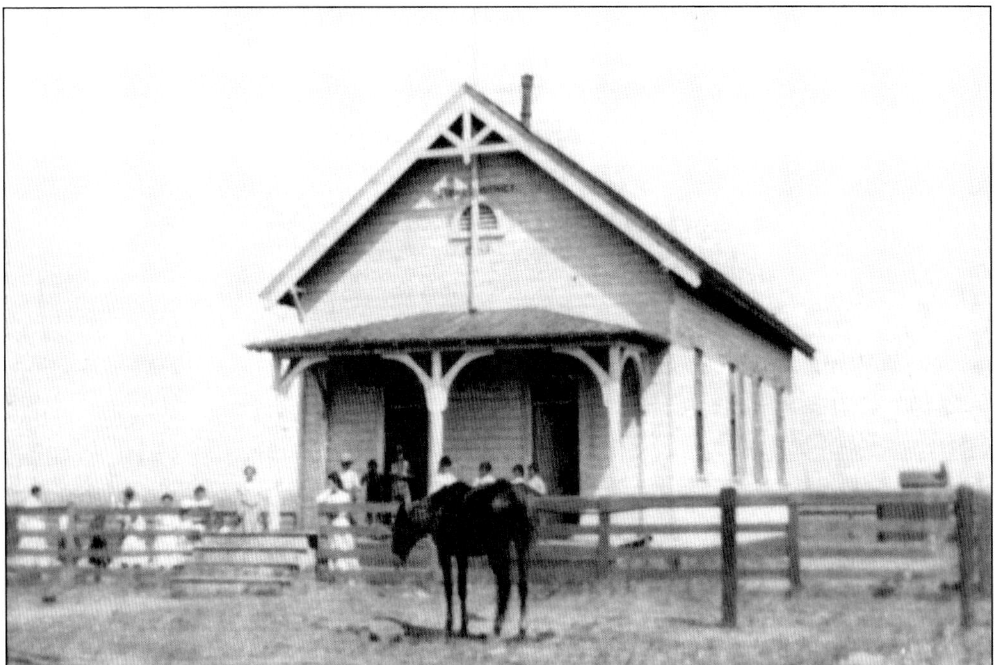

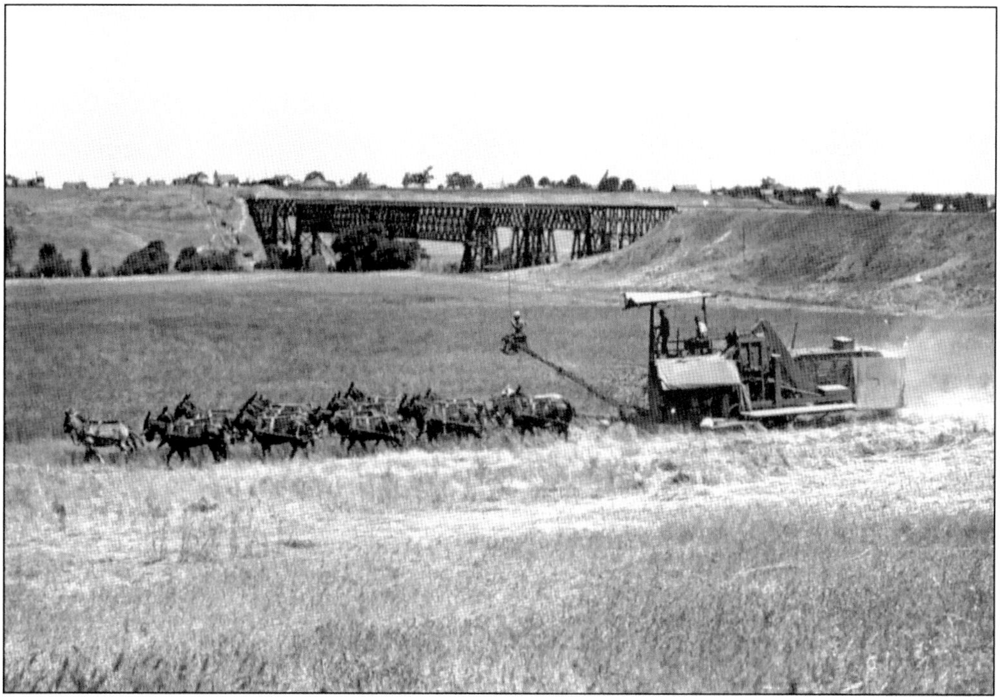

Although taken some time a century ago, this vista is recognizable as the Hickman side of the Tuolumne River looking northeast toward Waterford. This was Chandley Cogswell's property, planted in grain and harvested by a mule-driven combine. The Southern Pacific Railroad trestle in the background was razed in 1978. (Sandra Burley.)

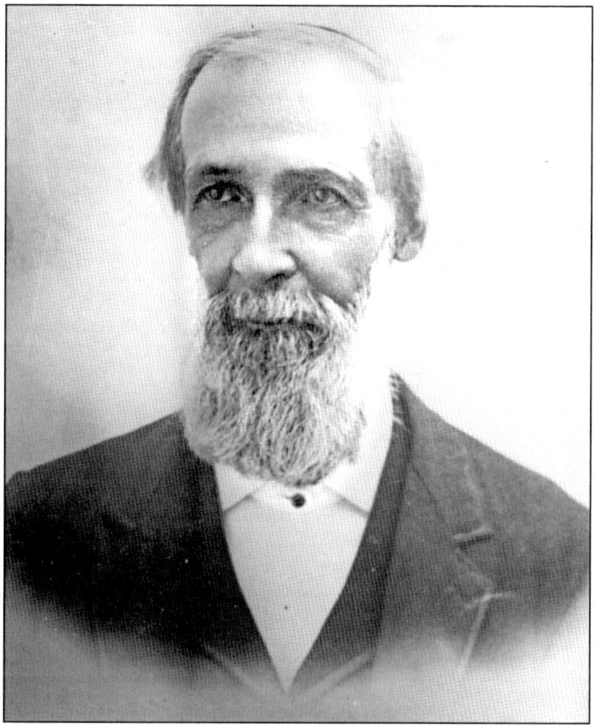

Cogswell Road south of Hickman was named for farmer Chandley Cogswell. He first came to California from New York in 1851 via the Isthmus of Panama, while brother Edison Cogswell took the Nicaragua route to San Francisco in 1853. Chandley ended up farming in Stanislaus County, where sister Ellen lived. Chandley returned to New York in 1860 to assist his dying father. In 1880 or 1881, Chandley brought to Hickman his mother, Prudence, wife Clarissa, and children Minnie, Hattie, and William. Cogswell died at age 78 in 1906. (Sandra Burley.)

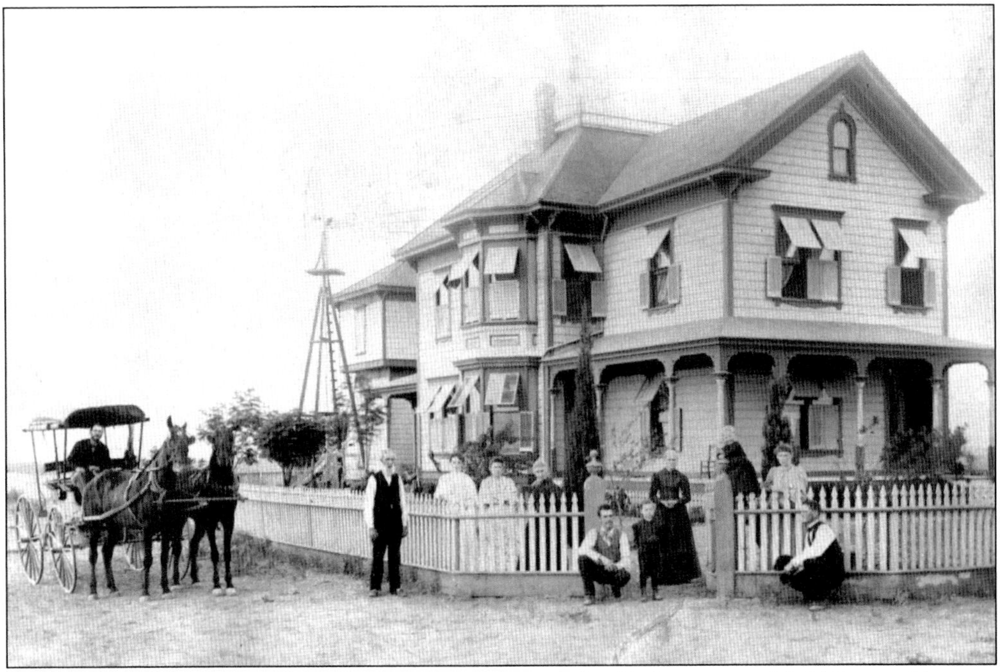

The 1889 Appling house was a prominent residence on the Hickman river bluff. Pictured here in 1894 from left to right are Appling and Cogswell family members Edward H. Appling, Chandley M. Cogswell, Beulah Bradley, Hattie Cogswell Jefferson, Ellen Cogswell Dallas, William Cogswell, William Raymond Appling, Clara Sykes Cogswell, Hugh Lester Appling, Minnie A. Appling, and Charles Jefferson. (Sandra Burley.)

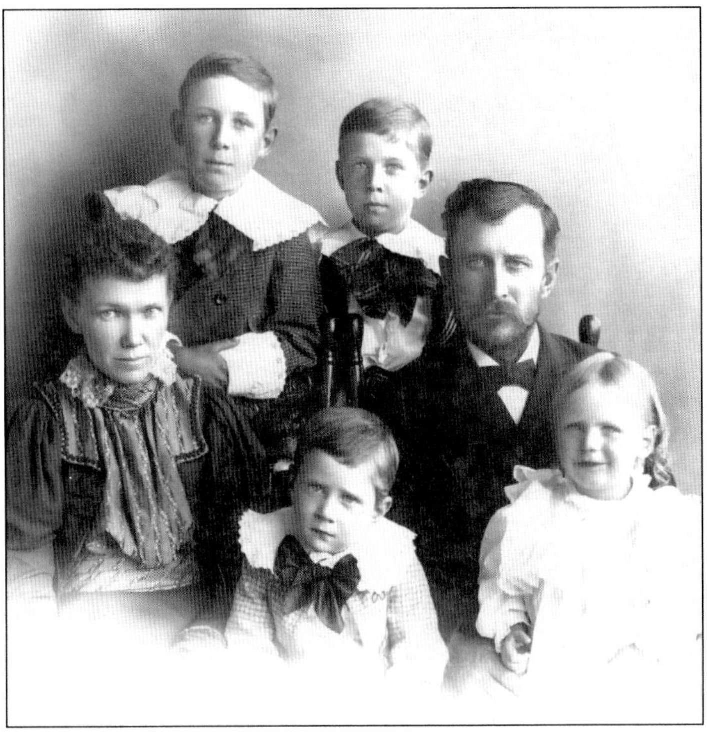

The Edward H. Applings of Hickman gathered for this 1899 portrait. Minnie Cogswell and Edward Appling married in Waterford on November 2, 1887. Pictured here from left to right are children (first row) Elmer and Clara; (third row) William Raymond "Ray" and Hugh. Born in 1855, Edward Appling came to California in 1875 and grew wheat on 640 acres rented from the Dallas ranch in 1887. A clerk of the Rowe School Board of Trustees, Appling died in 1915. (Sandra Burley.)

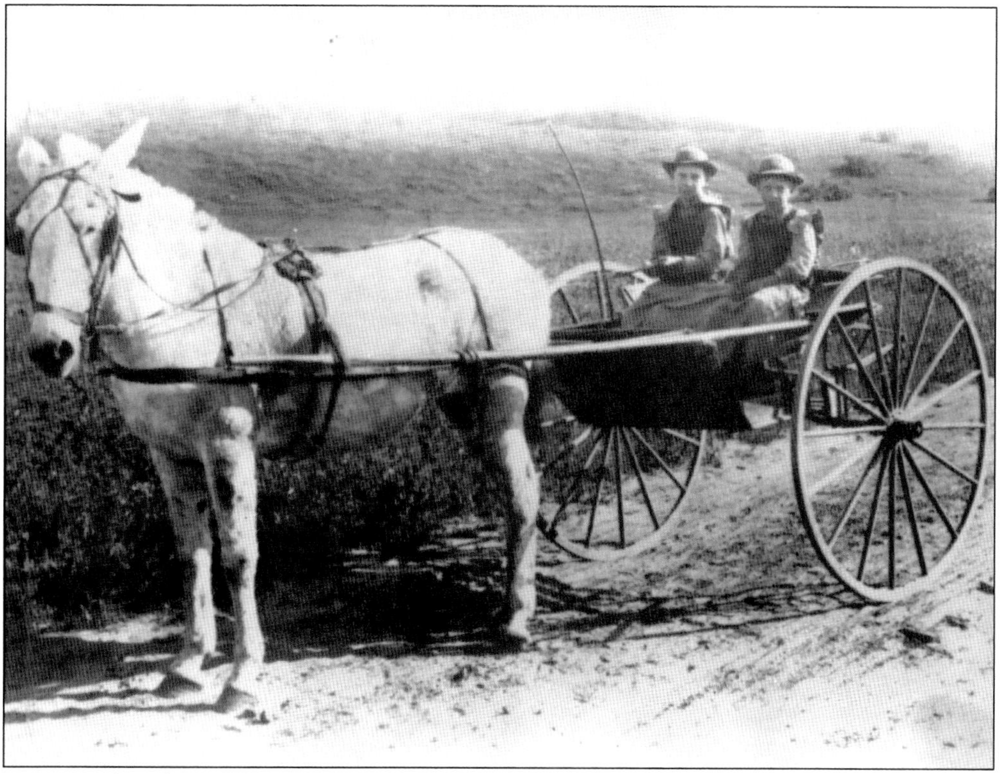

Many rural students relied on a horse and buggy to get to school. Seen here around 1905, Raymond and Hugh Appling stopped on the way to Tilden School so that a parent could take this picture. The Applings lived south of the Tuolumne River and attended Tilden School from 1902 to 1905. (Sandra Burley.)

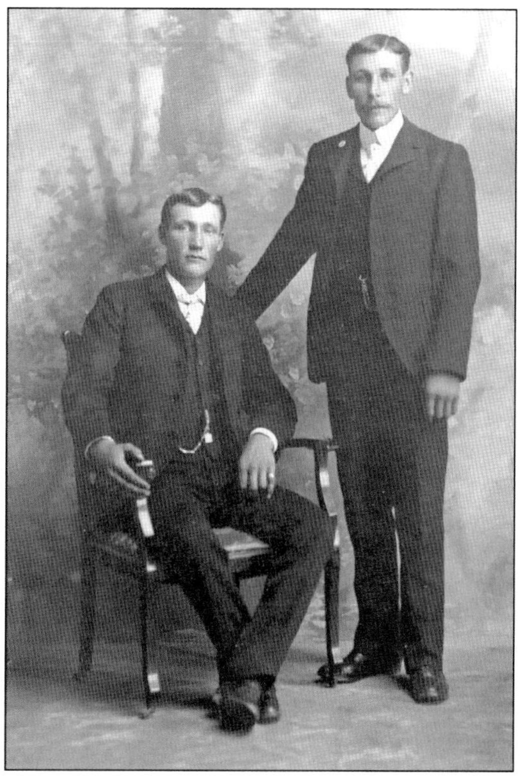

John Gilbertson (left) and brother Iver Gilbertson were Hickman-area grain farmers. The Denmark natives came to the area in 1902 through the efforts of John and Oline Roen and operated a farm near Roen Road off Lake Road. Between 1911 and 1918, John farmed rented property three miles north of Waterford on the Oakdale-Waterford Highway before moving onto 1,100 acres on Lake Road east of Hickman. (LaVerne Johnson.)

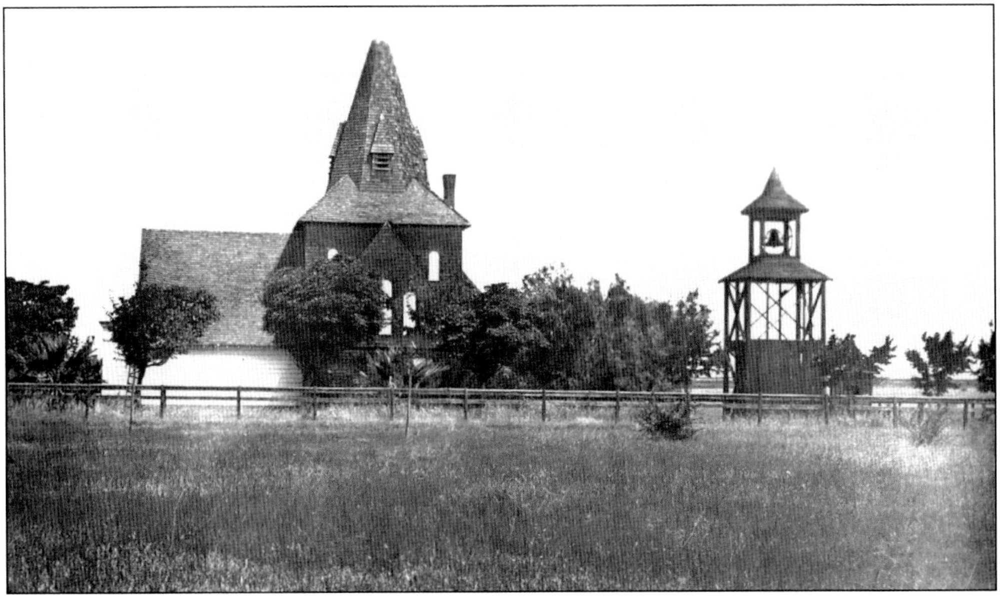

Built in 1891 by Louis and Mary Hickman, the Hickman Community Church is pictured here from the north, looking south. This image appeared on a card postmarked in Hickman on January 8, 1908, addressed to Alma Johnson (Prouty). The church building was designed after one in France. (Betty Roen.)

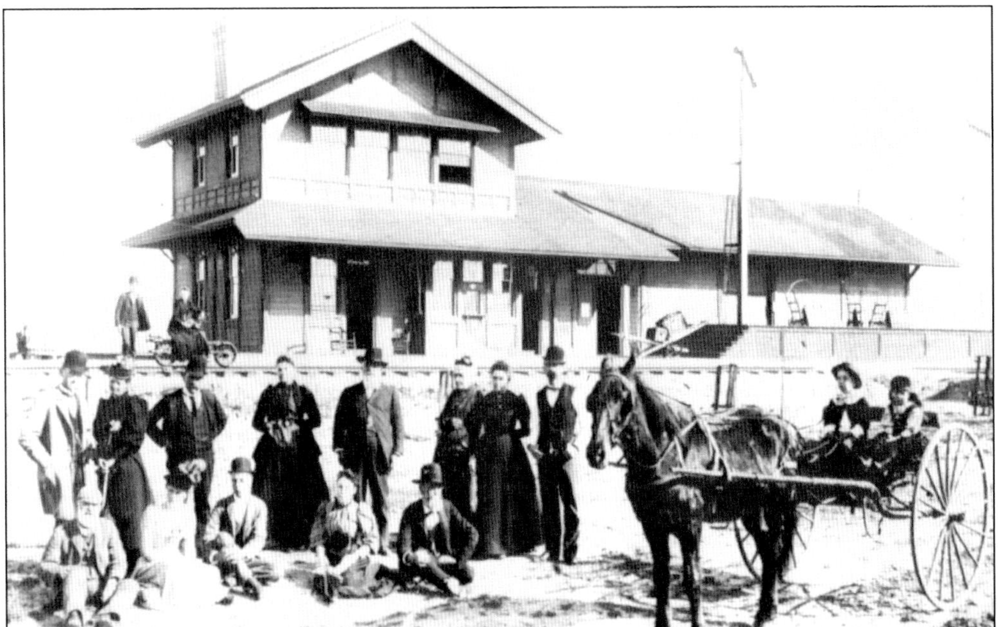

Hickman townsfolk gathered for this photograph in front of the Southern Pacific Railroad depot in Hickman around 1899. Sitting in the front are, from left to right, H. Trask, Mrs. R. Dallas, R. Dallas, R. Turner, and unidentified. Standing behind them are, from left to right, C.J. Jefferson, ? Brown, Louis M. Hickman, Clara Cogswell, O. Doolittle, Anna Grub, Annie Jefferson, and L.E. Grub. The couple on the railroad tracks are Mr. and Mrs. Frank Foster. Children Harry ? and Bernice ? are sitting in the buggy.

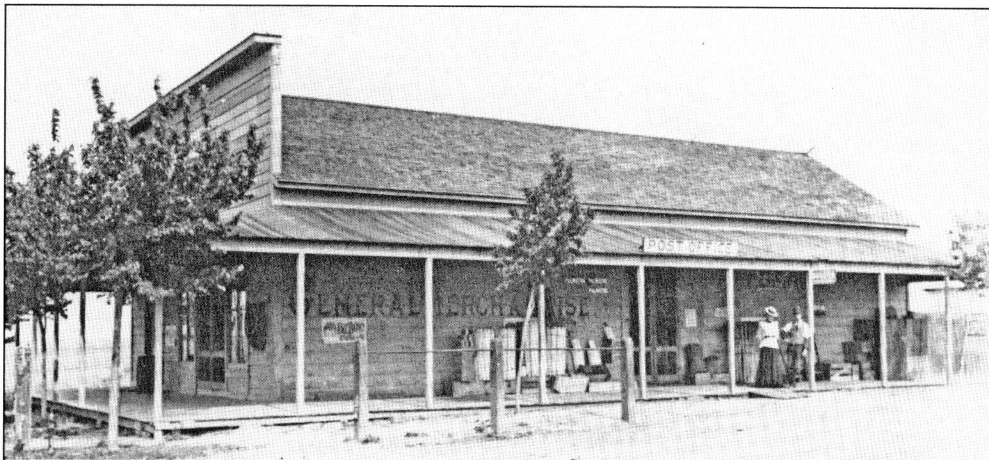

HICKMAN PAVILION

F. C. HALDEMAN, PROP.

BIG DANCE APRIL 24, 1915

Patronize the Hickman pavilion,
People go there by the million.

BEN EBEL

THE VILLAGE BLACKSMITH

HICKMAN, CAL.

Those mules and horses may kick like L,
But he'll shoe 'em up and shoe 'em well.

In 1899, the Hickman General Merchandise Store (above) doubled as the Hickman Post Office on Lake Road. By 1915, it was W.B. Warner & Co. Merchantile. A sign affixed to the side advertises Fat Boy cigars. Below are two advertisements placed by Hickman merchants in a 1915 Waterford publication. (Author's collection.)

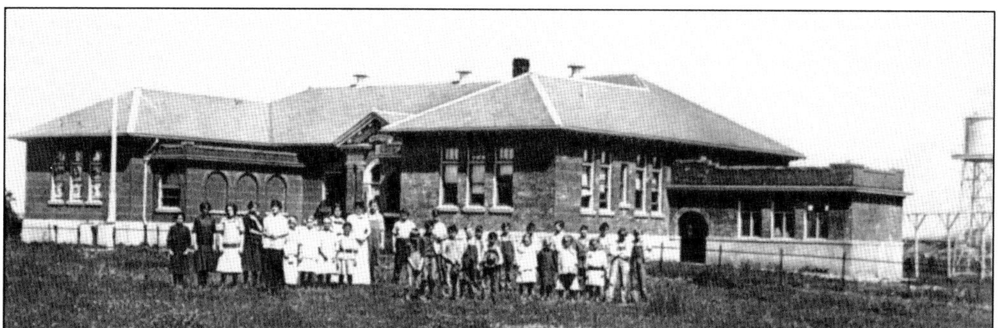

In 1911, this brick school opened in Hickman as Rowe School on its current site. (Author's collection.)

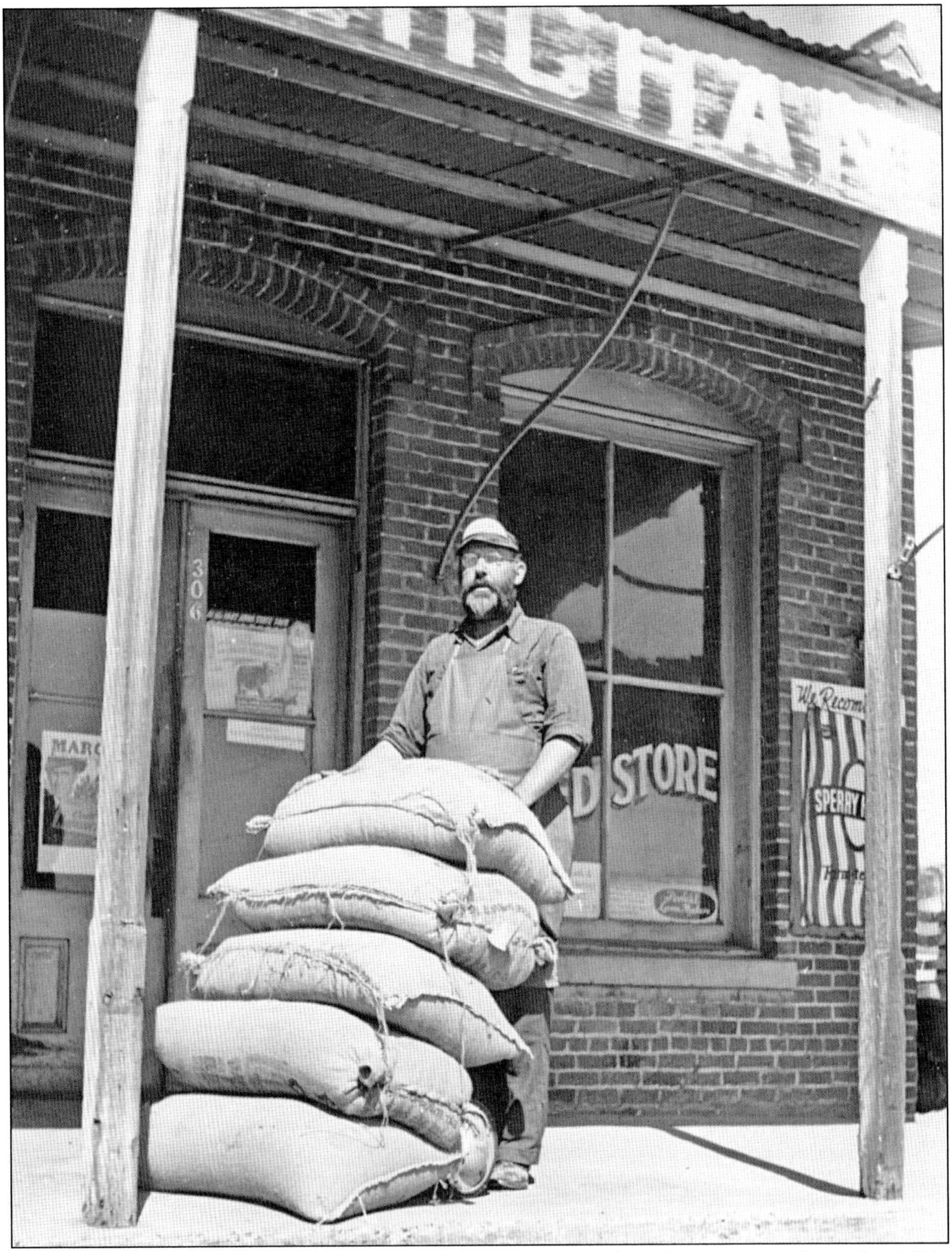

Hardy Monk stands outside of his Waterford Feed Store, which he operated from the 1930s through 1950s at the northeast corner of F Street and Bentley Street. The poster on the door has the Marco Theater in Waterford promoting Jimmy Stewart's *Call Northside 777*, released in 1948. This brick building was constructed in 1891 by John P. Harbert for a hardware and general store and closed upon his death in 1918. The building and its contents were sold in 1937; Monk purchased it and used it for the feed store. In the back of the store were living quarters used by Hardy and his father, Andrew Monk. The youngest of four children, Hardy barely missed being sent to fight in World War II when the war ended. (LaVerne Johnson.)

Five

Businesses of Long Ago
Merchants and Their Buildings

Waterford enjoyed a larger and more diverse business community in the first half of the 1900s than exists today. It hosted a varied collection of businesses in the 1920s and 1930s, including a lumberyard, a Ford garage where new automobiles were sold, and numerous grocery stores. In the 1930s, the upper floor of the Gordon Building at Bentley and E Streets served as the one-screen Marco Theater.

In 1945, Waterford was home to just 1,000 residents, and groceries were supplied by Leo Holzer at his Red and White Store on Bentley Street between D and E Streets; one block to the west was Rasmussen's Market, which succeeded Ballard's Grocery Store. Slaughter's Market on the ground floor of the Gordon Building became Calvin and Charlie Chu's Valley Food Center in the 1960s. The Chus moved their store in the 1970s to a metal building on F Street near Yosemite Boulevard. During the same time, Bill Gwin operated Sav-Mor Market at Yosemite Boulevard and Western Avenue (now site of Golden Bowl Chinese Restaurant).

In 1997, Valley IGA moved to its current location at Yosemite Boulevard and Western Avenue. Until the 1980s, Copeland Lumber operated at the site of the former United Lumber Yard at Bentley and F Streets (opposite the new post office). Other notable businesses over the years included Halbert's Store, Hardy Monk's Feed Store, Mark Royer's Blacksmith Shop, Ed Ludlow's Pool Hall, the Charlie Hall Restaurant, J.O. Armentrout's Livery Stable, Collins Meat Market, Elmer Mullin's furniture store, Kampen's Kitchen, Nolan Nickell's Bait Barn, Roy Rorabaugh's A&W Root Beer, the Waterford Auto Wreckers yard, Dizzy Dee's Dumpy Diner, and Cheap Jimmy's Cigarettes.

In 1982, Raul and Soledad Acedo opened Su Casita Mexican Restaurant at Yosemite Boulevard and Western Avenue. However, thousands remember Jimbo's Drive-In for fast food and ice cream cones between home and the lakes. It operated on Yosemite Boulevard near the main entrance to Riverpointe. Waterford Farm Supply—established by Phil and Myrna Stine—operated in the bricked Harbert Store building at the corner of Bentley and F Streets. The business is now located in the former site of the second Valley Food Center. From 1985 to 2004, Big Bear Park drew thousands of visitors to waterslides, a swimming lagoon, and RV camping.

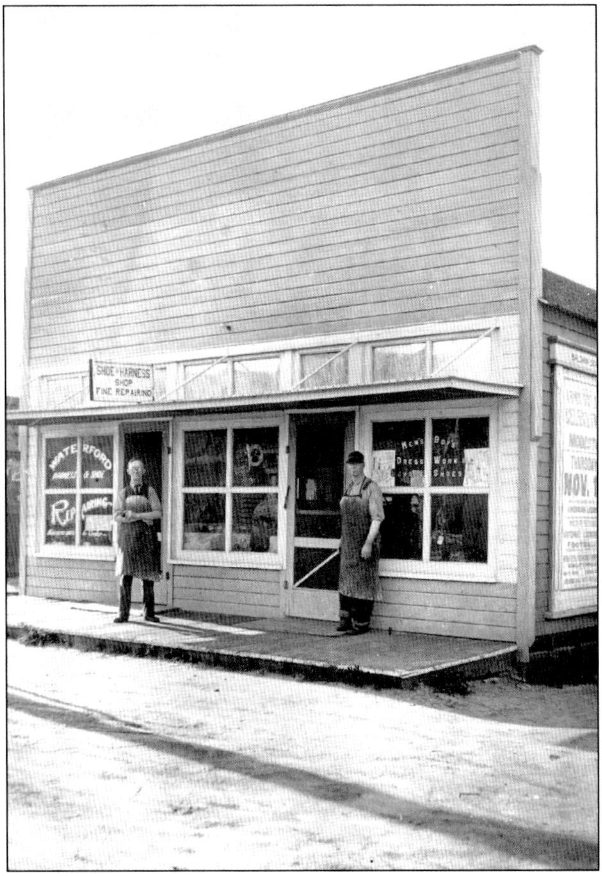

Royal Ballard operated his Shoe and Harness Shop on the north side of Bentley Street just east of F Street. Standing in front of the store in 1927 are Ballard (right) and George William Steffan. The building was a part of the Bentley Street commercial district from 1918 until 1930 and was moved to Albin Crabtree's ranch east of Roberts Ferry. Ballard died in 1956. (Waterford Historical Society.)

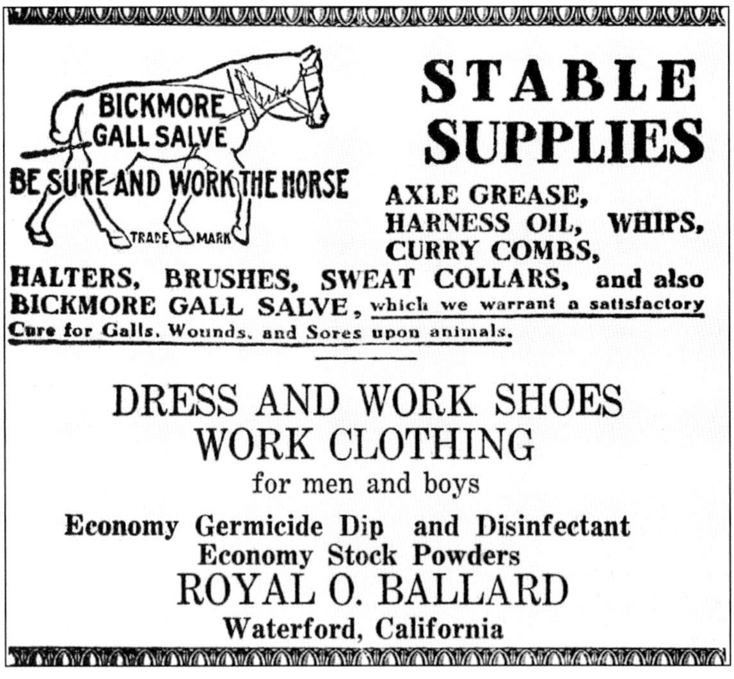

Royal Ballard took out this advertisement for his Shoe and Harness Shop in the March 13, 1931, edition of the *Waterford News* to advertise his products. (Waterford Historical Society.)

Charles Chester Horsley was a prominent businessman involved with the family's Red House Mercantile. Horsley attended Dry Creek School northeast of Waterford and went to Heald College. He helped organize and was a stockholder in the Commercial and Savings Bank in Waterford. Horsley also helped organize the Waterford Irrigation District in 1913 as its first secretary. He was postmaster from 1893 to 1897 and justice of the peace.

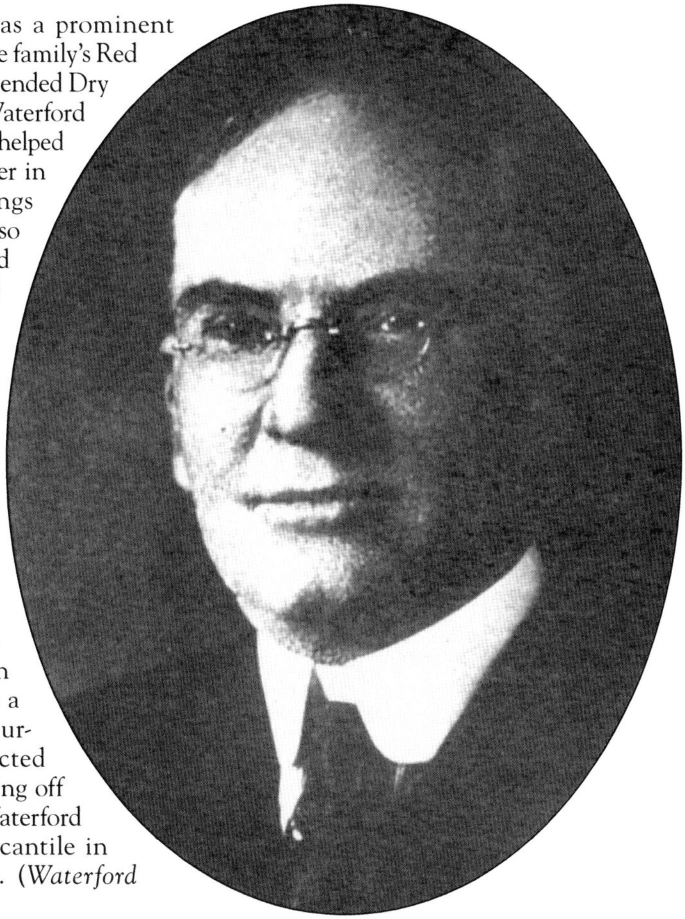

J.R. Horsley and Sons established their Red House store first at the northeast corner of Bentley and E Streets on July 4, 1892. The store had the advertising slogan of "Everything from a Pen to a Combine Harvester." A four-foot-tall porch was constructed to accommodate those stepping off of wagons or buggies. The Waterford store was a branch of a mercantile in Snelling. J.R. died in 1914. (*Waterford Centennial: 1857–1957.*)

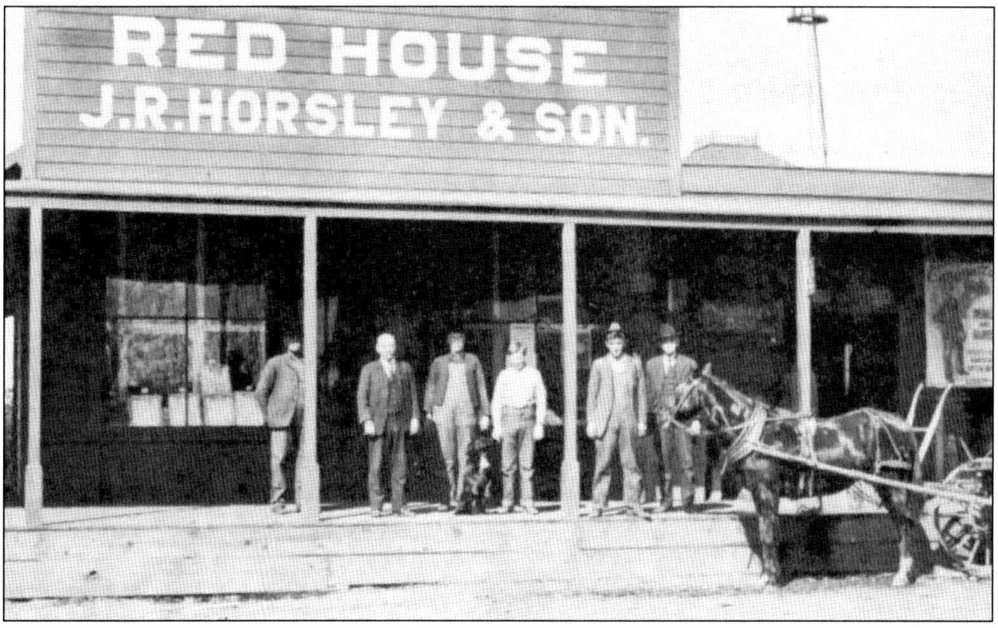

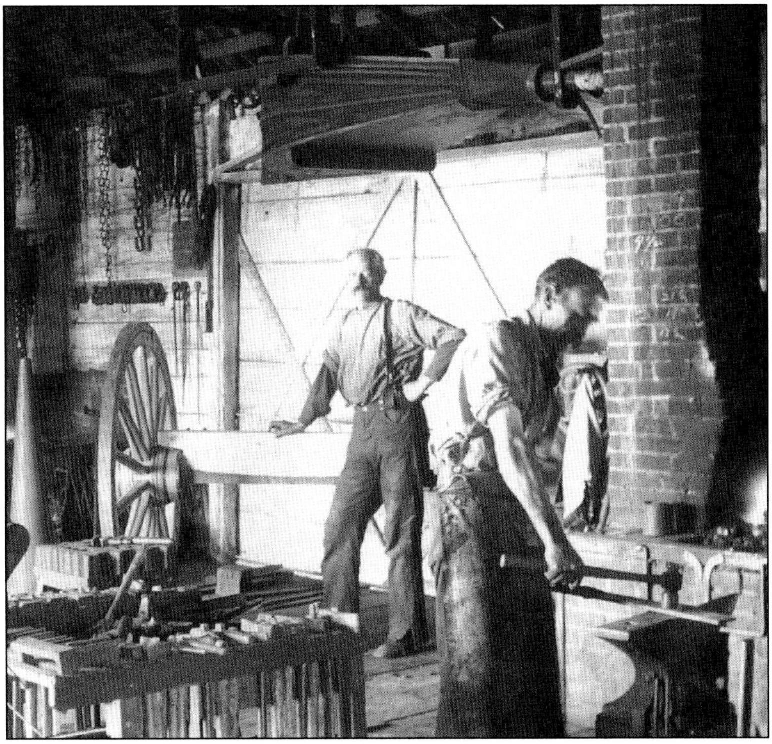

Joe Prouty was the blacksmith in Waterford. He first settled in Roberts Ferry in 1869 when he was just 17 years old with friend Edward Shaw. He opened his blacksmith shop in 1880 at Yosemite Boulevard and Old Hickman Road. Prouty and his men could shoe 50 to 60 horses and mules in one visit before the animals were put to use pulling harvesters. (Betty Roen.)

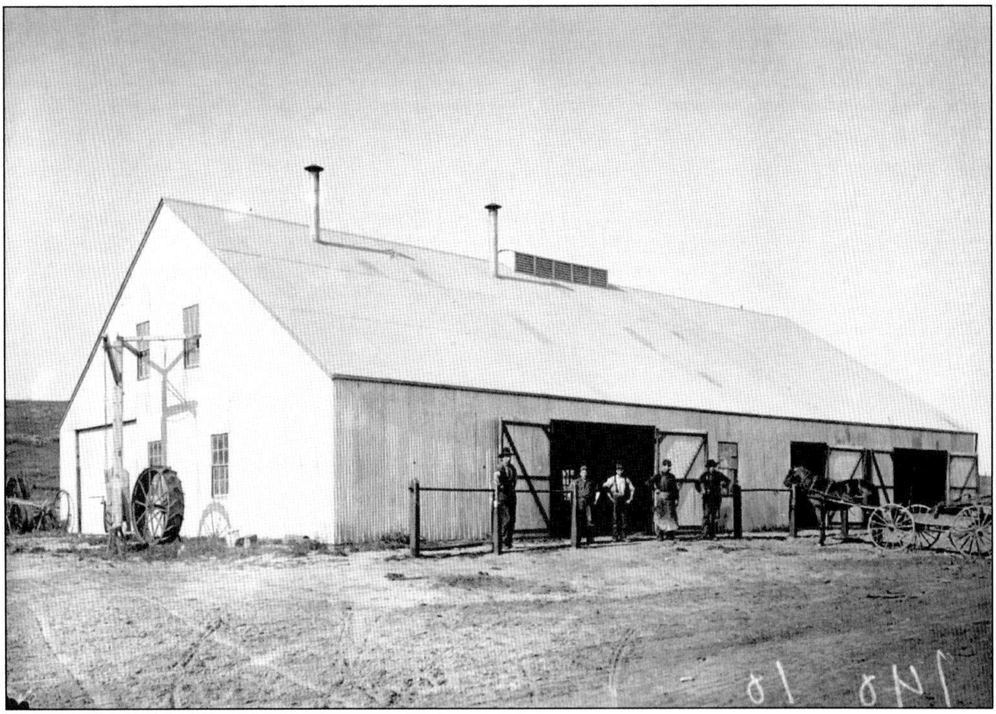

This was Joe Prouty's blacksmith shop, which was situated on Yosemite Boulevard east of Tim Bell Road. In this c. 1905 photograph, a horse and buggy are seen at right. The hill behind the metal shop is north of the old town site of Bakersville. (Betty Roen.)

WATERFORD LIVERY STABLE

J. O. ARMENTROUT

To show your girl what you're about,
Come get a rig from Armentrout.
And if you think a horse too slow.
He keeps a Ford now, don't y' know?

H. H. TURPEN

Waterford, Cal.

Contractor and Builder

Bungalow or Bungalhigh
He will build for you or I.

New Method Laundry

BERT COWDEN, AGENT

Waterford, Cal.

When you clothes are greasy and covered with dirt, just bring them around and leave them with Bert.

WATERFORD HOTEL

C. A. WALTHER

PROPRIETOR

When supper is o'er,
'Tis a good place to snore.

This space was reserved and paid for,
But the ad failed to come through,
Because the man found
That his button was all blue.
To tell his name, we couldn't to save us,
But we think, perhaps, it was Evie Davis.

NOTE—Evie says he can't cook much, but will help carry the water.

Mrs. T. BRESCIA

La Grange, Cal.

GENERAL MERCHANDISE

A great big store with a great big biz; everyone knows where it is.

EUGENE BRADFORD

LA GRANGE, CAL.

Pool Hall and Cigar Stand

Come roll the balls upon the table,
Or have a smoke of any label.

J. M. FINLEY

Waterford, Cal.

"Nothing to advertise," says he.
"Just take this coin, and let me be."

POOL HALL AND SOFT DRINKS

F. C. HALDEMAN

Hickman, Cal.

Welcome, men folks, young or shady; but Thursday nights you must bring your lady.

J. A. McMILLAN

Waterford, Cal.

Expert Harvester Repairer

Also Agent for the Harris M'f'g Co.'s Extras

For the best work this side of Boston
Don't forget to call on Austin.

W. B. Warner & Co.

Hickman, California

GENERAL MERCHANDISE

For things to eat, and prices low,
This is the place you want to go.

MISS LUCILE SQUIBB

TEACHER OF

VIOLIN AND PIANO

A little music in the home will lend good cheer and proper tone

---

This page of advertisement came from a Waterford Band Concert program of April 10, 1915. The event featured a three-act comedy-drama called *Diamonds and Hearts*. The brochure mentions that "They say that Waterford band (with the aid of the bull frogs and coyotes) is hot stuff." The program cost 5¢ apiece and were sold at Horsley's Store. (Betty Roen.)

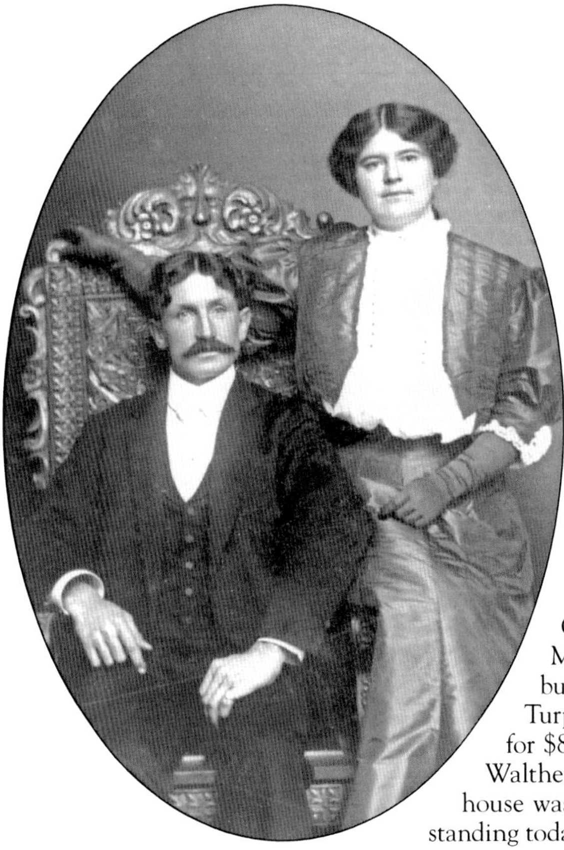

Contractor Henry Hampton Turpen built a number of early residences in Waterford. In 1906, he constructed the house (below) on D Street north of Main Street that later became the Baptist Church's first parsonage. Henry married Mary Susan Carmichael on June 6, 1906, but she died in childbirth on April 9, 1908. Turpen sold the house in 1908 to the church for $800. In 1915, Turpen married Ruth May Walther, and she bore him seven children. The house was used by the church for 36 years and is standing today. (Both, Valerie Turpen.)

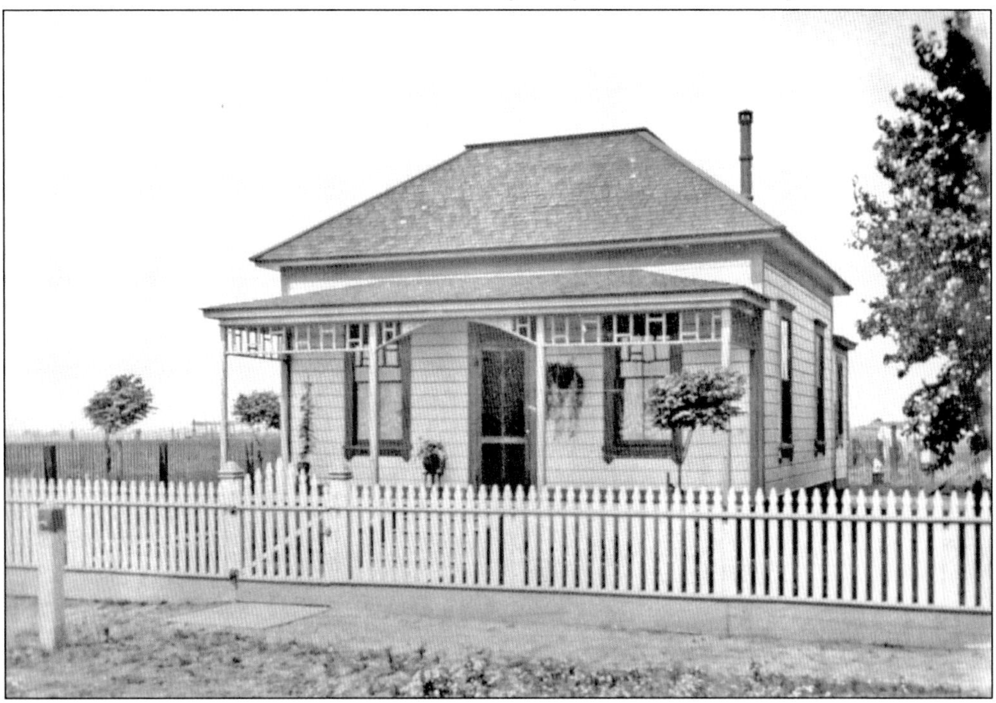

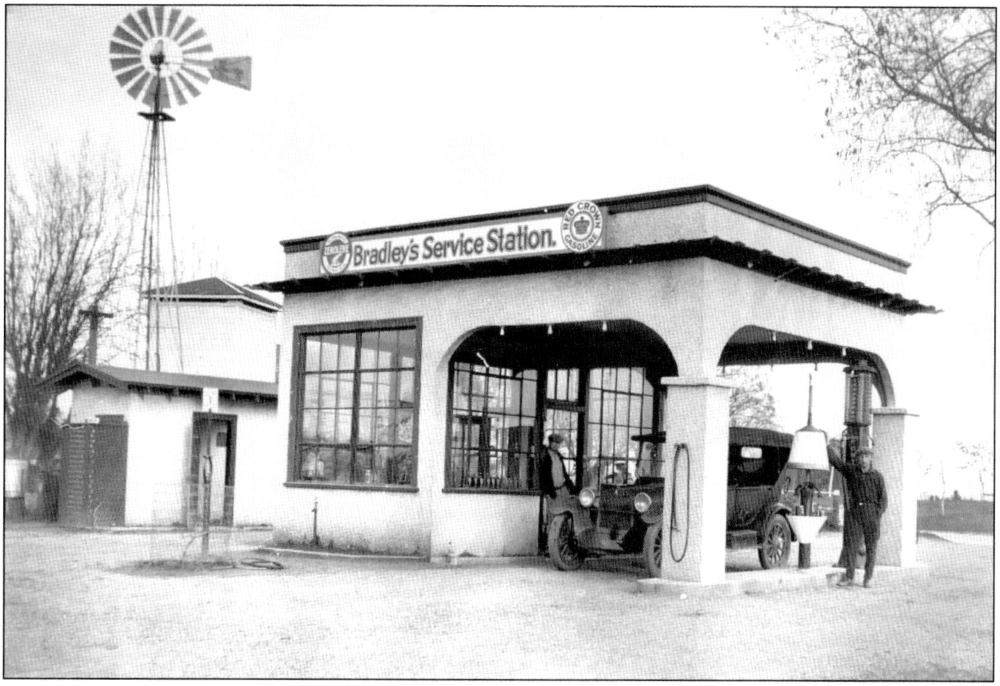

In 1927, Shorty Bradley operated this service station at the northeast corner of Yosemite Boulevard and E Street. Zerolene and Red Crown gasoline brands were offered for the first cars, all under the convenience of a canopy. Shorty was reported to have killed a sea lion that made its way to Waterford up the Tuolumne River. (Waterford Historical Society.)

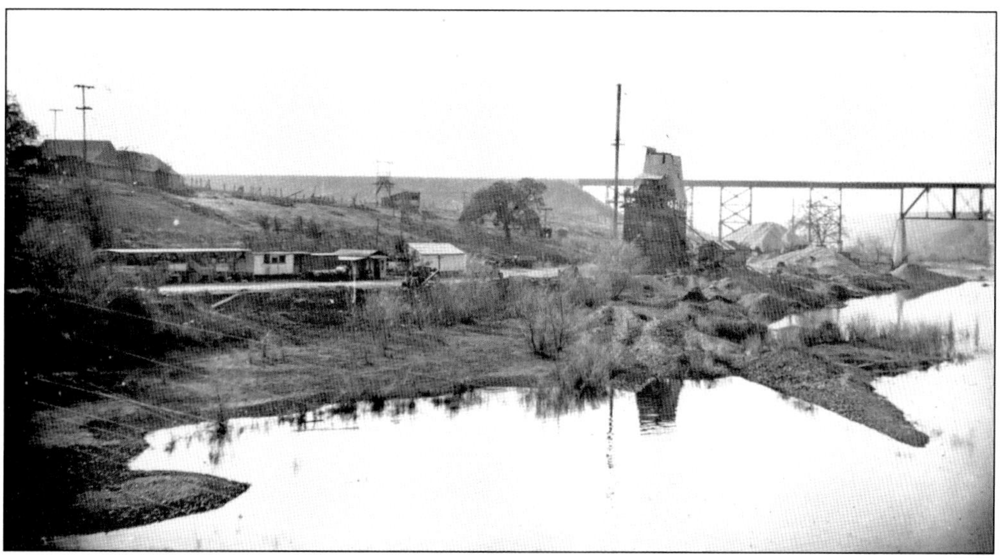

This 1927 photograph shows a gravel plant that operated on the Hickman side of the Tuolumne River east of the iron railroad trestle. The trestle came down in 1978. (Waterford Historical Society.)

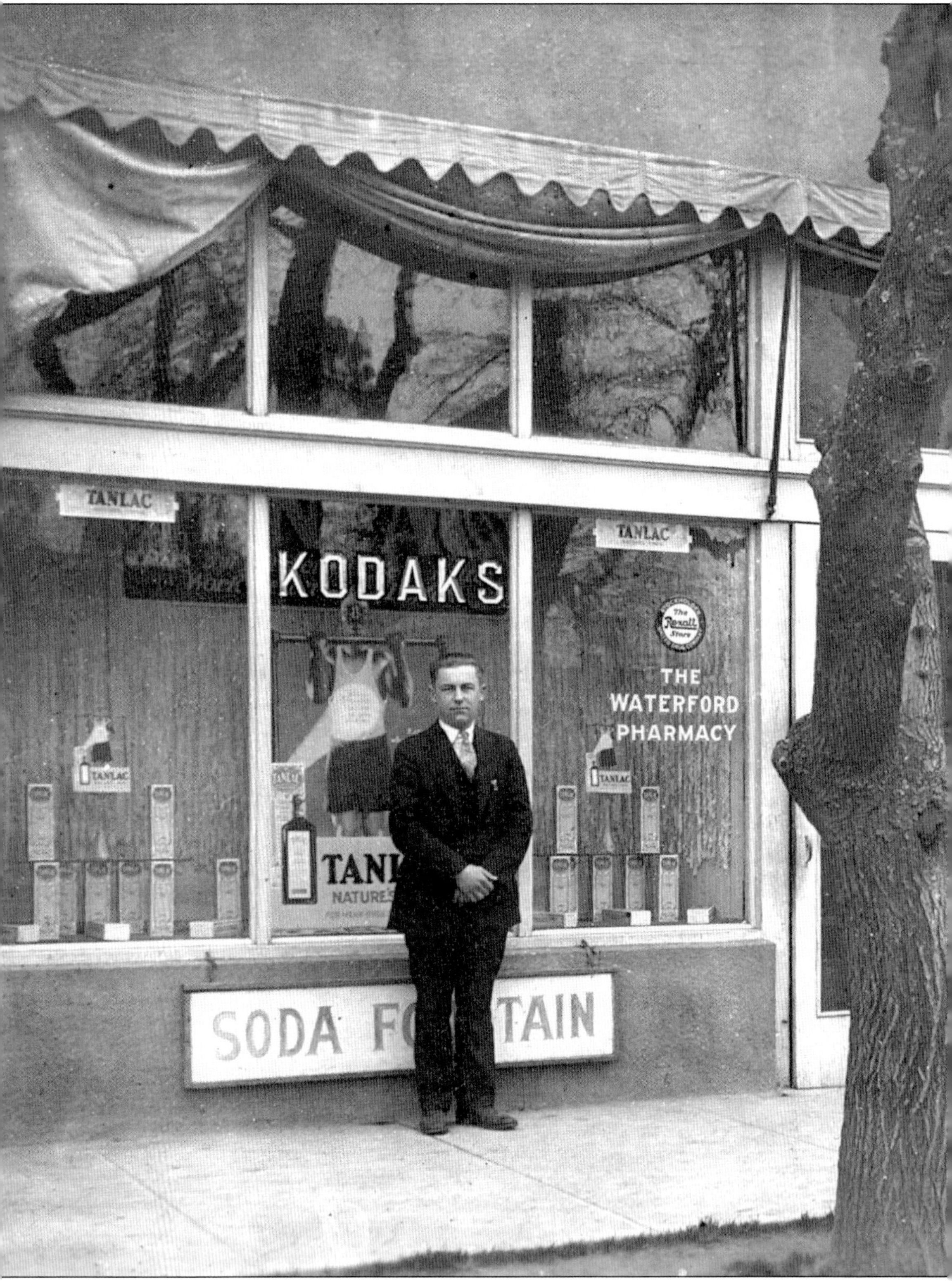
TANLAC
TANLAC
KODAKS
THE
WATERFORD
PHARMACY
TANLAC
TANLAC
SODA FO TAIN

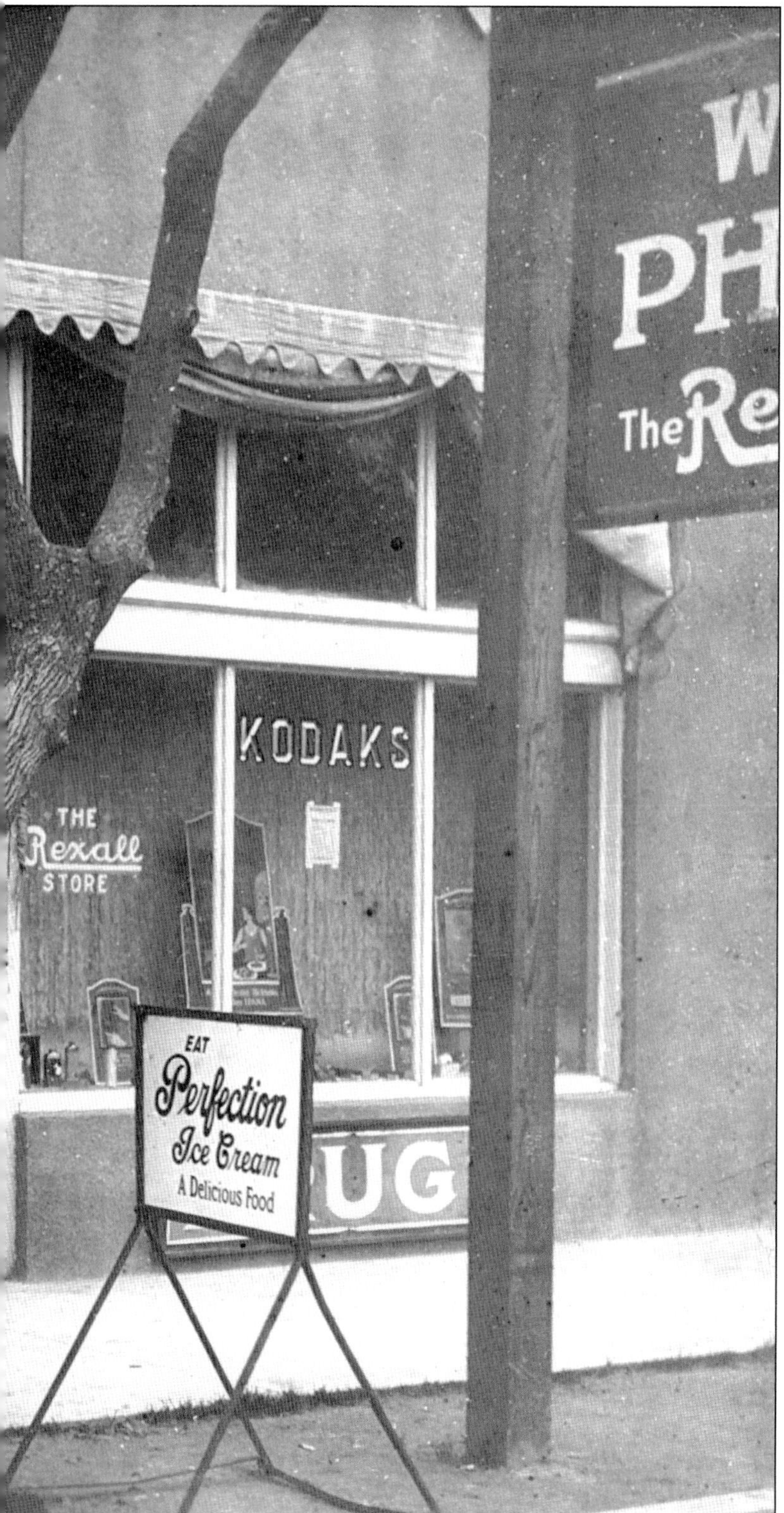

Maurice "Shorty" A. Rager served as the town pharmacist from 1923 to 1976. Rager first worked for town druggist J.L. Hennemuth and then opened his own Waterford Pharmacy, seen here in 1927. This business operated in part of the Ford garage building on the south side of Bentley Street, just east of F Street—approximately where Lyndale's and Shirley's Fabrics used to be. Rager's pharmacy included an ice cream and soda fountain. He later moved his pharmacy to the Wallis Hardware building across the street, where Quesenberry's Pharmacy operates today. Rager lived in the house on E Street between Quesenberry's and the Waterford fire station. Once a fire chief in Waterford, Rager was born in 1903 and died in 1987, leaving behind wife Evelyn Rager, also a drugstore employee. (Waterford Historical Society.)

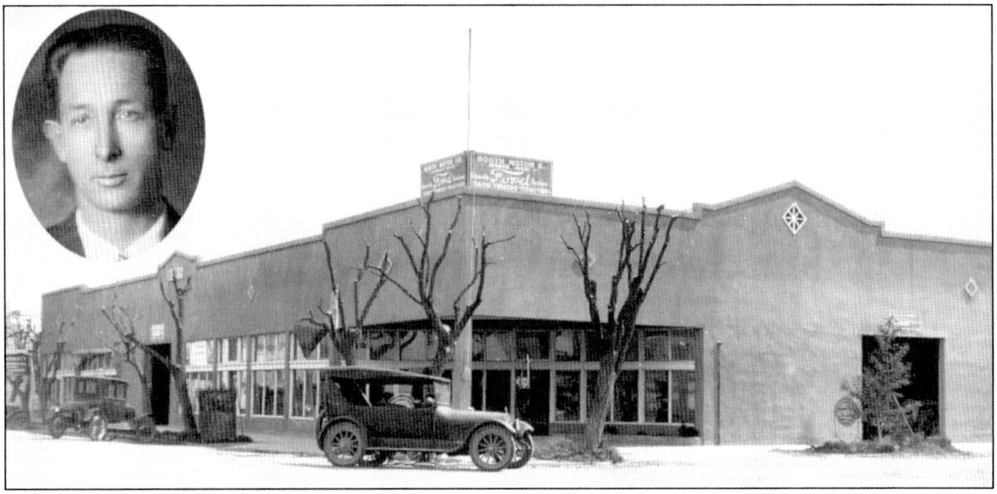

The Boothe Motor Company, or Ford garage, occupied the southeast corner of Bentley Street and F Street in 1927. Ralph Weichert (inset) and a Mr. Deaver were partners in a car dealership in 1931. In 1934, the Depression caused the business to fold. The blackboard advertises gas at 18¢ per gallon. Before the garage was built, a saloon sat on this corner. Chesley "Chet" Bentley, born in 1894, bought the garage in 1920. The building housed a radio shop in 1937, but it closed a year later. It was leveled in 1942 and replaced by a church. (Waterford Historical Society.)

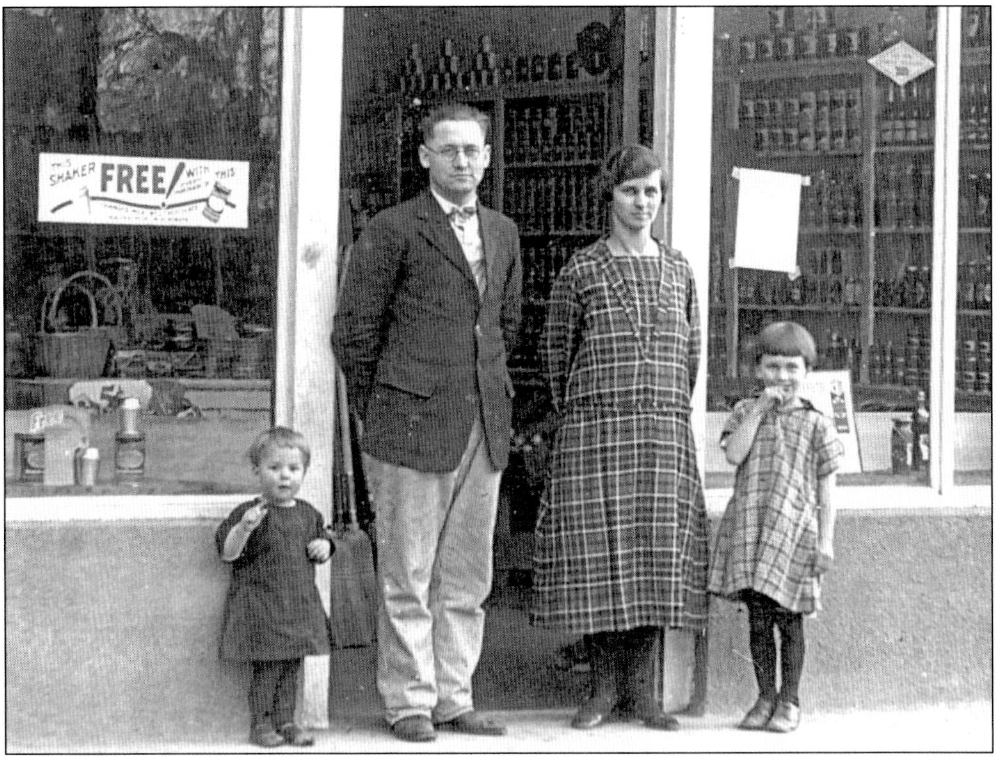

The Waterford Cash Grocery was operated by Judge Chapin, pictured here with his family. The store was operated in the eastern section of the Booth Ford garage building facing north on Bentley Street and just west of the alley. The store was later operated by A.J. Howard and Edna Kirkpatrick. (Waterford Historical Society.)

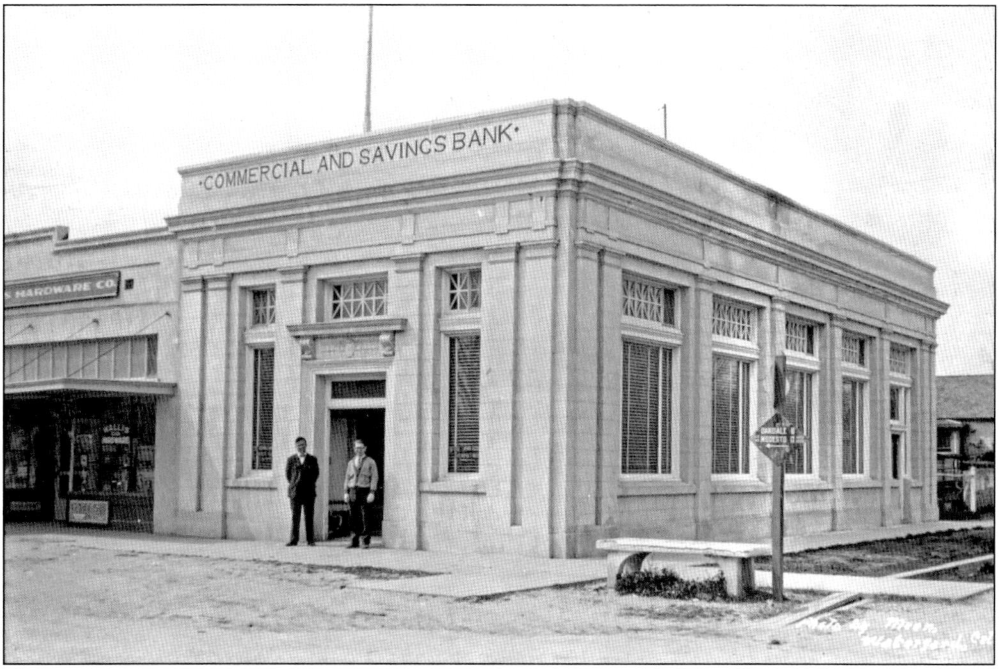

The Commercial and Savings Bank of Waterford was established in the 1920s at the northwest corner of Bentley and E Streets. The building was later used as the Waterford Court. The bank was robbed on February 16, 1931, when two robbers took $3,700 from cashier S.E. Ayer and clerk Virgil Spoonmore. Suspects Vaughn Coley and Francis Hardeman were apprehended in a small cave near Hazeldean Road after Sheriff Grat Hogin organized a manhunt. The bank folded in 1933, in part because of worthless Waterford Irrigation District bonds. (Waterford Historical Society.)

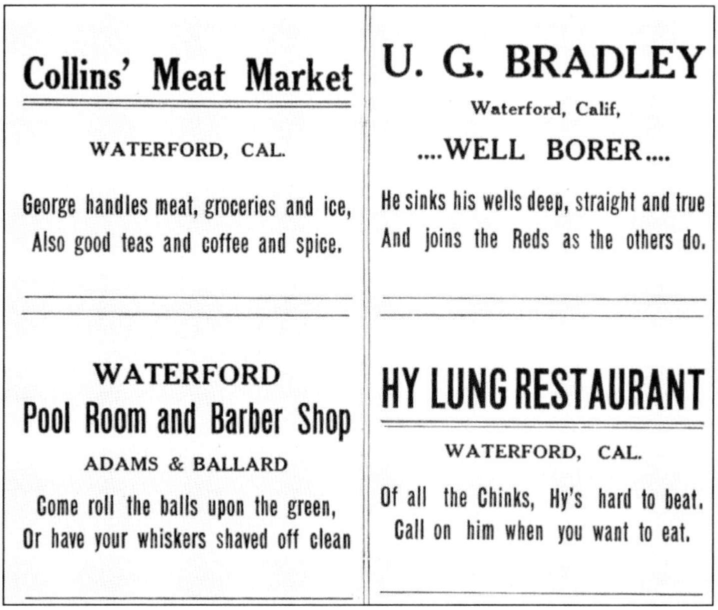

A section of advertisement from the 1915 Waterford Band Concert program shows advertisements for Collins's Meat Market, well-borer U.G. Bradley, the Waterford Pool Room and Barber Shop, and the Hy Lung Restaurant. Locals wrote the clever rhymes included in the ads. (Betty Roen.)

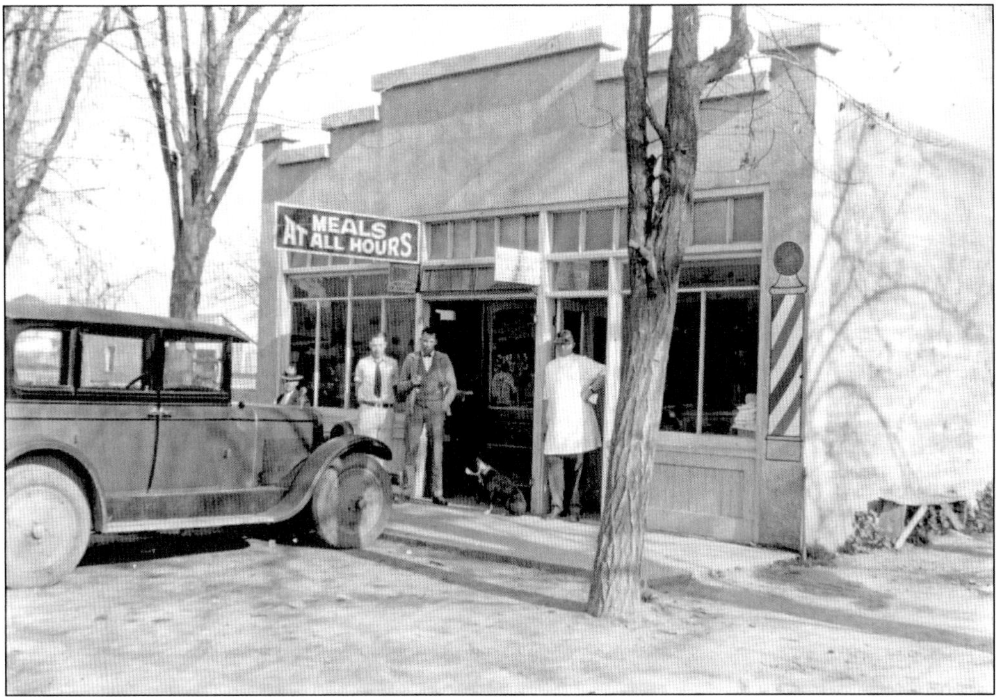

Ed Ludlow operated this barbershop, which still stands at 12634 Bentley Street between E Street and the alleyway at mid-block. Pictured from left to right in this 1927 photograph are Bill Keep, Elmer Mullin, and Ed Ludlow. The business, later operated by Ted Brooks, combined several services under one roof. Meals were offered, as were haircuts. A sign in front notes the services of Modesto Steam Laundry. (Waterford Historical Society.)

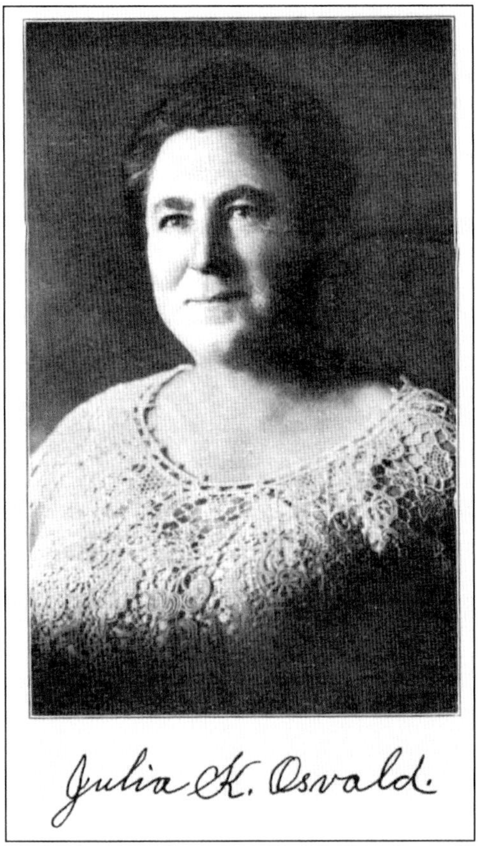

Born in 1864 in Bohemia, Julia Osvald was an early Waterford and Hickman businesswoman. She and her husband, Karel J. Osvald, owned lots on Front Street (later renamed F Street), and he managed a store and shoe shop while Julia ran a high-class rooming house. In 1907, they bought 83 acres in Hickman, where they ran a dairy. The story is told that she caught Chinaman George "fishing" for turkeys she kept penned up at her place.

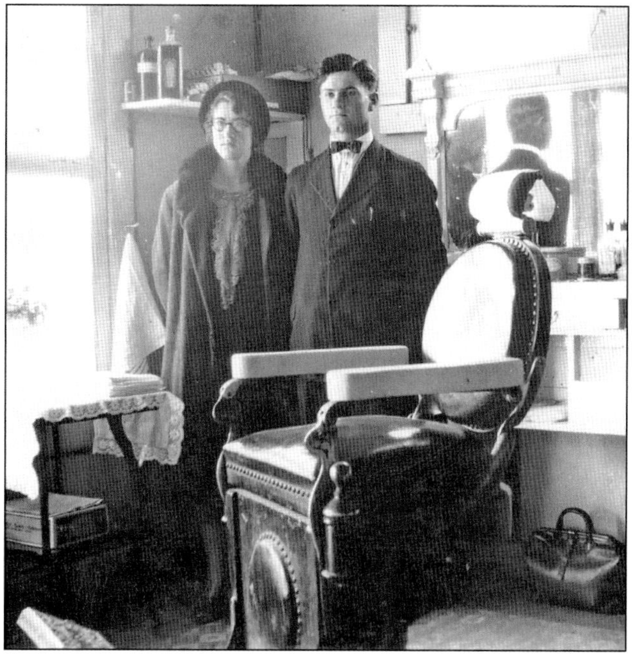

Glen Murrey stands inside his barbershop in Waterford with his wife, Beulah Peters Murrey, in 1927. The shop was located on the west side of E Street between Bentley and Welch Streets. (Waterford Historical Society.)

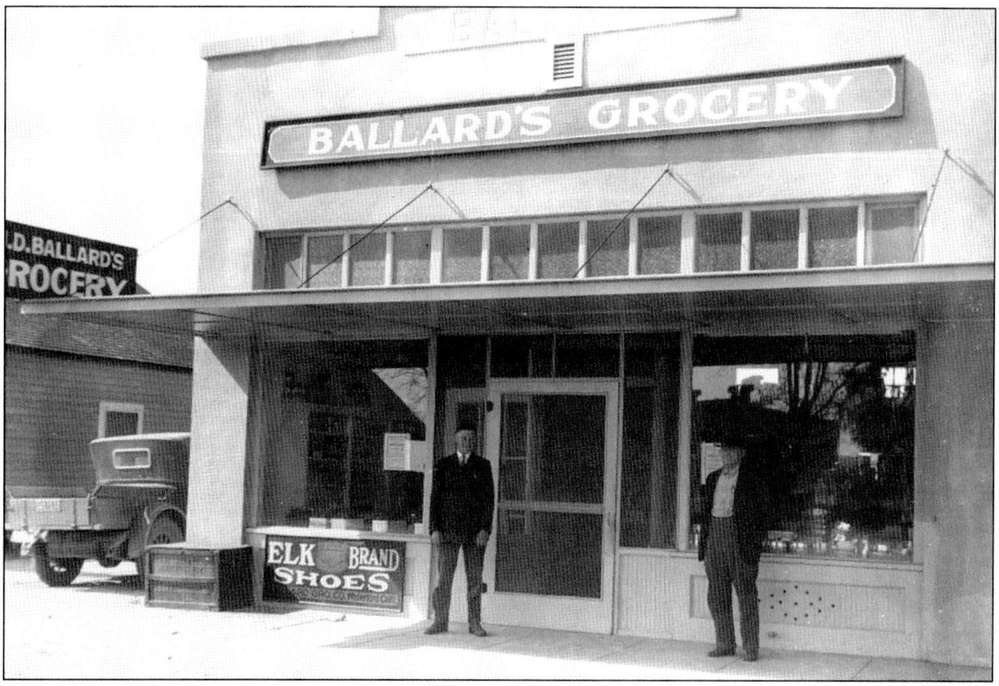

Ballard's Grocery was located on Bentley Street between E and F Streets in the western end of the commercial structure built a year prior. Owner Merton "Mert" Ballard and Earl Zimmer stand in front of the store here in 1927. A sign on front reads, "Elk Brand Shoes, Ballard Gro. Co., Waterford, Calif.," while the box is stamped San Joaquin Baking Company. Alfreda Ballard later ran the store after her husband's passing. In 1944, she sold it to Albert Rasmussen, who changed its name to Rasmussen's Grocery. Rasmussen became terminally ill, and when he took his life in 1955, the townspeople were shocked. (Waterford Historical Society.)

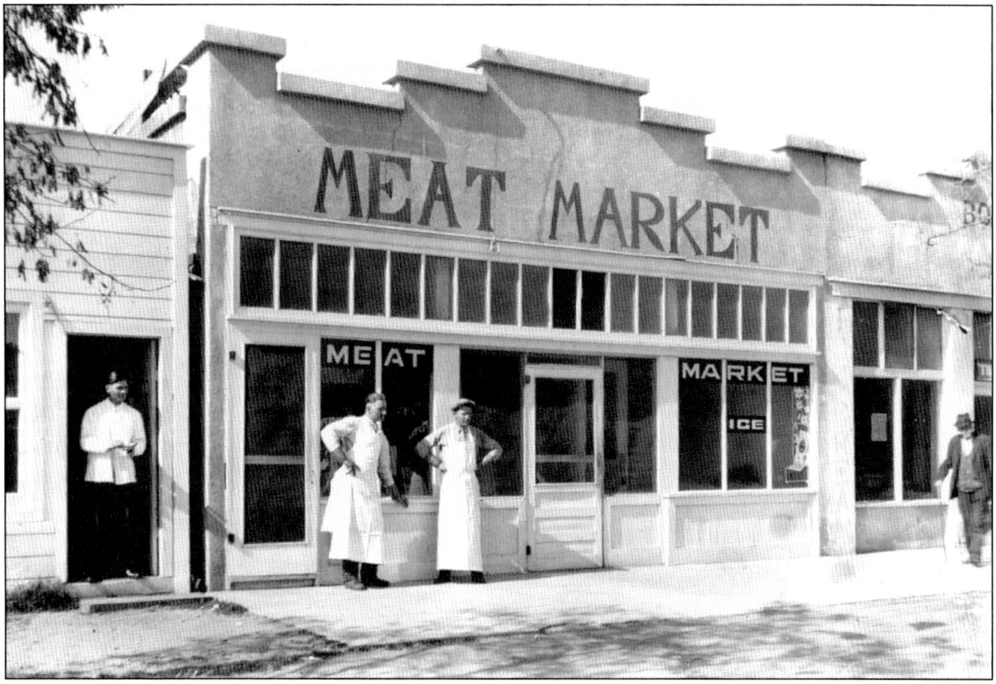

Brothers Oden (right center) and Pete Rudi (left center) operated the Waterford Meat Market on E Street in downtown Waterford. The market, shown here in 1927, also sold blocks of ice for original iceboxes before the days of refrigeration. Their father, Ole Rudi, came to Waterford from Norway in 1905. Oden Rudi later had a son named Joe Rudi, the famous Oakland A's baseball player. (Waterford Historical Society.)

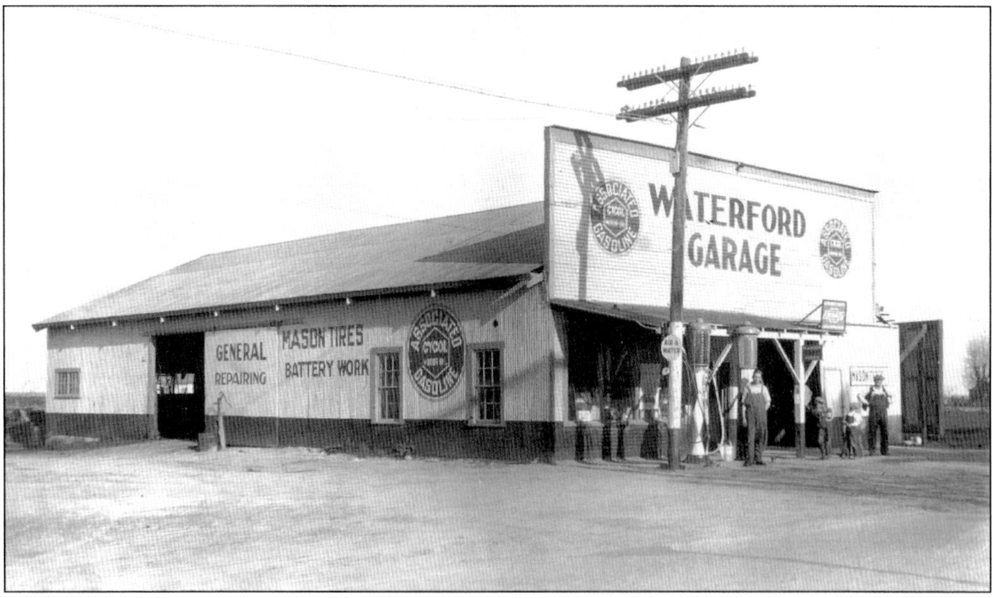

The Waterford Garage was constructed by Chet Bentley at E Street and Welch Street. The shop was owned by Noah Disler in 1927. Robert "Bob" Carpenter Sr., who came to Waterford in 1923 from Indiana, bought the shop with his brother Cecil "Si" Carpenter in 1929. Bob operated the garage until 1973. It was later Chuck Shepherd's Waterford Auto Parts. (Waterford Historical Society.)

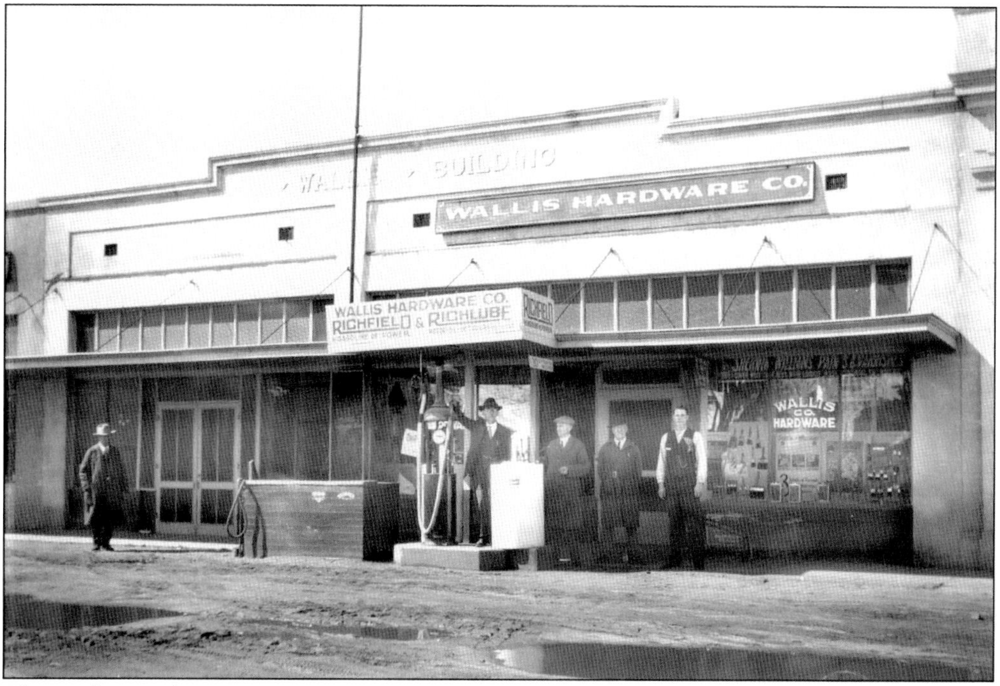

The Wallis Hardware Company operated in the Wallis Building, now site of Quesenberry's Pharmacy. The business, pictured in 1927, sold gas at the edge of the sidewalk. Pictured are Fred Wallis (center, with his hand on the pump) and two brothers with the last name of Cooper. The building was constructed in 1920 by Fred's father, James Wallis, who first came to Montpelier from Wisconsin in 1879 and permanently settled in 1906. (Waterford Historical Society.)

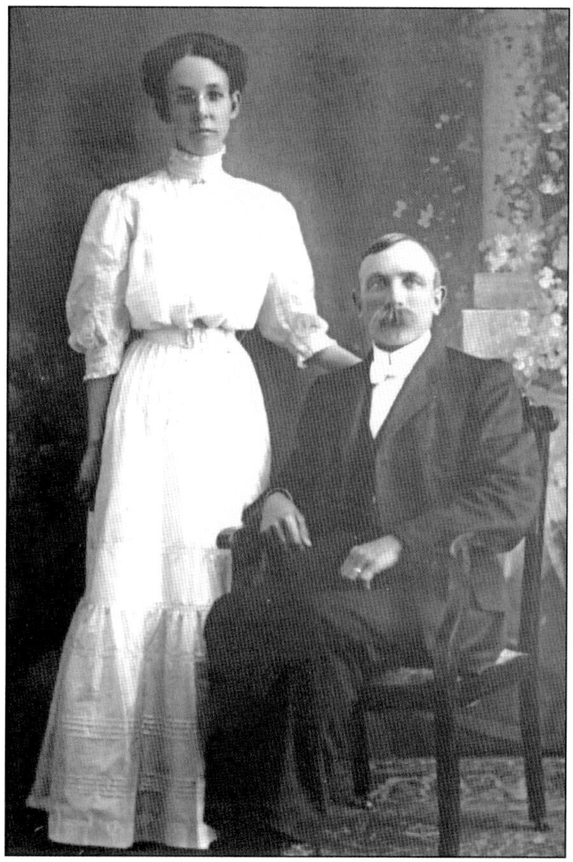

Charlie Nielsen and Carrie Monk were married on November 2, 1908, in Waterford. Born in 1875, Charlie immigrated from Denmark in 1898. He took over father-in-law Andrew Monk's grain farm north of Dry Creek in 1910. He farmed grain and had a dairy herd. In 1941, the pair became caretakers of the Modesto Reservoir for about 10 years. His trademark bushy mustache and smile were familiar in the Waterford business community. (Carl Nielsen.)

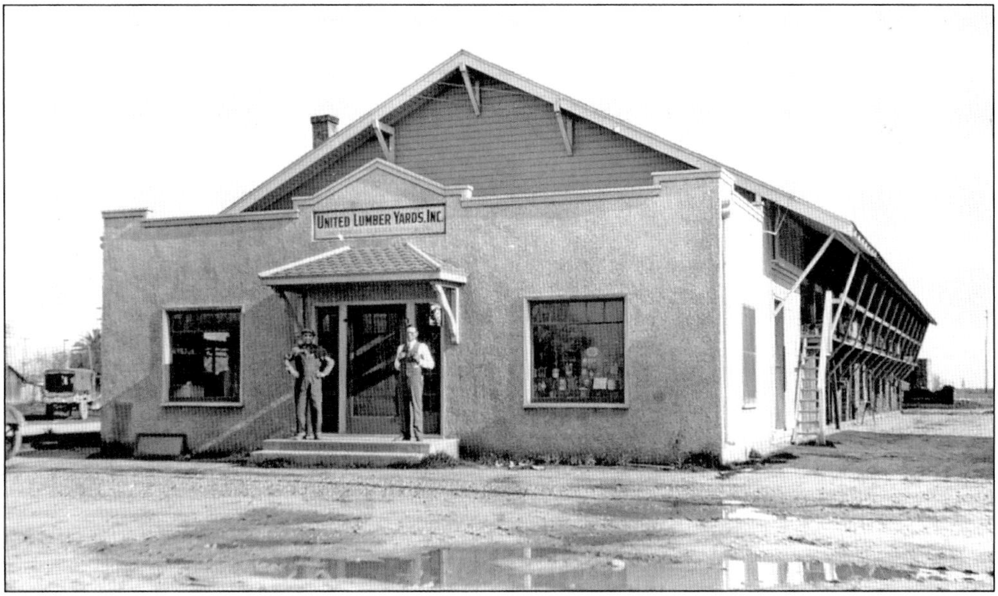

United Lumber Yards, seen here in 1927, operated at the southwest corner of Bentley and F Streets. It was later operated as Copeland Lumber. Standing outside the business are Charlie Switzer (left) and George Thomas (some accounts say P.O. Osvald.) The building is used to this day. (Waterford Historical Society.)

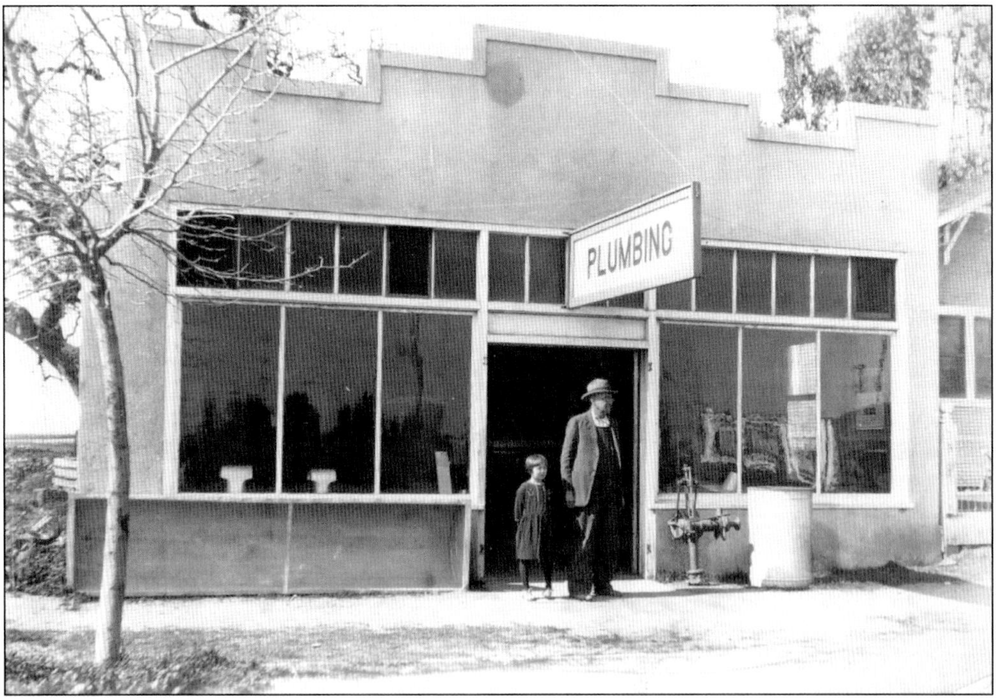

Bob Fike ran his plumbing shop on E Street south of Welch Street in the 1920s. Fike lived in a room in the back of the shop. Later, this building was used for the *Waterford News*. In the 1980s and 1990s, this building was used as a laundromat. (Waterford Historical Society.)

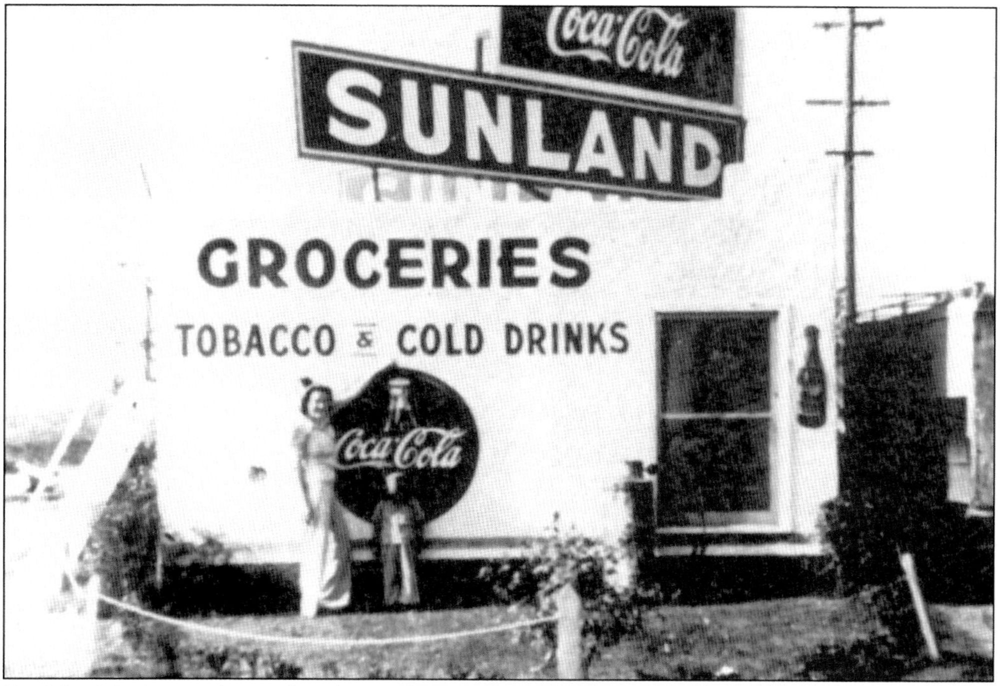

Sav-Mor Market was located at the southeast corner of Yosemite Boulevard and Western Avenue. Standing in front are owners Edna and Daryl Howe. The store went through different hands, first to Buel Brooks and then to Chick Brooks, who owned it up until 1944. Last operated by Bill and Betty Gwin, the market was later razed. The lot now bears a small shopping center that includes Golden Bowl Chinese restaurant. (Walt Switzer.)

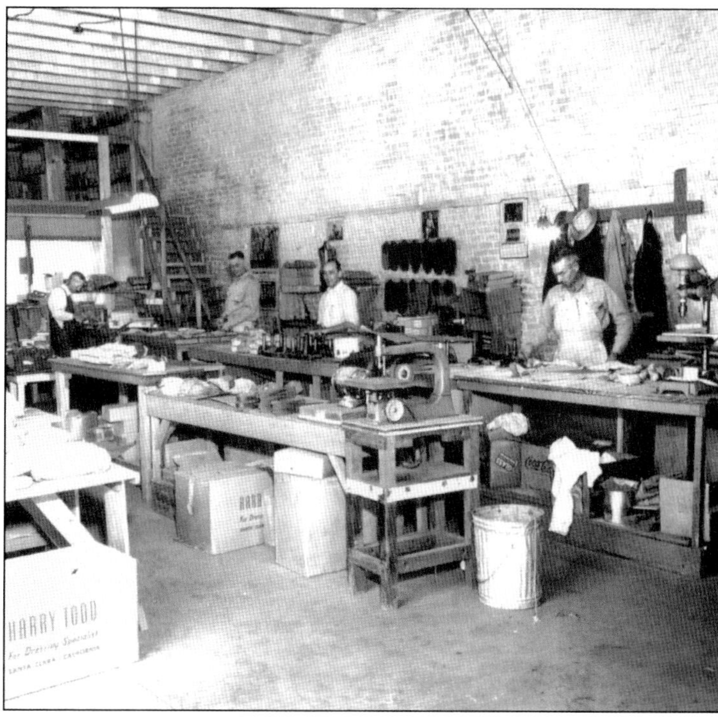

The Tilco Glove Shop was located in the old bank building at the corner of Bentley and E Streets during the 1940s. The company made leather gloves, moccasins, jackets, and cobbler aprons. Pictured are owner John Tilman (second from right) and Jim Word (right). The identity of the others is unknown. (Waterford Historical Society.)

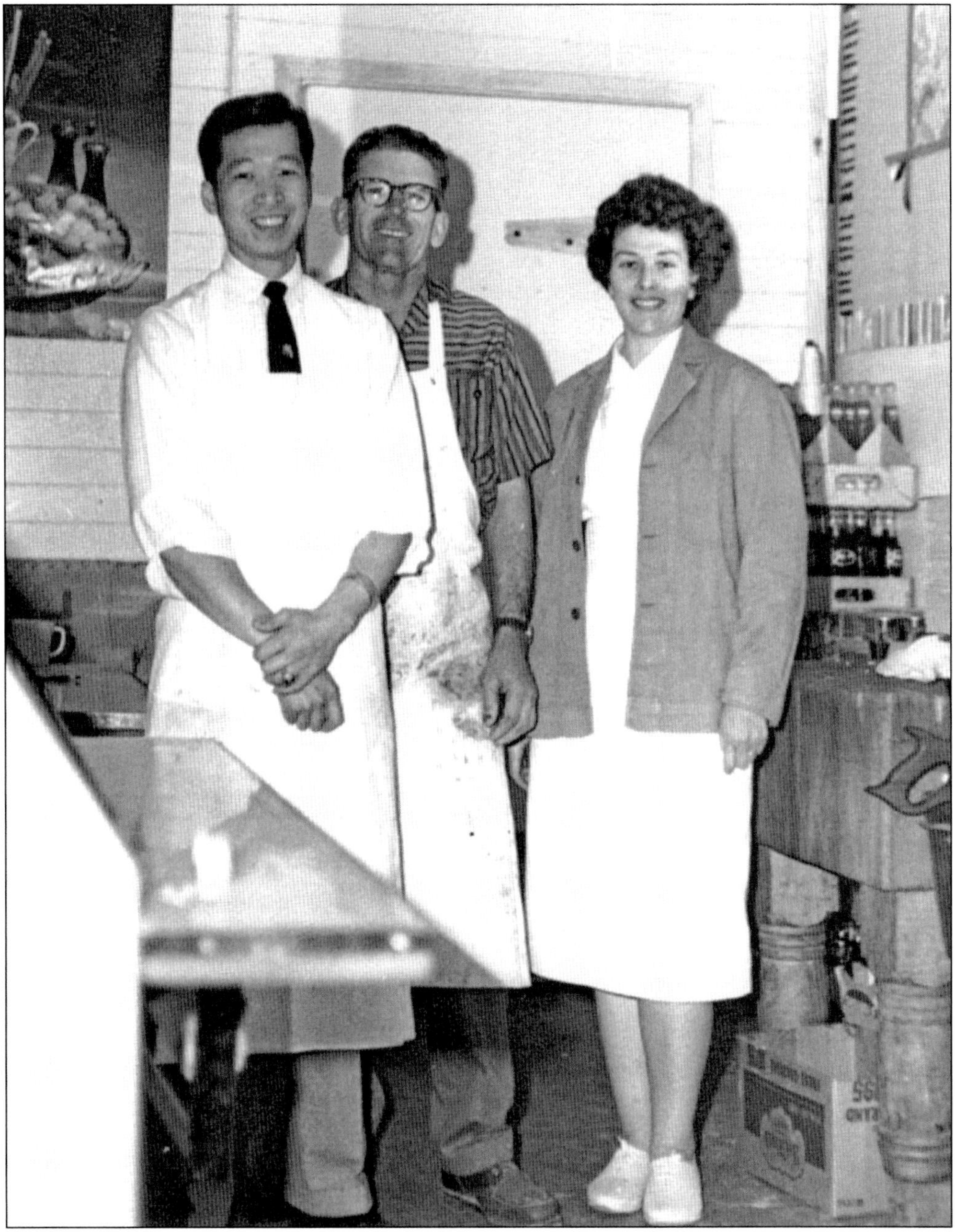

Calvin Chu (left) and brother Charlie Chu (not pictured) purchased Slaughter's Market in 1960 from Waterford butcher Curtis Slaughter (center) and his wife, Allene (right). Born in 1908, Curtis Slaughter came to Waterford in 1936 and sold ice in the Waterford area for City Ice and Fuel Company. He purchased a meat market from Lyle Couchman in 1955 and sold the business in 1960 to the Chus. Slaughter continued working as a butcher for the Chus until he decided to build his own meat locker in 1964 in the adjacent lot. Slaughter was a butcher until a year before his death in 1971. (Calvin and Peggy Chu.)

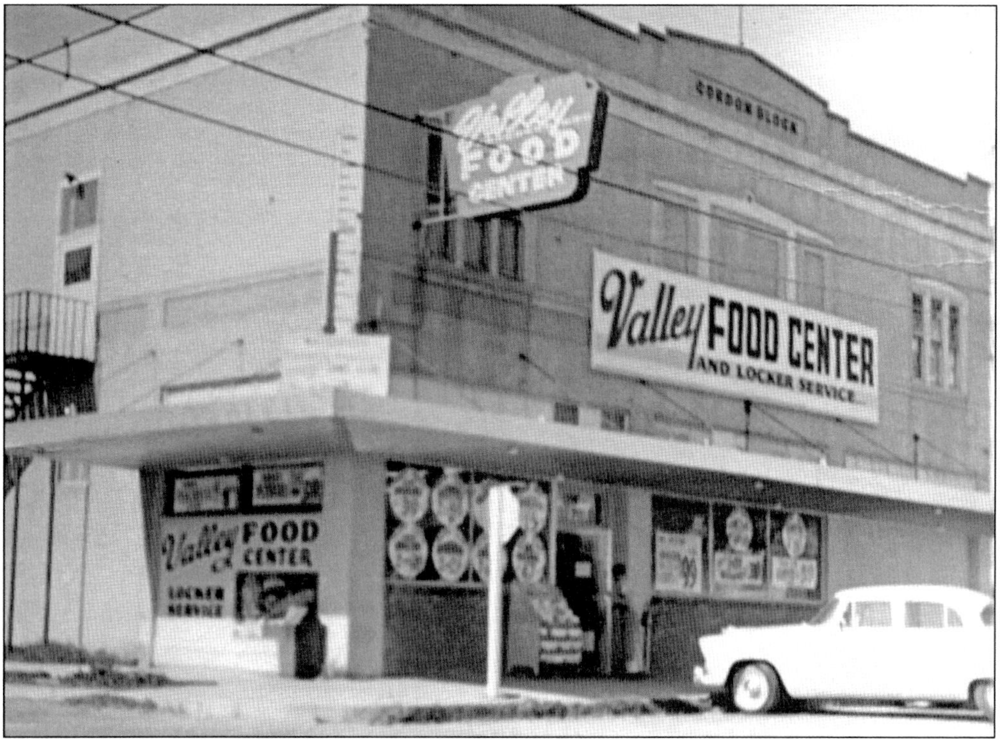

Brothers Calvin and Charlie Chu opened Valley Food Center and Locker Service in 1960 in the Gordon Building, then 30 years old. The Chus lived in the second floor above the 5,000-square-foot market during that time. In 1977, the market moved to the 14,000-square-foot metal building at the southeast corner of Yosemite Boulevard and F Street. In 1997, the store moved to its current location on Yosemite Boulevard, expanding to 32,500 square feet. The Bentley Street commercial building looks almost the same today, minus the wide awning and the fire escape staircase at left. (Calvin and Peggy Chu.)

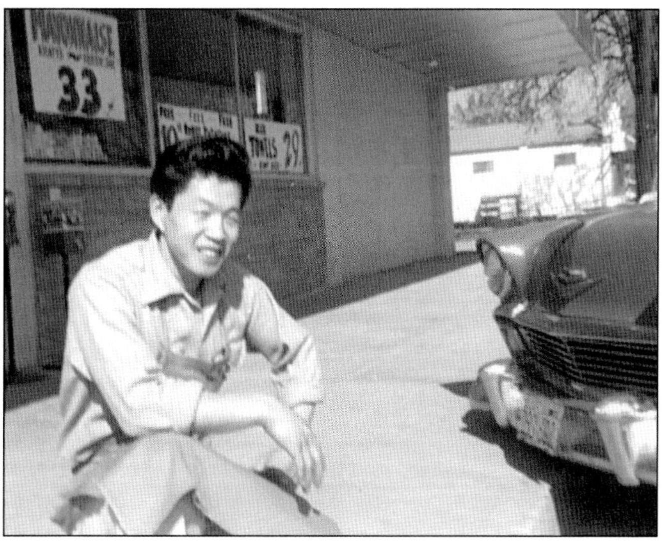

Donning his grocer's apron, Charlie Chu pauses for a pose in front of Valley Food Center at its first location shortly after its 1960 opening. Charlie and brother Calvin Chu, both born in China, came to Waterford from Patterson to run the market and remained for decades. The market operated in the Gordon Building at Bentley Street and E Street (now Pizza Plus). Visible in the background is Leo Holzer's Red and White Store. (Calvin and Peggy Chu.)

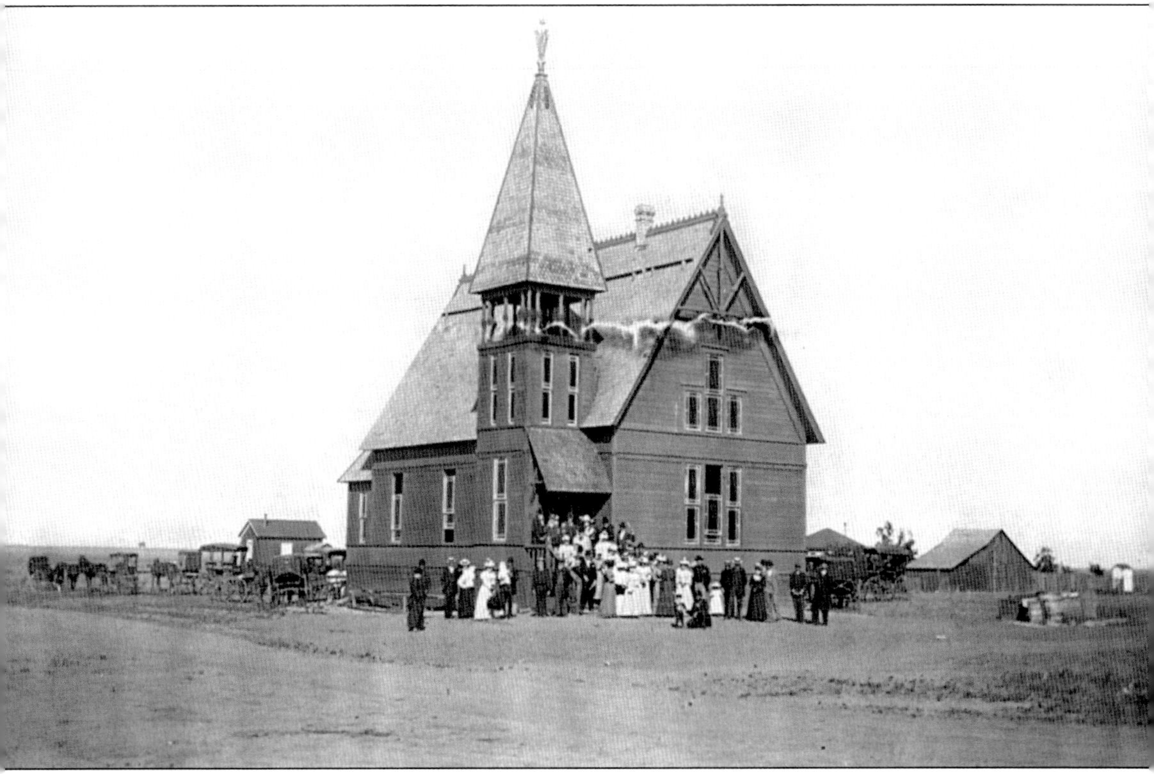

With few houses and trees around it, Community Baptist Church was dedicated on May 5, 1897, at the same spot it is today—on the corner of D and Main Streets. The church had organized on May 11, 1893, with four charter members: Martha "Mattie" Pinkston, James G. Hudelson, George W. Nelson, and W.C. Collins. This first church sanctuary was designed by Pastor W.R. Connelly, who traveled back and forth between Merced and Waterford by train. Skilled in carpentry, Connelly also helped construct the building. Rev. F.W. Webster was the pastor on dedication day. It was built debt-free for $2,675. (Donna Dugo.)

Six

Waterford Worships
Buildings and People of Faith

Although Waterford had a reputation as being rowdy in its earliest beginnings—no doubt encouraged by its abundance of saloons—the forces for good came from Christians who shared a vision for improving others' lives while serving God.

The first missionary outreach in Waterford involved a circuit rider from the Southern Methodist Church of Snelling who conducted services in town. However, the first organized congregation in Waterford, the First Missionary Baptist Church (now Community Baptist Church), owes its founding to Martha "Mattie" Pinkston. On January 11, 1891, Pinkston started Sunday School classes in the White Oak School at the corner of Tim Bell Road and Covey Street. A church grew from that effort in 1897 with founding church members Pinkston and James Gresham Hudelson, George W. Nelson, and W.C. Collins. With the guidance of itinerant preacher W.R. Connelly of Merced, the group spearheaded the building of a church sanctuary, dedicated on May 5, 1897, at the southeast corner of D and Main Streets.

The "Little Brown Church," built at the southeast corner of Bentley and C Streets, was first used by a group of Methodists. In 1917, the building was rented out to the Brethren church, which officially formed on July 15, 1918. The Brethren church used this facility until Rev. Levi Winklebleck and elder John W. Deardorff led construction efforts in 1925 on Church Street.

Waterford experienced a church expansion in the 1920s. The Brethren were growing, and the Baptists were bursting at the seams, prompting an annex. Pinkston turned the first ceremonial shovel of dirt for the 1924 building project. In the early 1950s, the Baptists decided that their dilapidated 1897 church building had to go. They continued worshiping in the old church while a new two-story structure was built in an L-shaped footprint to the east and south. On October 5, 1952, the new church hosted its first service, and the historic church was razed.

In 1947, the Baptist church suffered a split as members left to start First Southern Baptist Church on E Street near Yosemite Boulevard. For many years, the church operated Byron F. Todd Preschool.

Later, other churches in town included Calvary Baptist, Seventh-day Adventist, Landmark Missionary Baptist Church, the Church of Christ, and Assemblies of God.

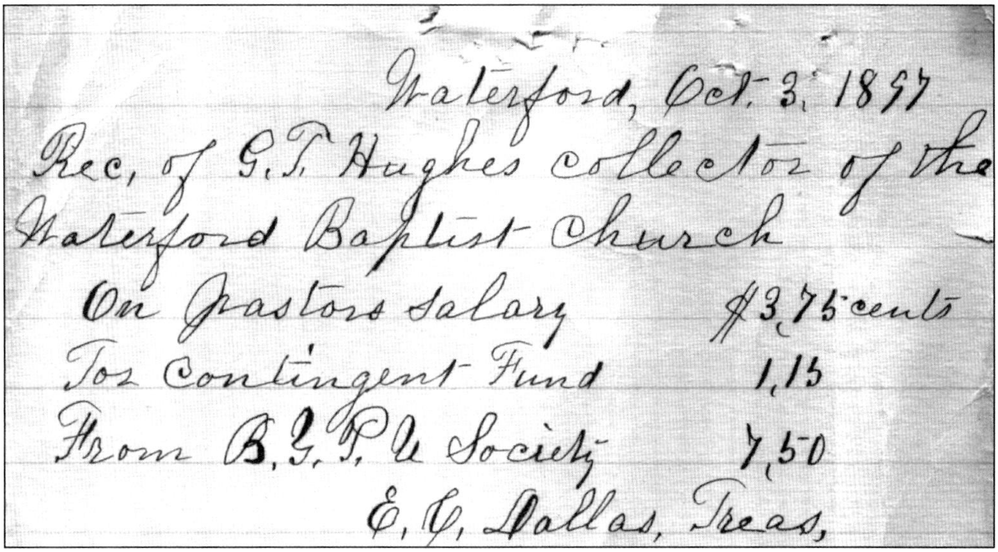

Waterford, Oct. 3: 1897
Rec, of G.T. Hughes collector of the
Waterford Baptist Church
On pastors salary $3.75 cents
Tos Contingent Fund 1.15
From B.Y.P.U. Society 7.50
E.C. Dallas, Treas,

This early document, dated October 3, 1897, shows that E.C. Dallas, treasurer of the Baptist church, paid $3.75 for the pastor's salary, $7.50 for the BYPU (Baptist Young People's Union) Society, and $1.15 for the contingency fund. (Community Baptist Church.)

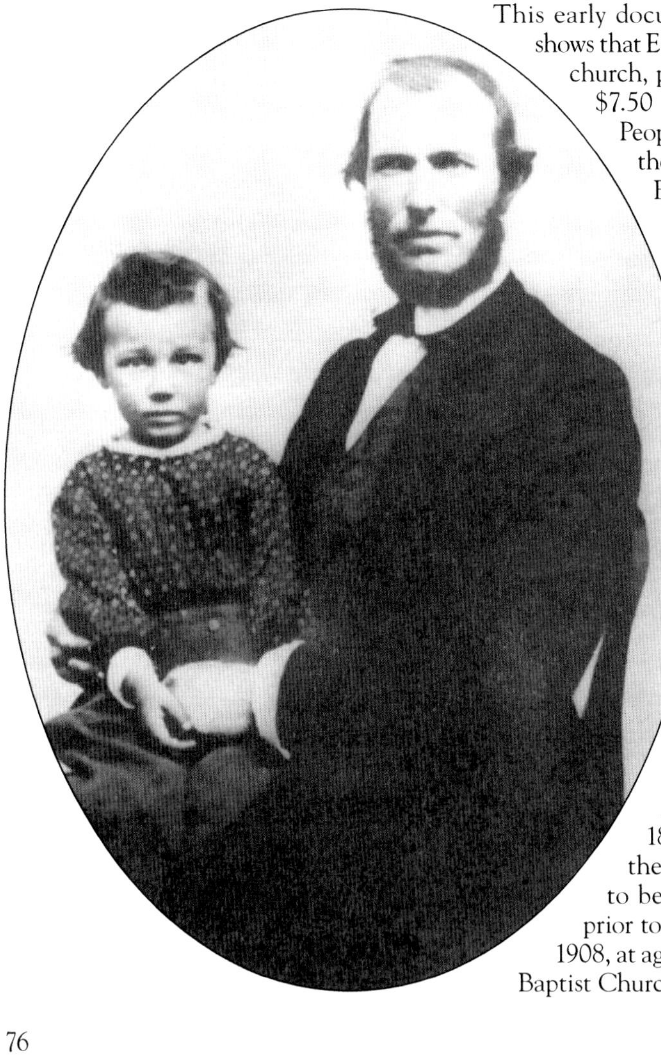

James Gresham Hudelson was one of the five founding members of First Missionary Baptist Church, now called Community Baptist Church. Here he holds son Aaron Gresham Hudelson. James Hudelson came to Stanislaus County from Missouri in 1850. After his first wife, Mary, died in 1855, he married Louvisa Turpen, the sister of Maj. A.M. Turpen, said to be first postmaster in Waterford prior to 1872. J.G. died on December 2, 1908, at age 83, in Waterford. (Community Baptist Church.)

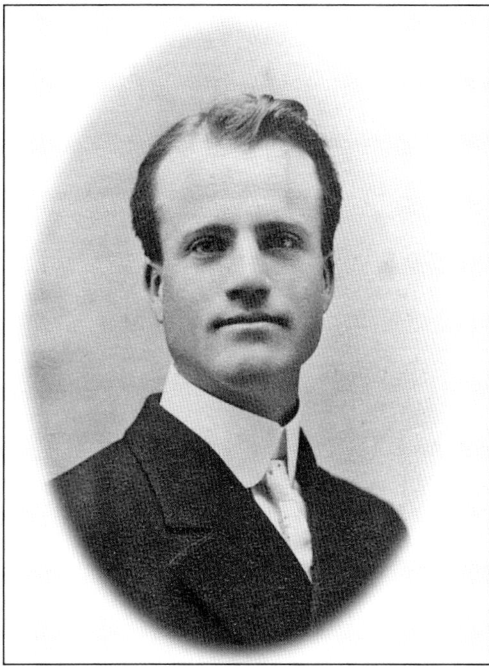 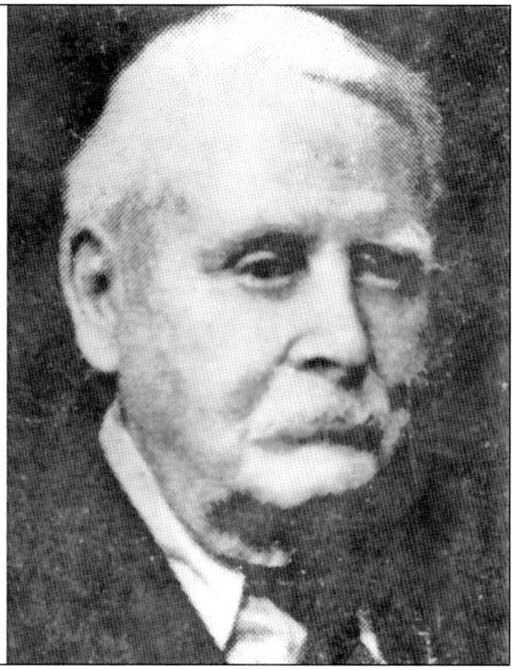

These men served First Missionary Baptist Church (later Community Baptist Church) in its early days. R.G. McIntyre (left) proclaimed the gospel of Jesus Christ from March 1912 to May 1916. Rev. Homer Newberry (right) was pastor from December 1918 to January 1921, during a time of growth. By 1920, his church logged 55 members, but that number doubled after a six-week Grace Car Chapel railroad revival took place, and the church changed its name to Community Baptist Church. From that point on, members of different denominations were welcome into the fold. Newberry lived in the county until his death in 1952 at age 96. (Community Baptist Church.)

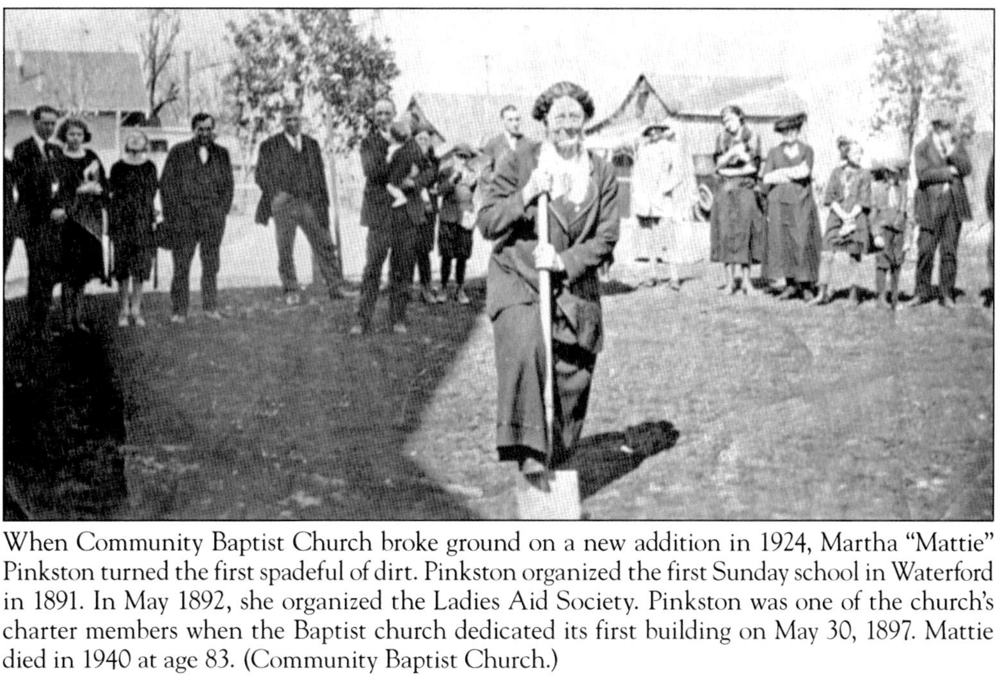

When Community Baptist Church broke ground on a new addition in 1924, Martha "Mattie" Pinkston turned the first spadeful of dirt. Pinkston organized the first Sunday school in Waterford in 1891. In May 1892, she organized the Ladies Aid Society. Pinkston was one of the church's charter members when the Baptist church dedicated its first building on May 30, 1897. Mattie died in 1940 at age 83. (Community Baptist Church.)

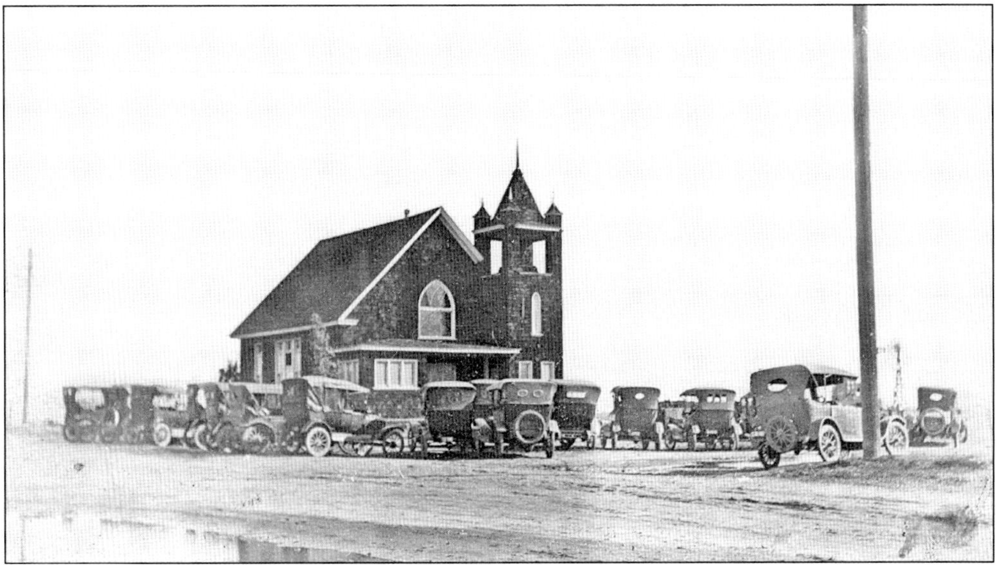

The Little Brown Church, seen here around 1920, was located at the southeast corner of Bentley Street and C Street, on what is now the schoolyard of Waterford Elementary School. It was a Methodist church at first but became inactive. Starting on September 16, 1917, the building was rented for $1 a week for Sunday gatherings of the Brethren church. The Brethren used this facility until 1921. In 1925, they built their own church on Church Street. (Waterford Historical Society.)

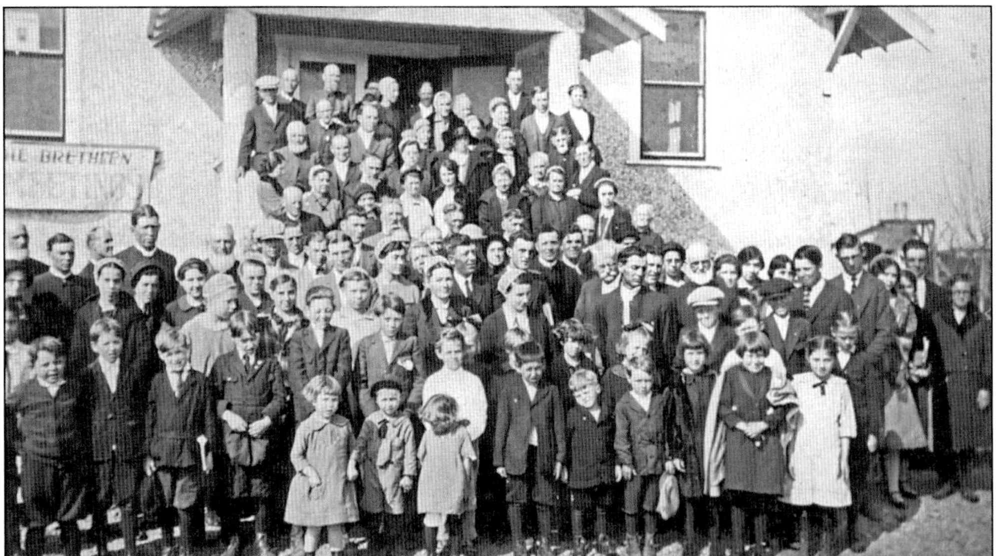

On dedication day in 1925, the Brethren church of Waterford was open for worship at the corner of Church Street and Pecan Avenue. Rev. Levi Winklebleck and J.W. Deardorff were instrumental in leading the construction effort. Visible at left are early pastors Robert Kennedy and John Deardorff. (Waterford Church of the Brethren.)

John Peters was the first paid pastor of the Waterford Church of the Brethren. In May 1933, the church called Peters from Washington State, offering him a salary of $50 per month and use of the parsonage. Under his pastorate, the church added a social hall in 1935. When he left in 1940, Peters stated: "The congregation did the work of pushing the church wagon, and all I had to do was hold up the tongue." (Waterford Church of the Brethren.)

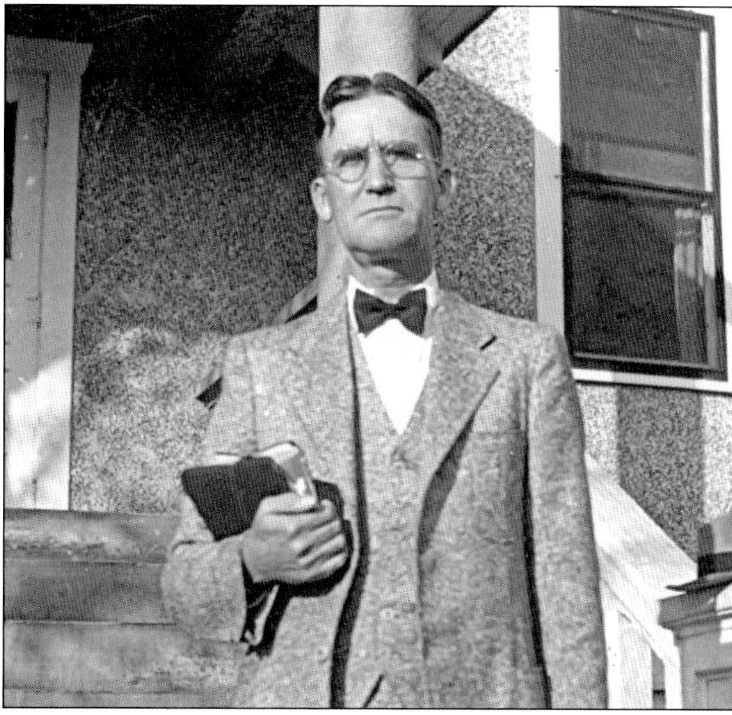

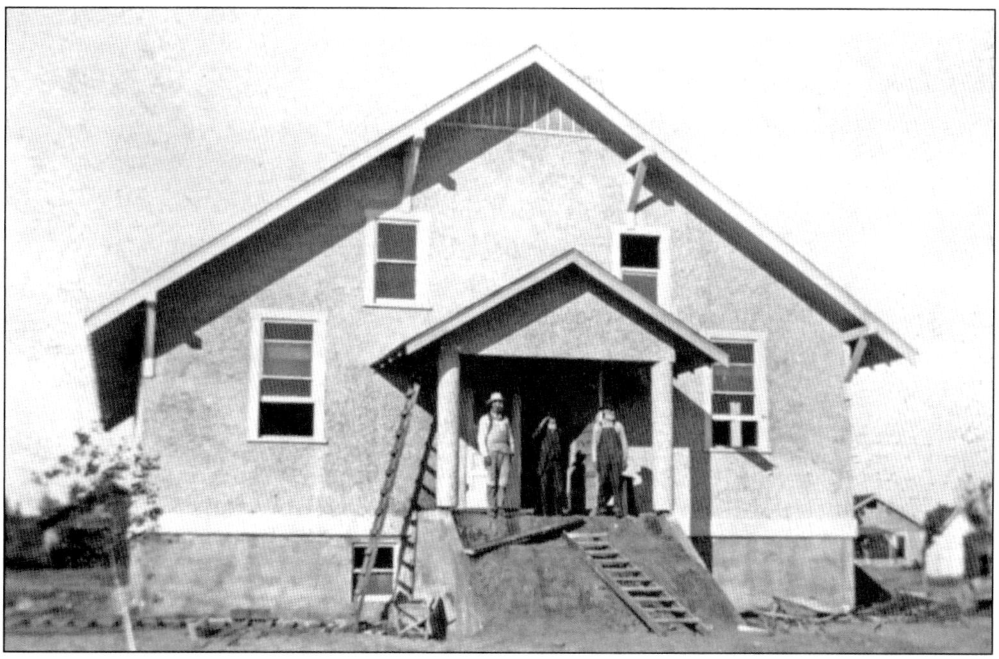

Workers finish the cement steps leading up to the Brethren church in 1925. The church still stands at the corner of Church Street and Pecan Avenue. (Waterford Church of the Brethren.)

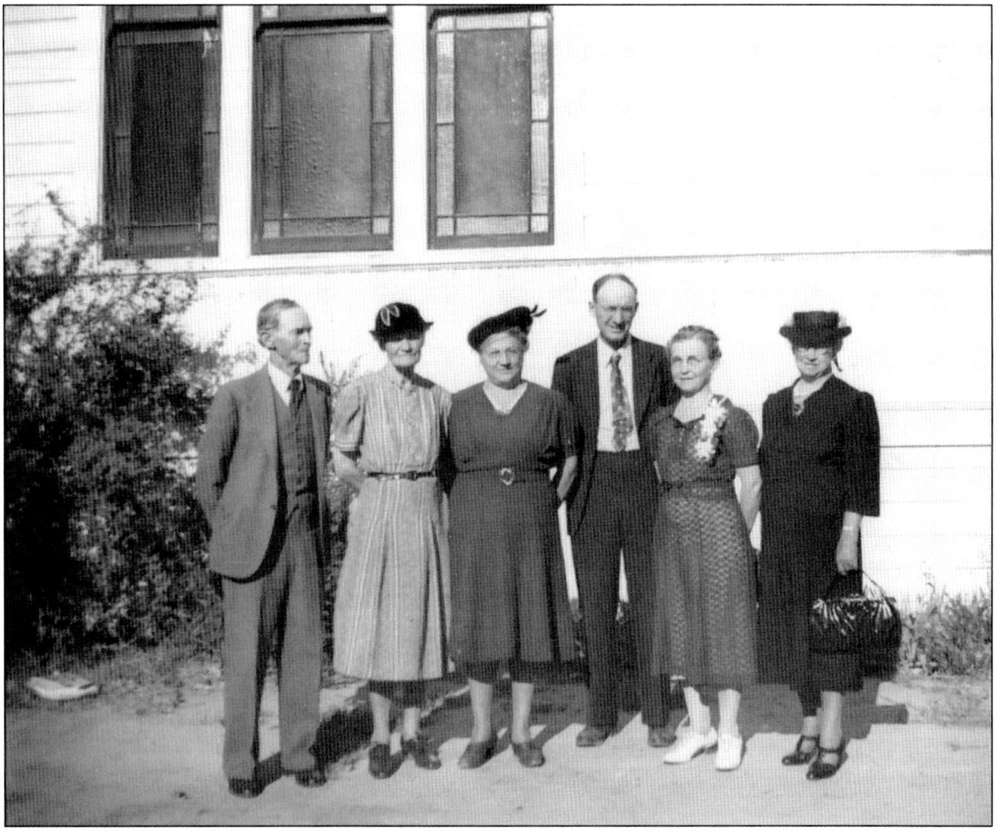

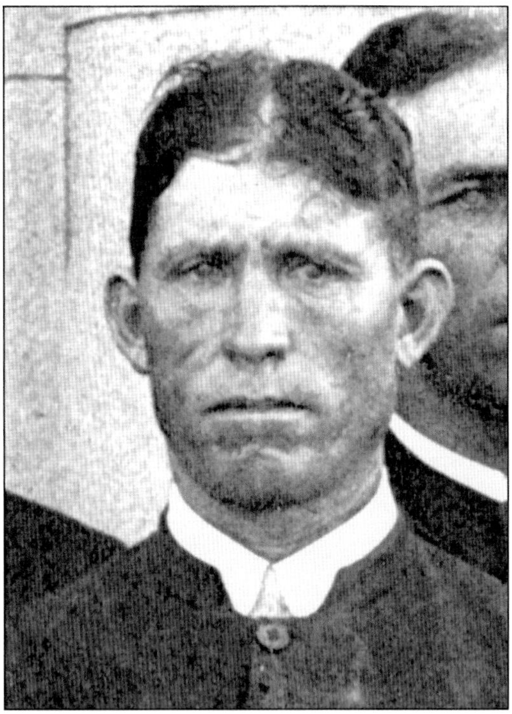

Gathered on the west side of the first Community Baptist Church are, from left to right, a Mr. and Mrs. Andrews, Vivian Haushaw, Raymond and Jesse Appling, and an unidentified woman. The building seen here was added in 1924 and demolished in 1952. Today, the ground on which they are standing is the lawn of the current Community Baptist Church at D and Main Streets. (Sandra Burley.)

Robert Kennedy was a deacon of the Brethren church in Waterford. He and wife Iva Kennedy moved from Kansas to Waterford in July 1919. Thomas K. Beard hired Kennedy to level the site that was to become the new church. (Waterford Church of the Brethren.)

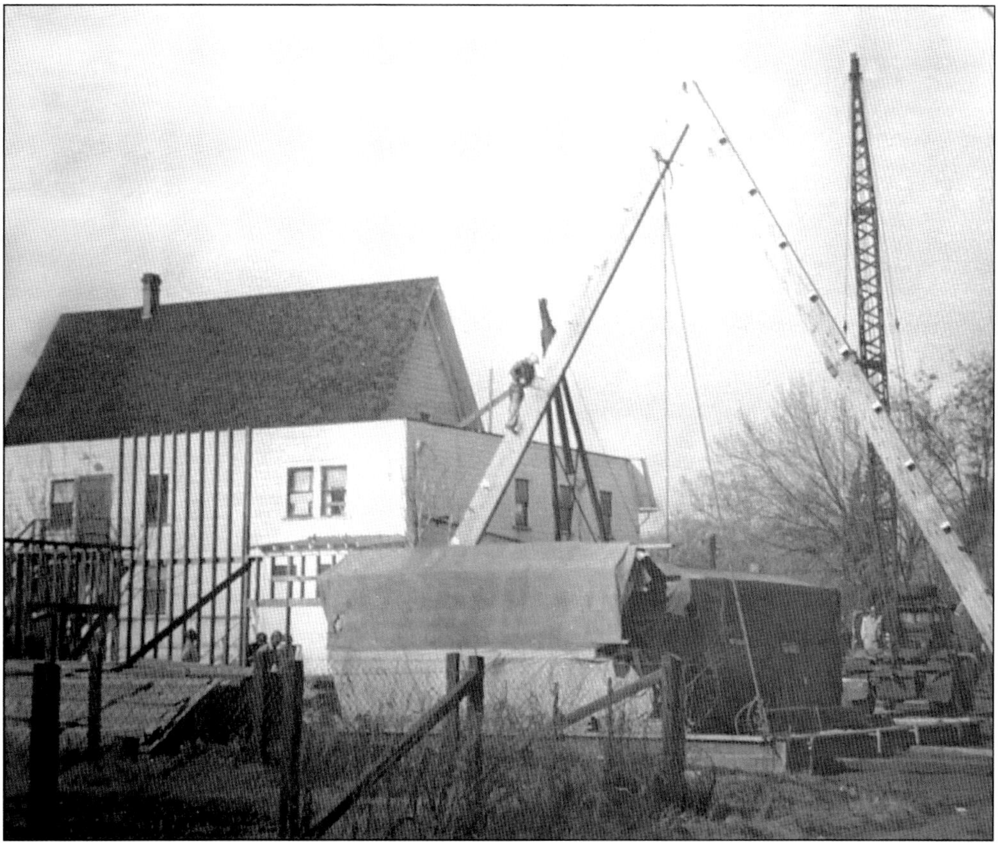

Giant beams go into place in 1952 to form the sanctuary of Community Baptist Church. This scene was taken from the alley looking northwest toward the building site. The white building at left is the back of the 1924 church annex, which partially obscures the original 1897 church. This photograph captures all three of the church's building projects over a 55-year span. (Donna Dugo.)

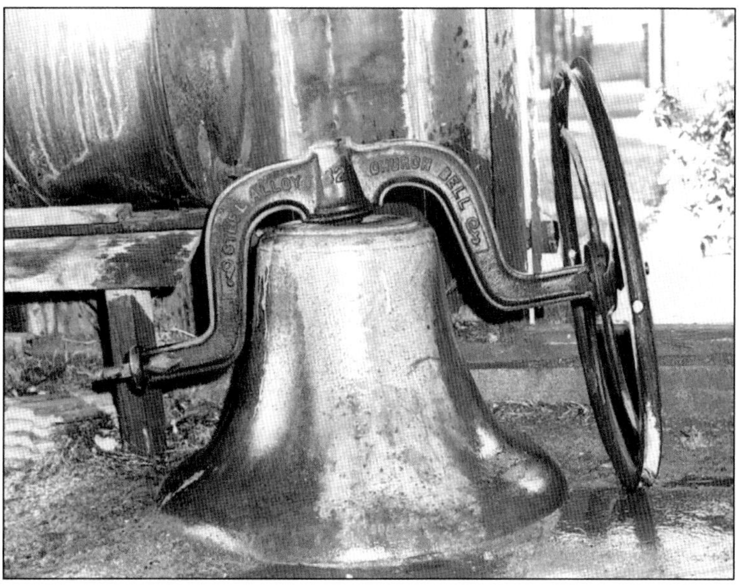

This steel alloy bell rang in the belfry of the Baptist church in 1897 after $69.75 was raised for it. For over a century, its ring was heard through Waterford alerting all to the start of Sunday school and worship. Bell ringers included Raymond Appling, who crafted the church constitution in 1915. The bell now hangs in a bell tower on the church lawn. (Community Baptist Church.)

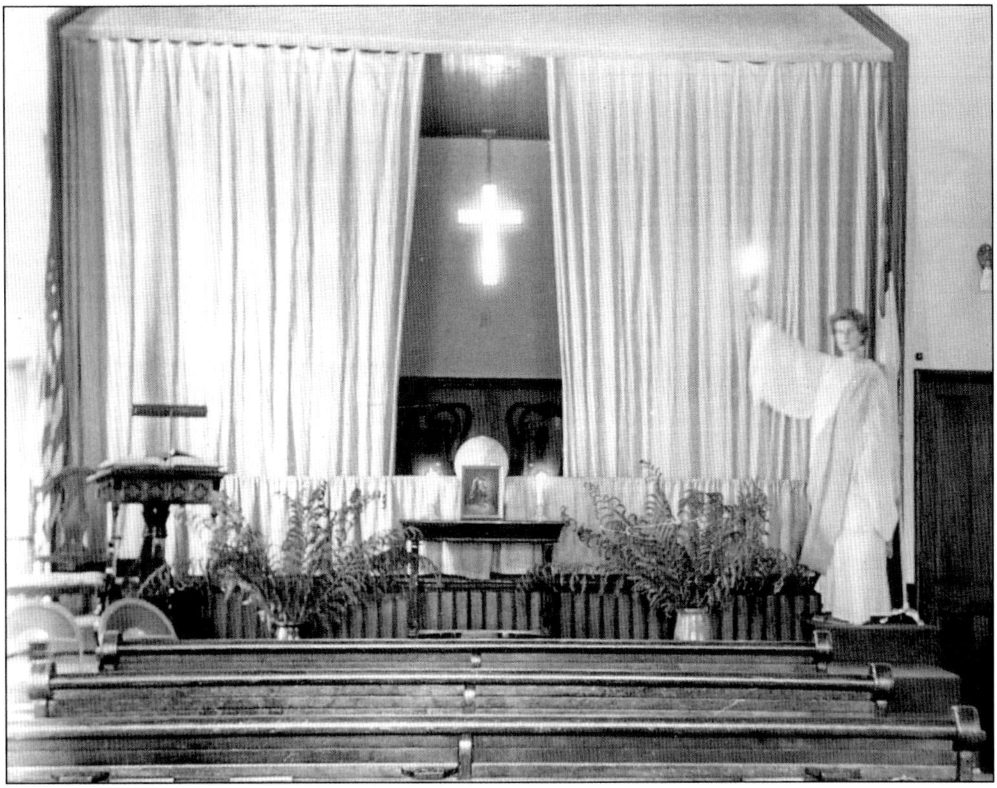

Longtime Waterford resident Allison Bodes posed inside the old Community Baptist Church for a dramatic presentation. The church was torn down in 1952 after the new church was dedicated and opened. (Community Baptist Church.)

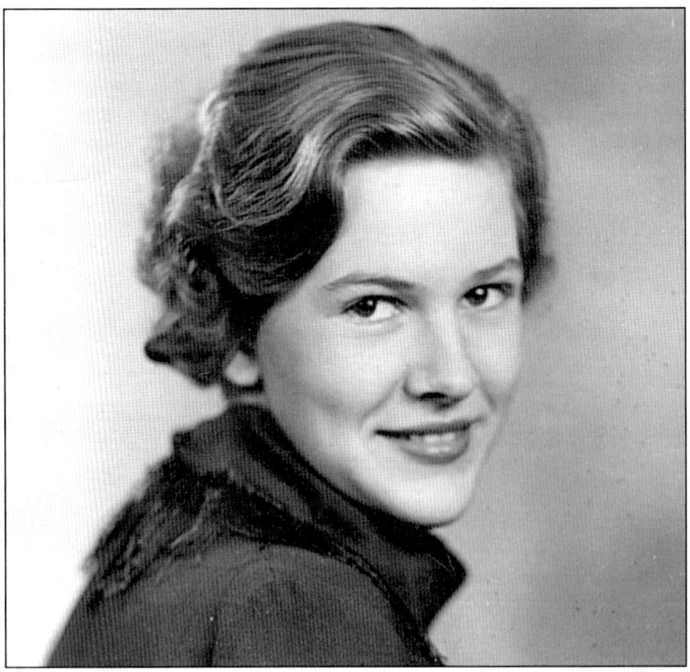

Minnie Sawyer Richards was a faithful servant of God in Waterford for more than three decades. Born in 1918 and raised in the Roberts Ferry area, Minnie was choir director at Community Baptist Church for 30 years. After cancer claimed Minnie in 1985, her daughters, Jeanne Kampen and Lee Clipper, continued in the music ministry. Son Russ Richards became county fire warden, and son Bill Richards is a Hickman teacher. (Bob Crabtree.)

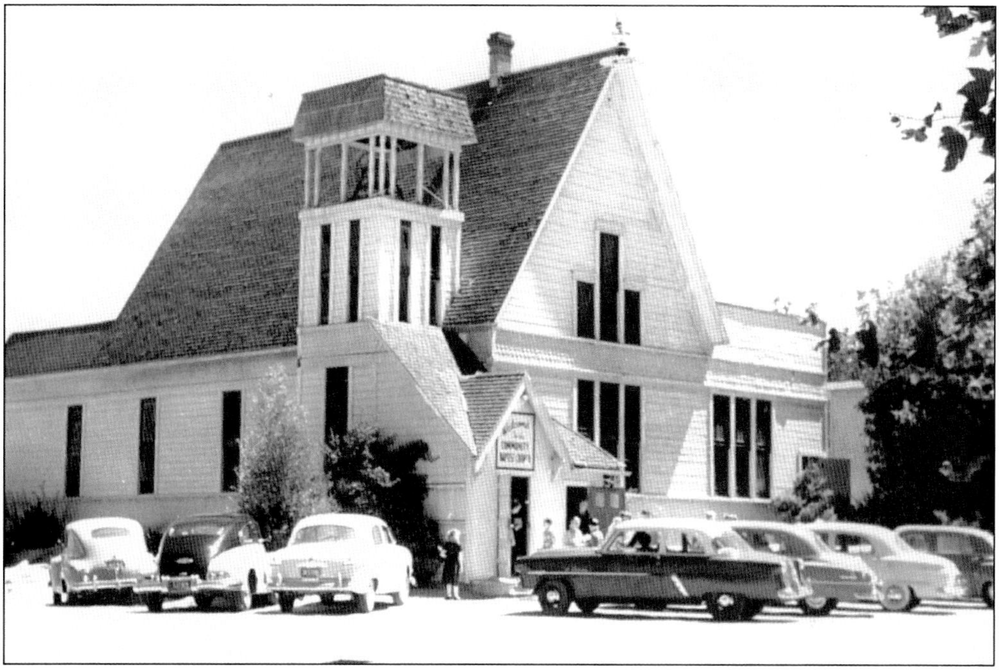

The first church in Waterford, the First Missionary Baptist Church, was dedicated on May 5, 1897, at the southeast corner of D Street and Main Street. Space was added onto it in the 1920s, and the grand steeple was lopped off. Community Baptist Church decided to build a newer and larger facility in an L-shaped pattern around the original church. It was last used in September 1952. (Community Baptist Church.)

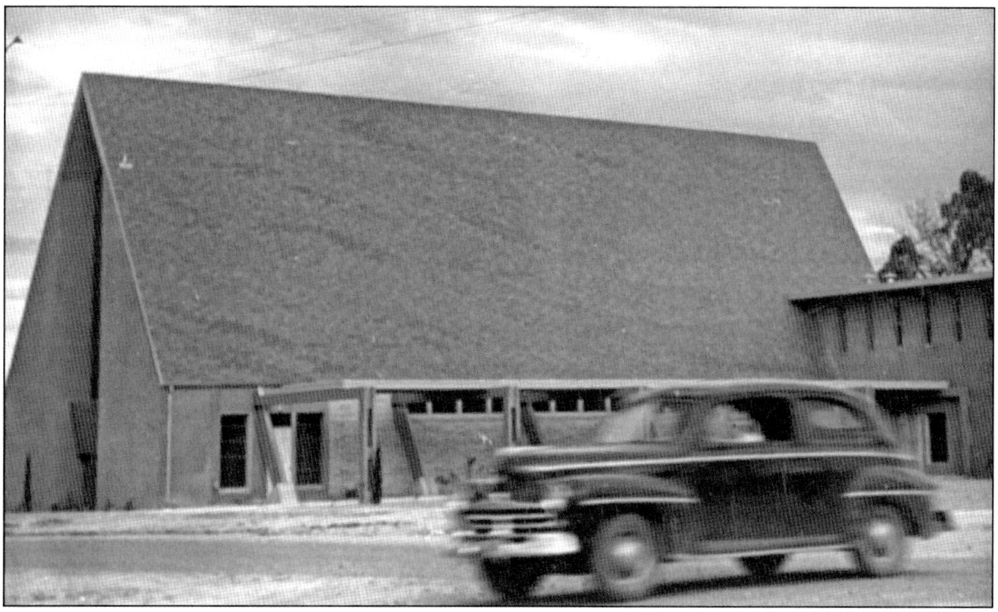

A vintage car rolls past Community Baptist Church in 1953, a year after this building was completed. The project broke ground on October 7, 1951, with Pastor John Moletti leading the service. It was completed a year later on October 5, 1952, with church members doing most of the labor. (Community Baptist Church.)

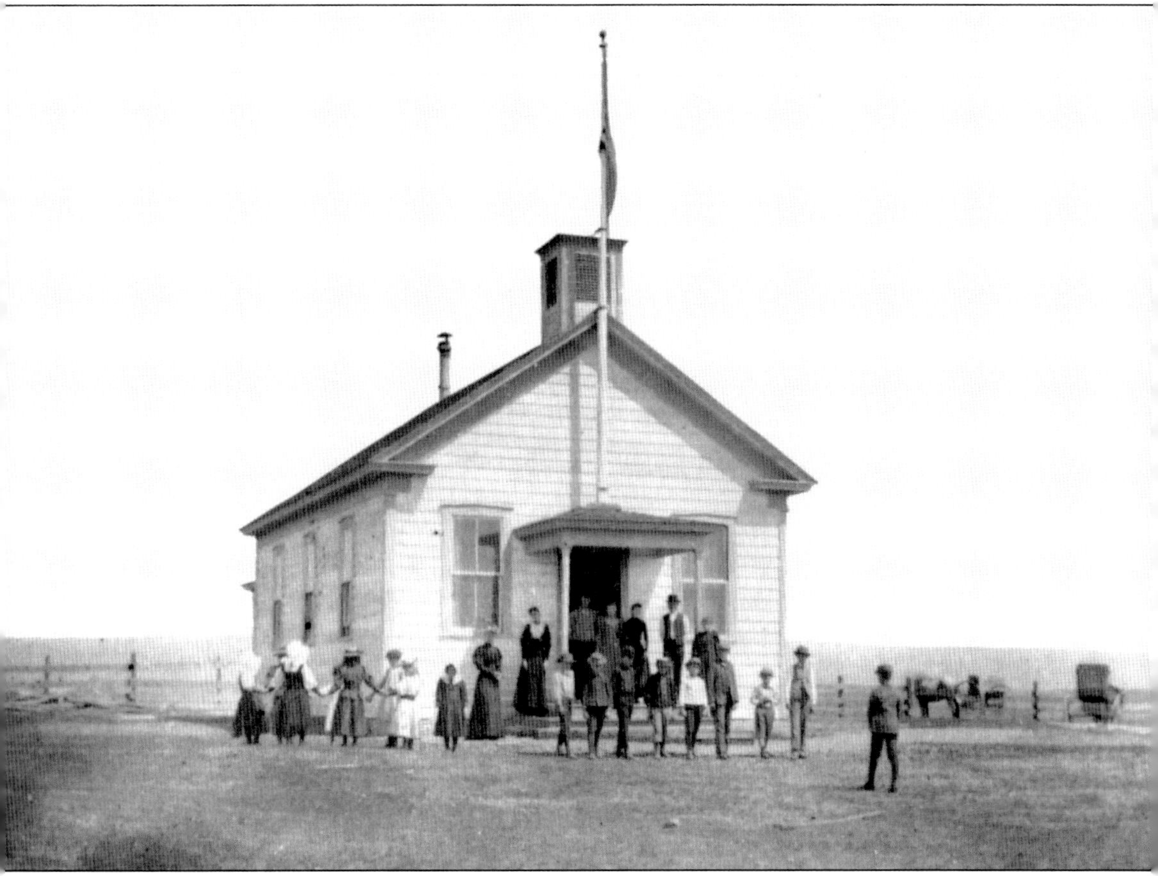

Seen here in 1893, Dry Creek School was located near Warnerville Road and Crabtree Road. Established in 1863, the one-room schoolhouse was established to educate the children of the farmers of the Warnerville and Cooperstown areas north of Roberts Ferry. Cooperstown was a freighting community before the Sierra Railroad tracks came through in June 1897. W.F. Cooper ran a store and saloon there. A post office opened in Cooperstown on July 27, 1901, and served until August 31, 1932. (Author's collection.)

Seven

School Days
Education in Waterford

As soon as Waterford was settled with families, there became a pressing need for formalized schooling.

In 1865, the Grant School District was formed, and a school was constructed on the Hickman side of the Tuolumne River, directly south of Reinway Avenue, about 500 feet from the river's edge. Grant School burned and was replaced by Rowe School, which was later moved the southeast corner of Whitmore Avenue and Hickman Road. By 1880, the school had 18 boys and 22 girls and offered class only six and a half months per year.

A competing school came about the following year. On August 16, 1866, the White Oak School district was created and offered schooling for children living in Waterford and as far north as Claribel Road. Waterford's first school was built at the northwest corner of Tim Bell Road and Covey Street. White Oak School was a typical one-room schoolhouse with a bell to call the students. It was in operation from 1866 to 1907, when a new school was constructed on Bentley Street between C and D Streets. A brick schoolhouse was constructed in 1920 on the current school campus. This building was damaged in the March 15, 1946, Walker Pass Earthquake, and students were displaced for weeks.

In 1946, Waterford constructed its current elementary school.

Richard Moon Elementary School was constructed on Reinway Avenue in 1976. Waterford parents increasingly grew tired of sending their high school students to Oakdale and then later Riverbank.

For the sake of community spirit, Waterford demanded its own high school, and a number of community members led its organization, including Wayne Long and Superintendent Allen Gordon. Several sites were considered, but ultimately, a 40-acre site owned by farmer Howard Martin at the southwest corner of Yosemite Boulevard and Reinway Avenue was selected. Waterford High School opened in 2001 and graduated its first class on June 7, 2002. In August 2008, Waterford opened Lucille Whitehead School south of the Moon School campus.

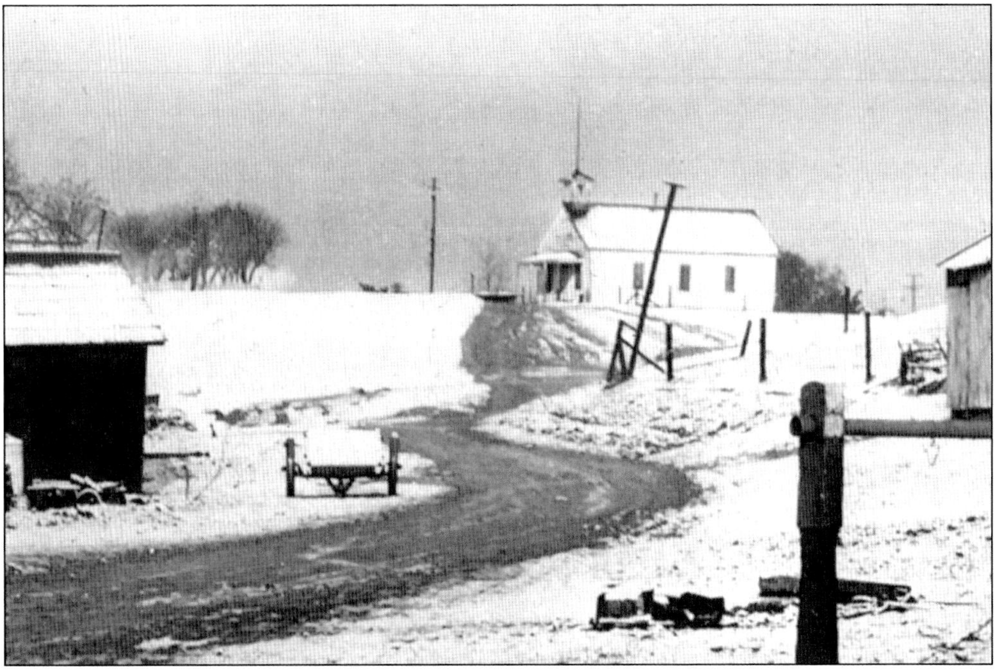

At its low elevation, Waterford is rarely dusted with snow, but it happens. This photograph was taken at the old horseshoeing building behind the Prouty Blacksmith Shop looking toward the west. Atop the hill is the White Oak School building, which sat on the corner of Tim Bell Road and Covey Street. (Betty Roen.)

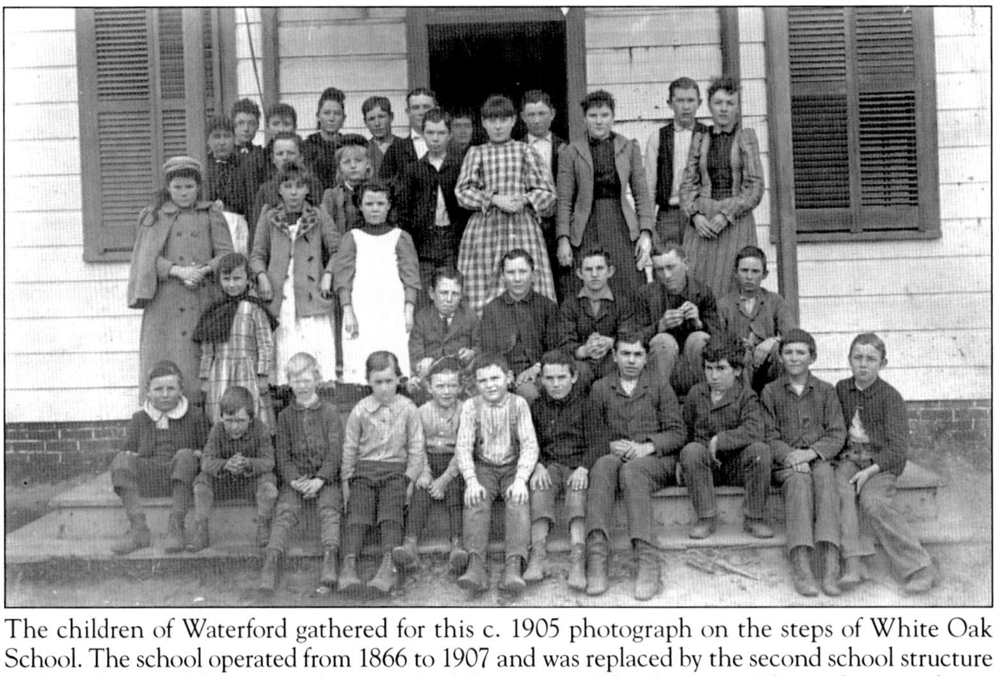

The children of Waterford gathered for this c. 1905 photograph on the steps of White Oak School. The school operated from 1866 to 1907 and was replaced by the second school structure built on the site of the present-day Waterford Elementary School campus. The students are facing the Tuolumne River from the school perched on the bluff at Covey Street and Tim Bell Road overlooking the town. (Betty Roen.)

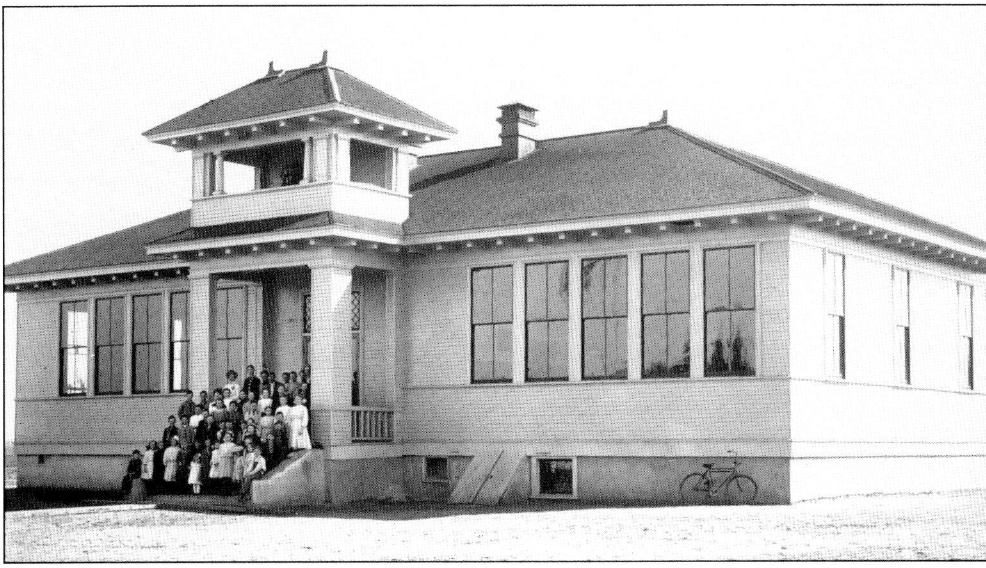

Built in 1907 and 1908, this was the second elementary school to serve Waterford. It replaced the White Oak School, which is seen in the background. This school was located on the grounds of the existing school campus but was later leveled. The school was initially called White Oak School as well but was officially named Waterford Elementary School on March 10, 1908. (Waterford Historical Society.)

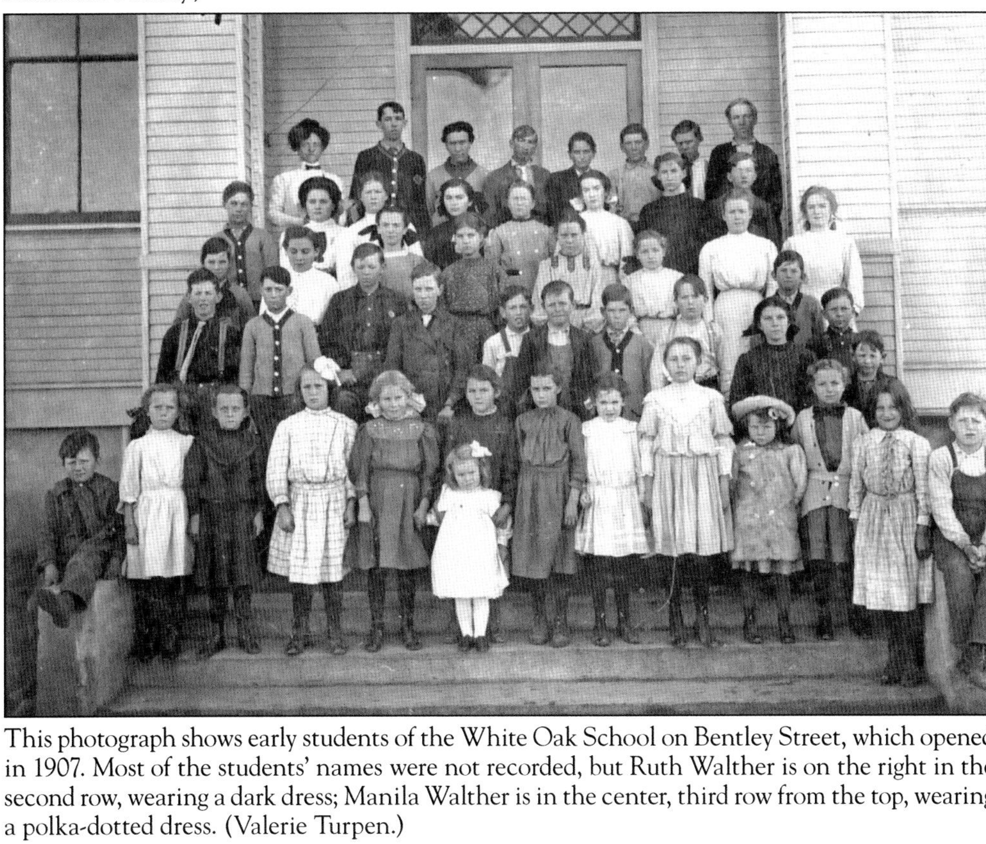

This photograph shows early students of the White Oak School on Bentley Street, which opened in 1907. Most of the students' names were not recorded, but Ruth Walther is on the right in the second row, wearing a dark dress; Manila Walther is in the center, third row from the top, wearing a polka-dotted dress. (Valerie Turpen.)

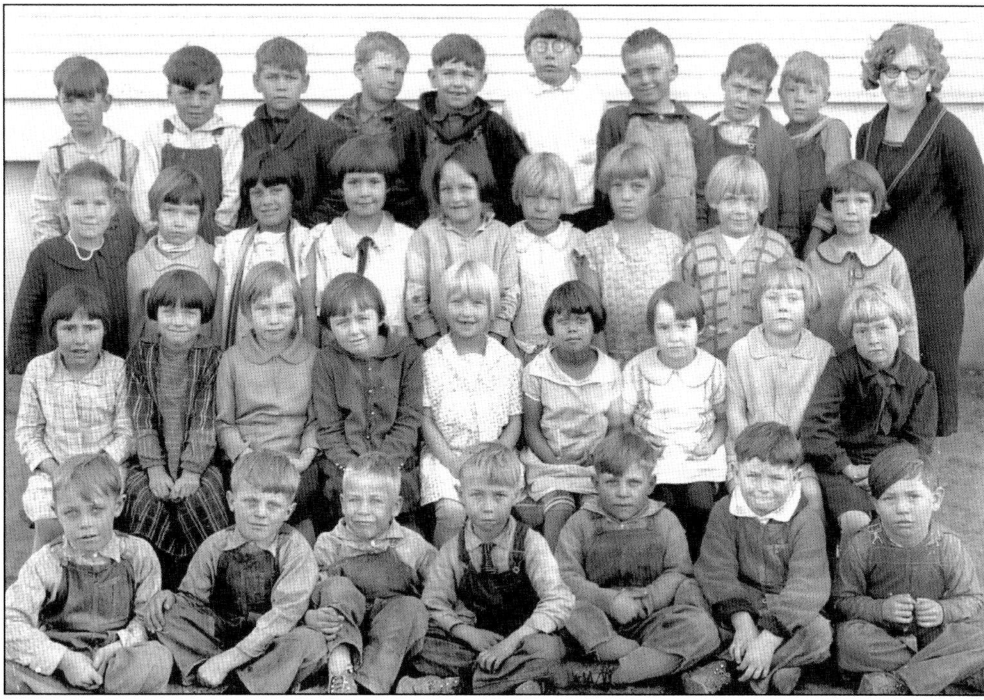

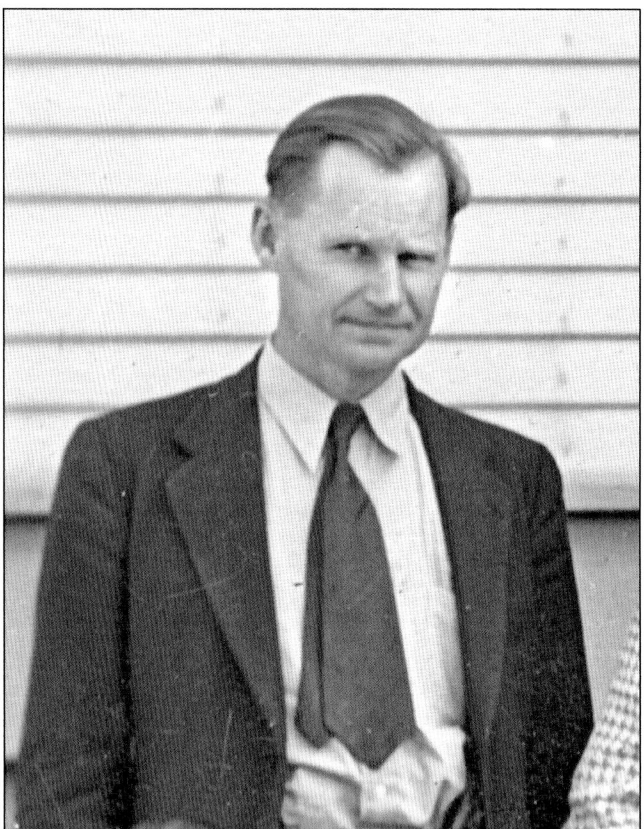

Mabel McEwen Dow Quick (upper right) taught first-graders at Waterford School during the 1927–1928 school year. The group is in front of Waterford's second elementary school building. One of Quick's students was Lucille Bishop (Whitehead), who became a well-known and well-loved teacher. Lucy, daughter of Henry and Charlotte Bishop, sits in the second row, third from left. (Lucille Whitehead.)

This image of Walter Hastings was taken from his eighth-grade class photograph at Waterford School. A sixth-, seventh-, and eighth-grade teacher from 1932 to 1938, Hastings was tapped to serve as principal in 1938. Four years later, he left Waterford School to enlist in the military at the height of World War II. (Waterford Historical Society.)

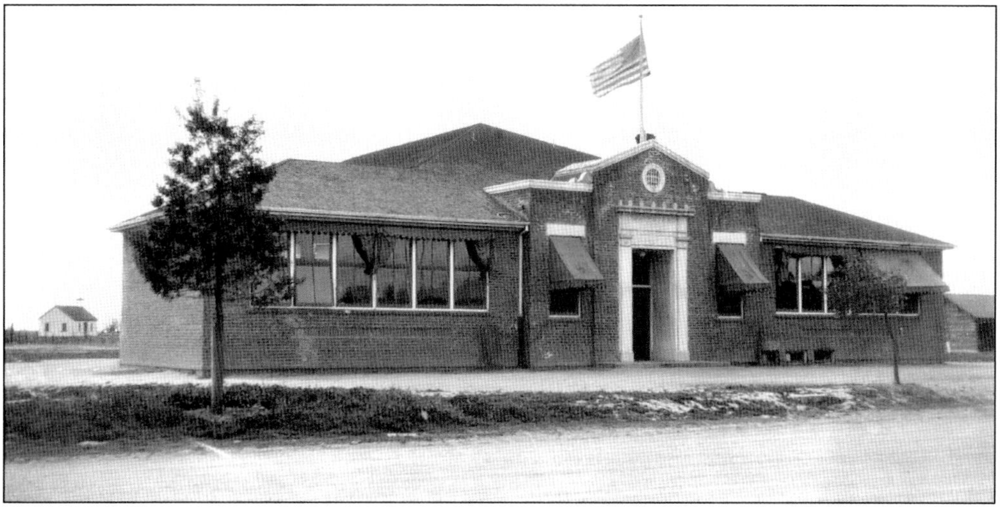

This brick building was Waterford's third school, constructed in 1920 on the site of the current Waterford Elementary School on Bentley Street. In 1921, Clara Bashor was principal, Alma Fisher was the intermediate teacher, and Jennie Dillwood taught the primary grades. Visible in the background at left is White Oak School, the town's first school building, which sat on the northwest corner of Tim Bell Road and Covey Street. (Waterford Historical Society.)

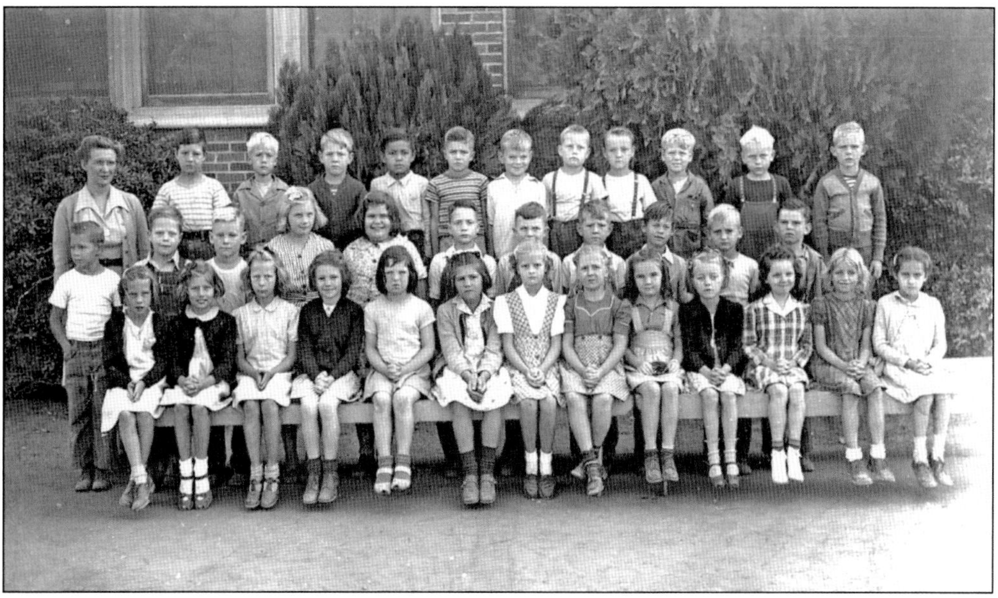

Waterford students gathered for this photograph around 1943 next to the brick school on Bentley Street. The only student that could be identified is Ted Casey, who is in the back row, third from the teacher. History has recorded that the brick school was removed because of damage sustained in the March 15, 1946, Walker Pass Earthquake, which shook the Central Valley floor. Students were displaced for weeks. Richard Moon organized the demolition and reconstruction effort through a one-year tax of $5 per $100 of assessed value levied on Waterford parcels. (Joe Casey.)

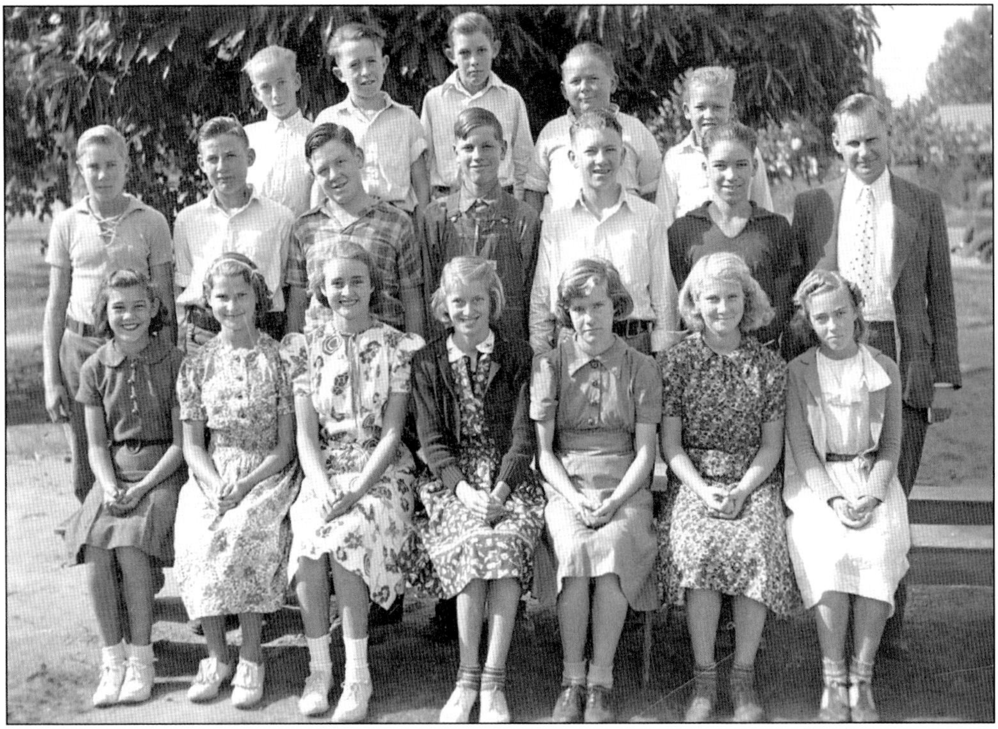

Seen here is the 1938–1939 eighth-grade class of Waterford Elementary School. From left to right, they are (first row) Donna Mae Allen, Mary Reasy, Naomia Root, Mildred Dunegan, Fern Beghtel, Lessie Rorabaugh, and Irene Menteer; (second row), Juel Cupp, Eugene Tallent, Bobby Raye, Ray Cunningham, Russell Turpen, Allen Bennett, and Walter Hastings; (third row) Robert Menteer, Jack Scouel, Marion Quesenberry, Elmer Thomas, and Richard Nielsen. Quesenberry became the town pharmacist. (Mildred Dennis.)

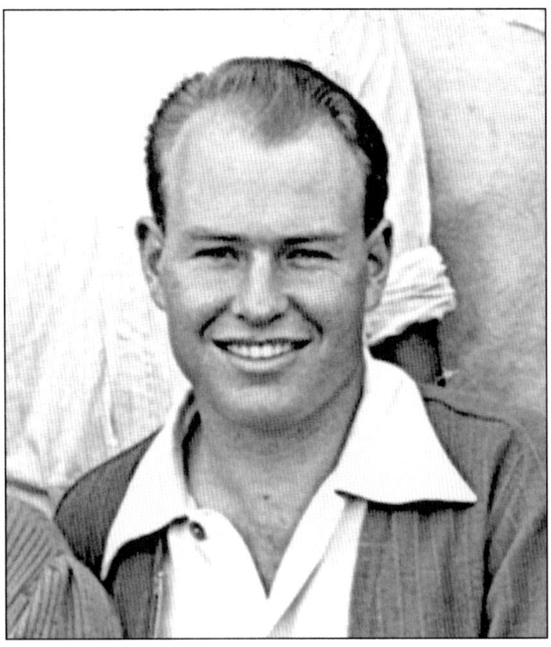

A youthful Richard Moon, who later became principal, helped to educate the eighth-grade class of 1940. Moon was first hired in Waterford to teach the 1938–1939 school year. He later became Waterford's first mayor. (Waterford Historical Society.)

Lucille "Luci" Whitehead taught school at Waterford Elementary School for 43 years, from 1941 to 1984. With husband Roland "Whitey" Whitehead, she also raised their son, Stephen. In August 2008, she was honored by having her name attached to the Lucille Whitehead School south of the Moon School campus. From small girl to senior citizen, Whitehead lived her entire life in the same Eucalyptus Road house where she passed away on January 1, 2011. (Lucille Whitehead.)

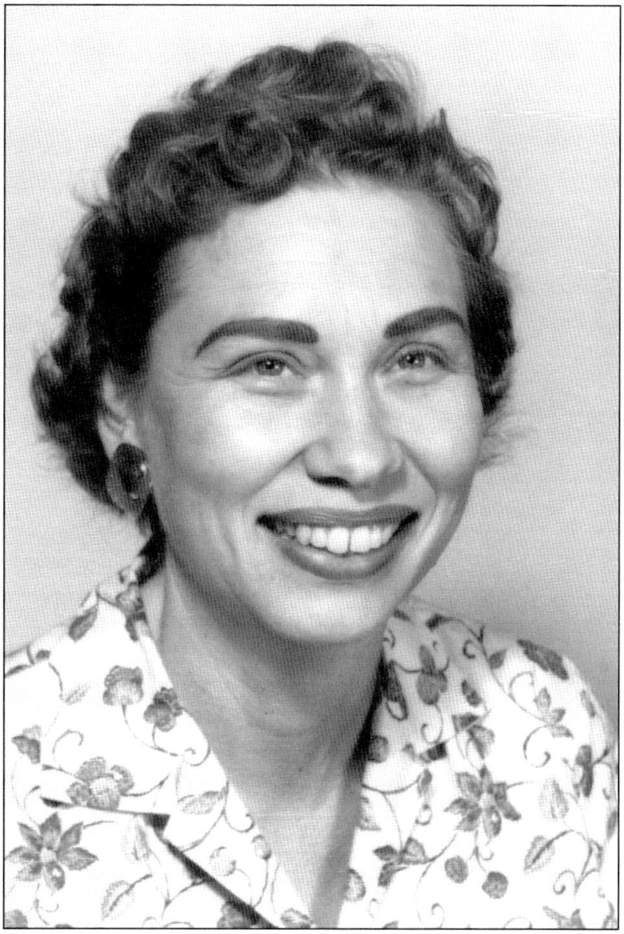

In this photograph, the much-loved teacher Lucille Whitehead poses with her 1943 class of second-, third-, and fourth-graders. (Lucille Whitehead.)

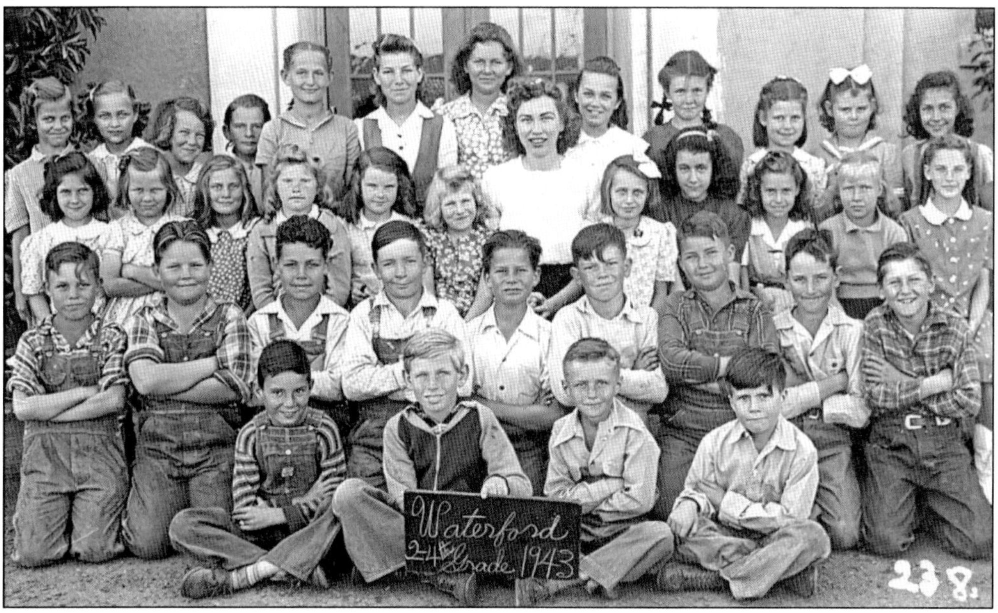

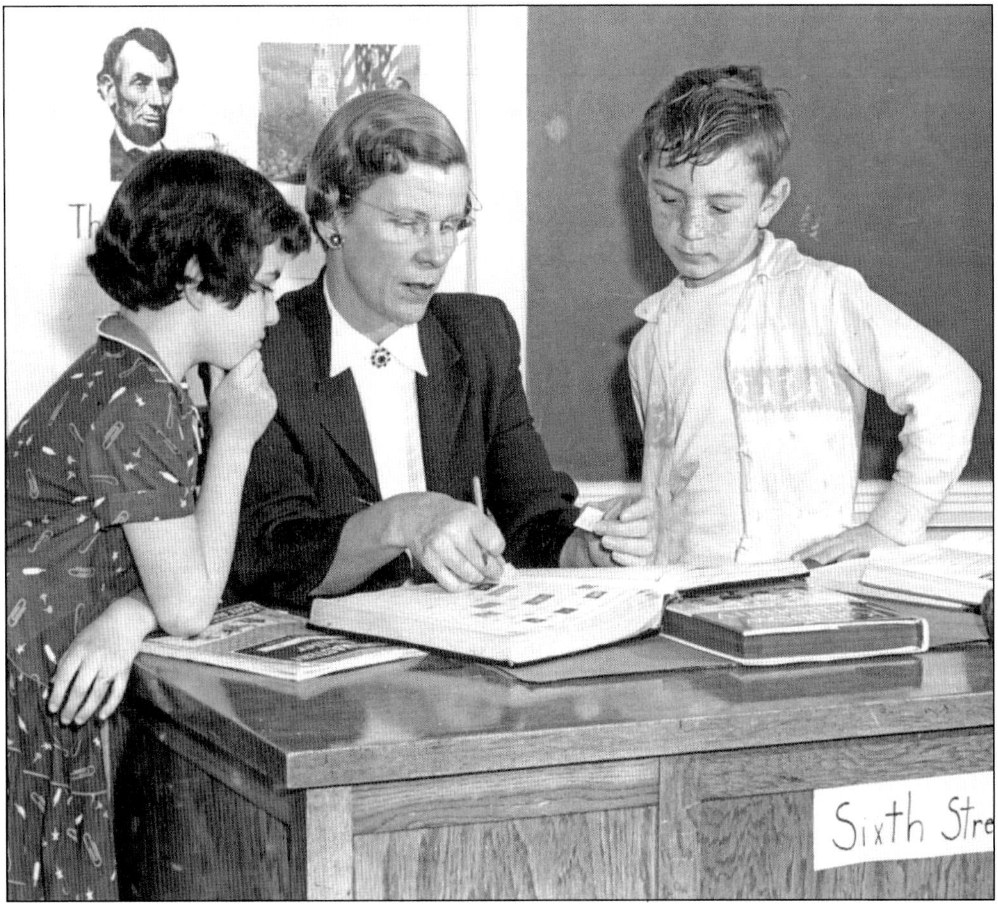

Third-grade teacher Helen Anderson is shown here instructing two unidentified students on American history. This c. 1957 photograph was taken for the Stanislaus County Office of Education. (Waterford Historical Society.)

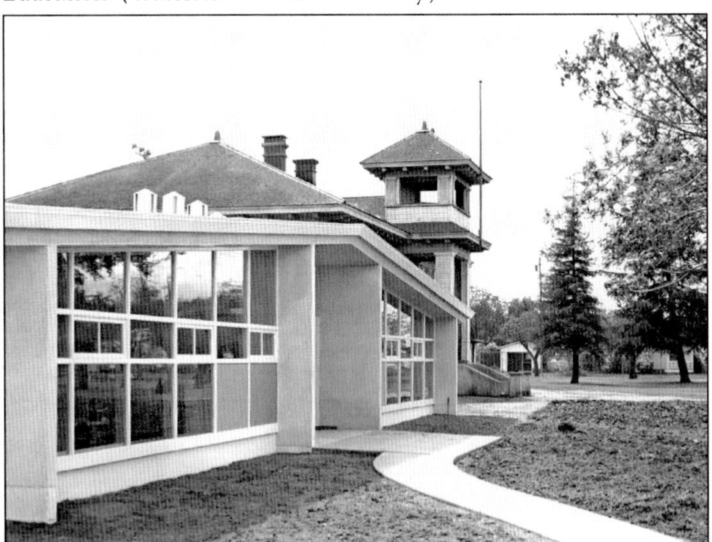

This photograph bears testimony to the location of Waterford's second school, now razed. It appears behind the kindergarten wing built in 1955. The old school was built in 1907 and demolished in the late 1950s. (Waterford Historical Society.)

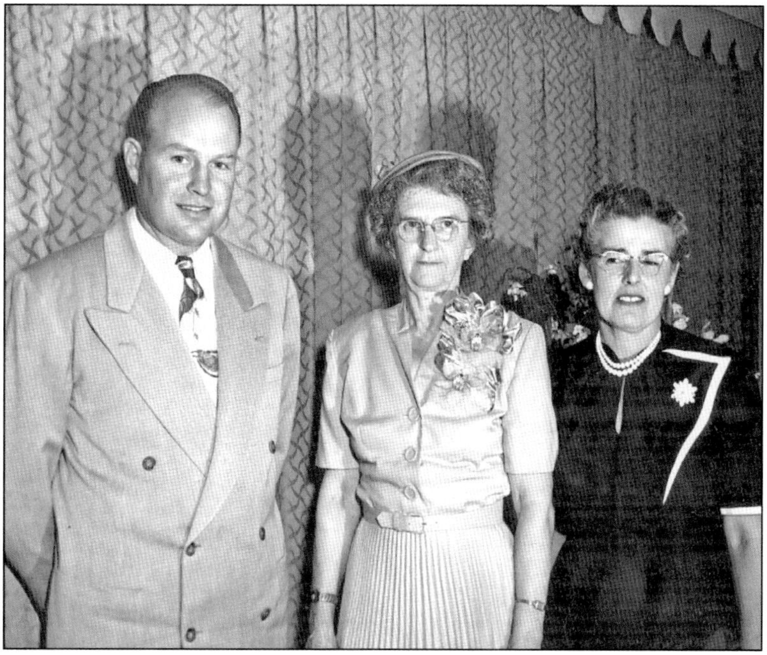

A longtime teacher at Waterford School, Edna Weichert (center) was honored during a retirement dinner on May 5, 1953. Standing with her are principal Richard Moon and Laura White. Weichert taught in the 1930s, 1940s, and early 1950s. She died in 1987 at age 97. (Waterford Historical Society.)

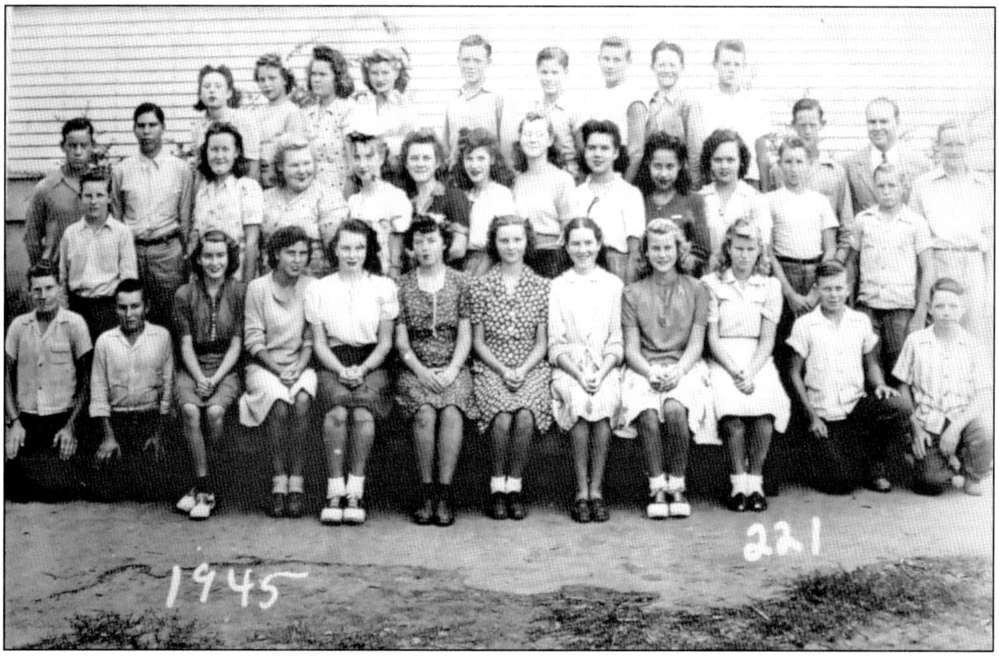

Seen here in 1945 are students of Waterford Elementary School. From left to right, they are (first row) Ted Hansen, Roger Coleman, Marvis Cole, Shirley Longmeyer, Louise Porter, Reha Weymant, Pearl Esterbrook, Helen Bishop, Reta Pane, Twila Bishop, Carl Wallers, and Doyle Swikard; (second row) J.C. Pace, Charles Fuller, Gladis ?, Lucille Coffey, two unidentified girls, Hilva Myers, unidentified, Ersel Root, Evelyn Gibbons, ? Moore, Buddy Turpen, R.L. German, and Charles Maddock (squeezed in behind them are Doyle Crafford and teacher Richard Moon); (third row) Dorothy Anderson, Dorris Bullard, Loreta Rash, unidentified, Buddy Small, Gene Atkins, Bobby Pane, Calvin White, and Robert Coffer. (Waterford Library.)

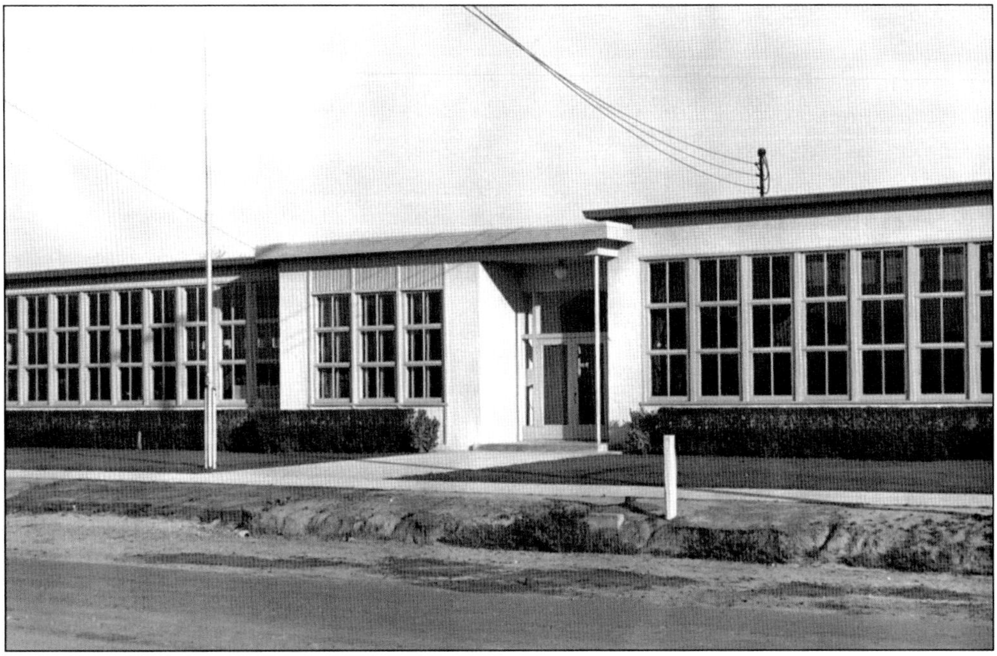

This is how the Waterford Elementary School appeared when it opened in 1946, just as America entered its post–World War II population boom.

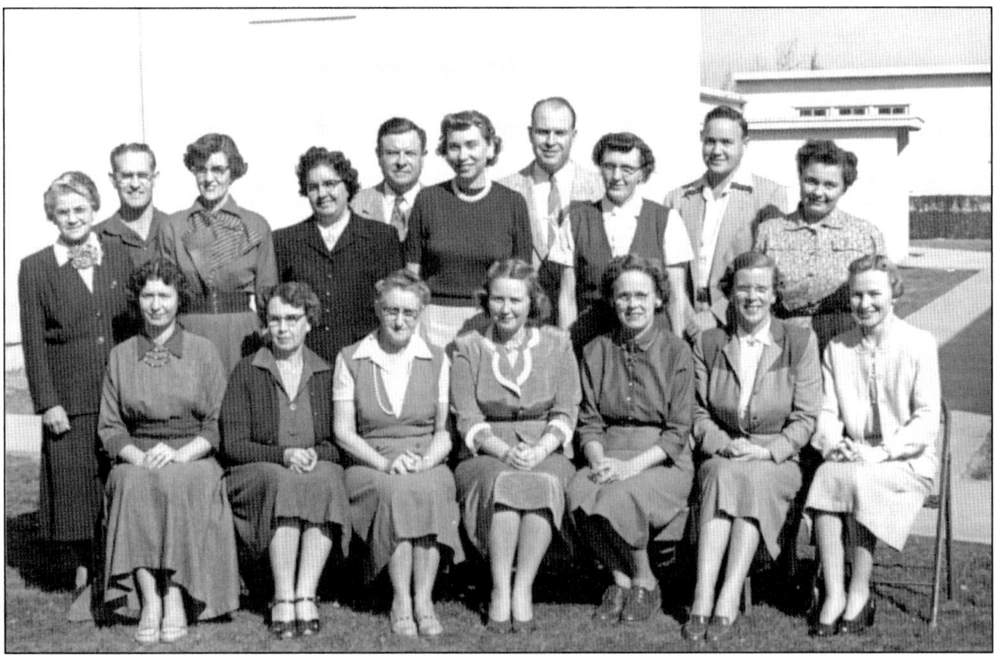

The Waterford Elementary School staff gathered for this photograph in 1955. From left to right, they are (seated) Lorraine Cederlind, Esther Kline, Merle Wine, unidentified, Esther Ashton, Helen Anderson, and school secretary Marilyn Switzer; (standing) May Weems, Cecil Fager, Marian Sargent, Mintee Francis, Jim Worthington, Lucille Whitehead, principal Richard Moon, Irma Muth, Bill Forbus, and Kathleen Chafin. The school had about 525 students at the time. (Waterford Historical Society.)

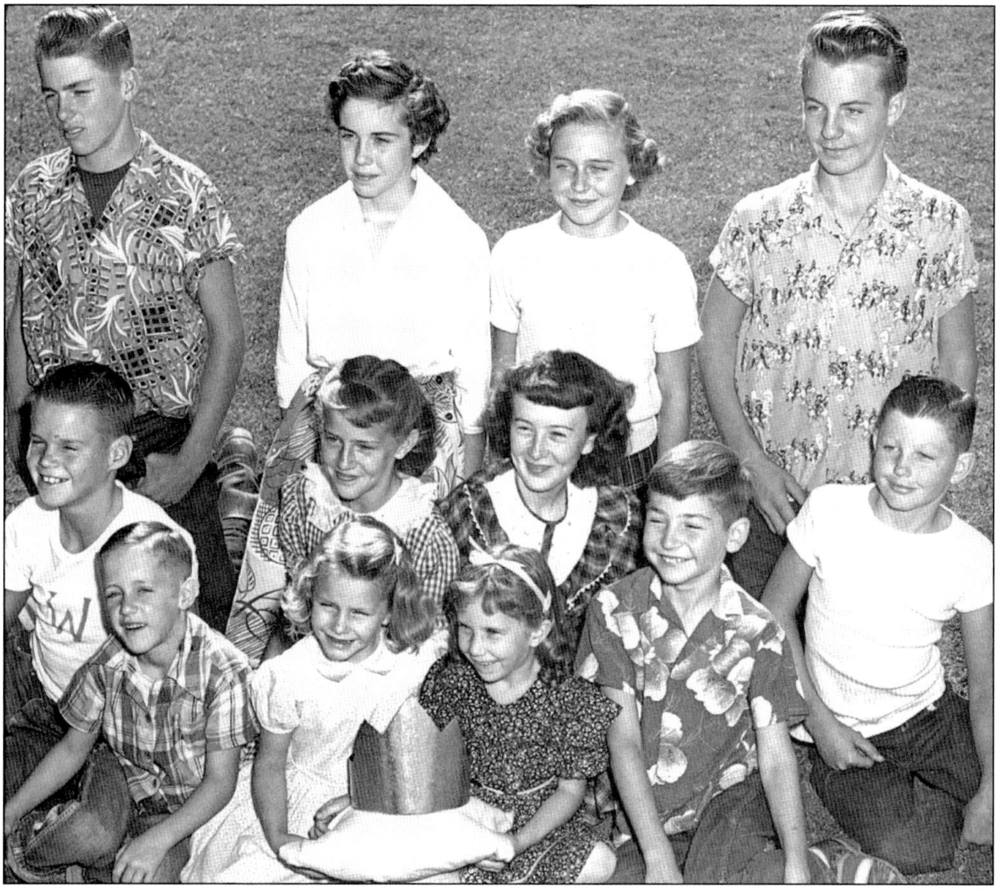

These Waterford Elementary School students were ace spellers who made it to the Stanislaus County Spelling Bee in the 1950s. From left to right, those pictured here are (first row) Phillip Jones, Meredith Hawkins, Ivalyn Miller, and Loren Baker; (second row) Denton Todd, Barbara King, Kathy Roberts, and Charles "Chuck" Shepherd; (third row) Artie Howe, Marie Allen, Linda Peavson, and Marvin Kaufman. (Waterford Historical Society.)

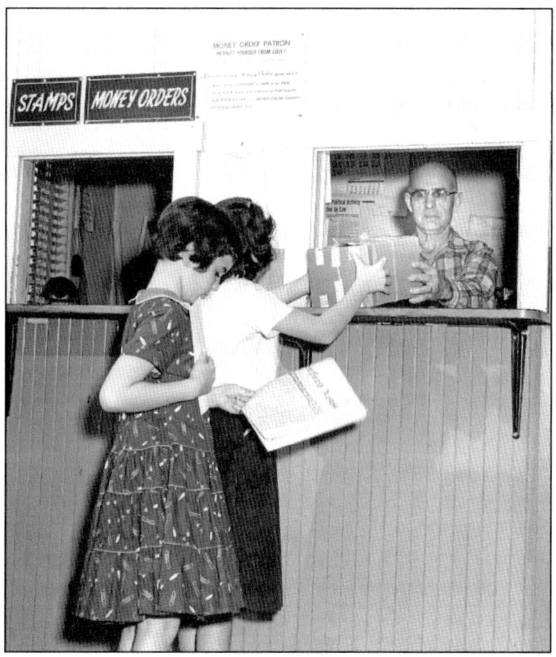

Waterford postmaster Schuyler Fager assists Waterford Elementary School girls in their study unit on the mail system in March 1956. Fager served as postmaster from 1945 to 1967. At the time of this photograph, mail was brought in on the train. One of the girls is holding a copy of the *Waterford News*. (Waterford Historical Society.)

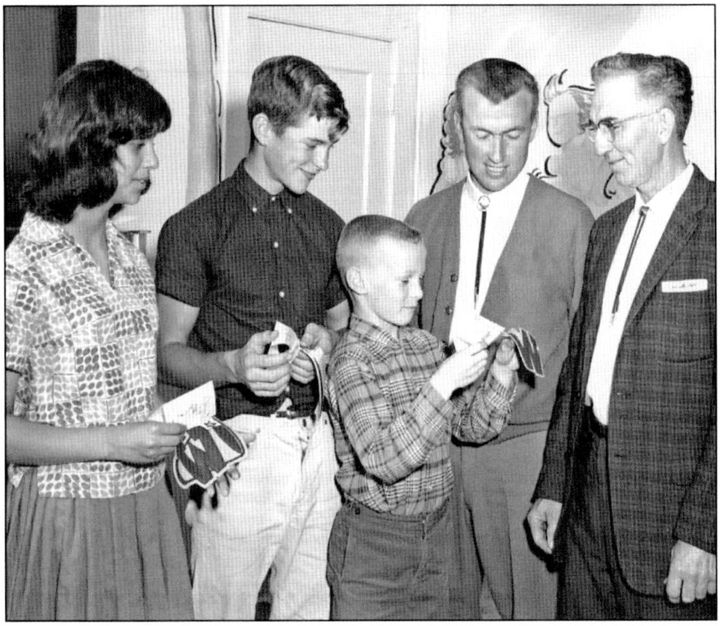

Sixth-grader Rob Weichert (center front) was presented a W letter by teacher Bill Interbitzen (second from right) and school board member Otto Price (right) in 1964. Also pictured are eighth-graders Mary Franca and Steve Cosner. This was a Stanislaus County Schools publicity photograph. (Waterford Historical Society.)

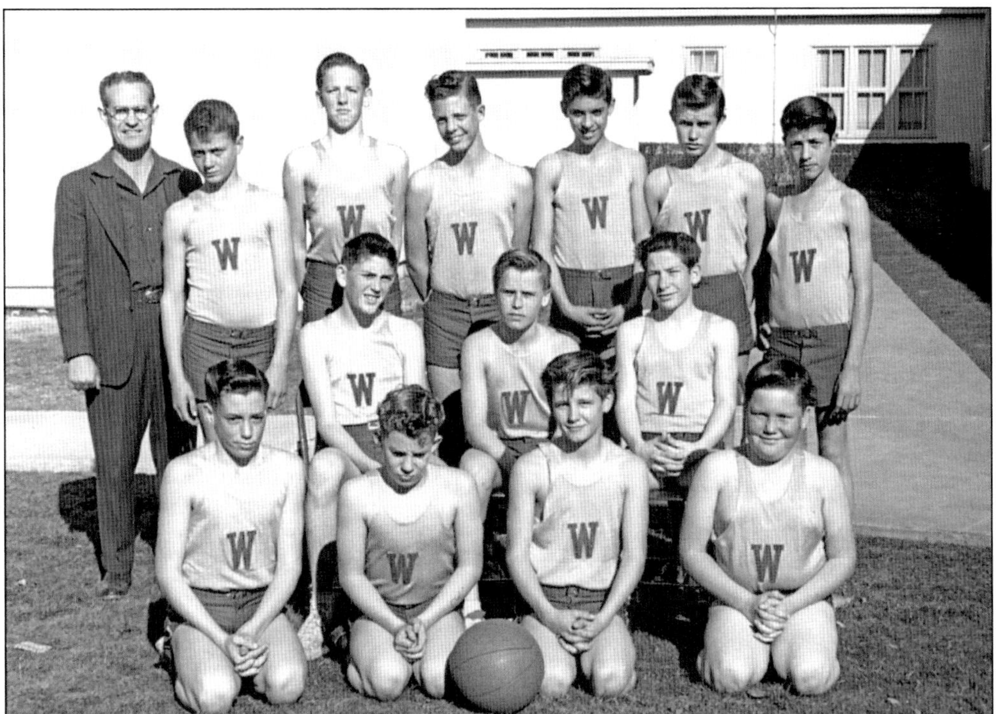

PE teacher Cecil Fager posed with this group of athletic students around 1954. Fager taught at Waterford Elementary School from 1954 to 1979. He served on the Waterford City Council from 1982 to 1984. (Waterford Historical Society.)

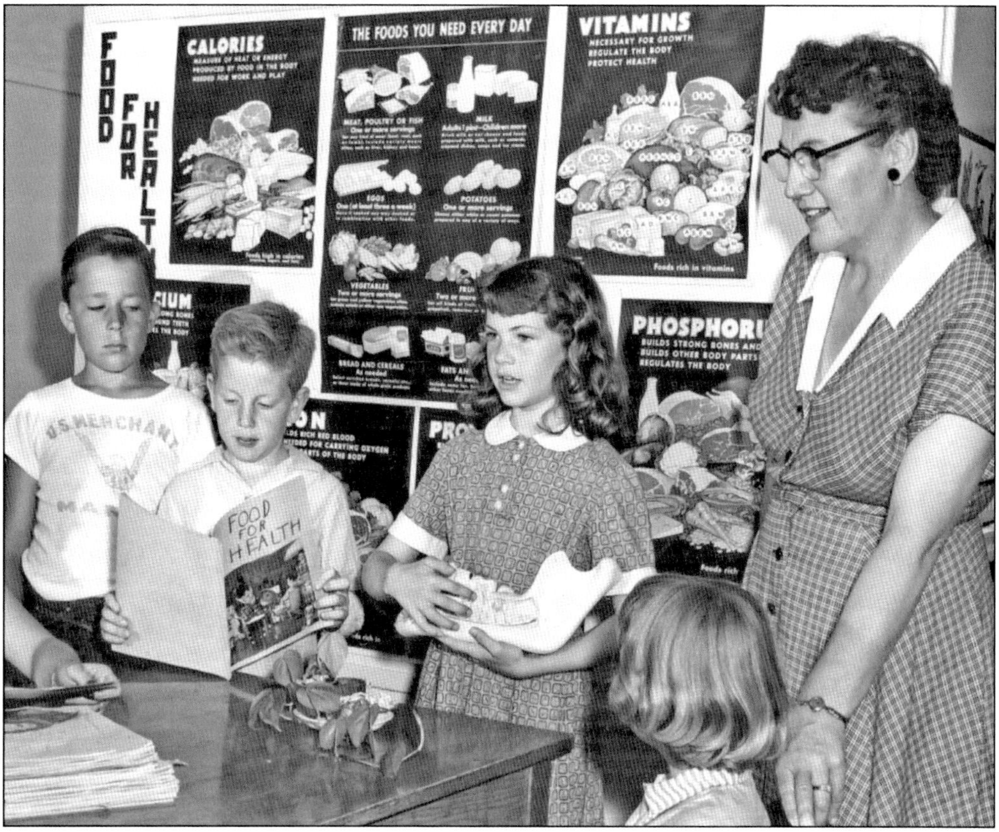

School nurse Freda Reneau took an active role in 1954 in educating Waterford kids about good nutrition. With her are, from left to right, Don Stackhouse, Raymond Jones, Susan Weichert and an unidentified girl. (Waterford Historical Society.)

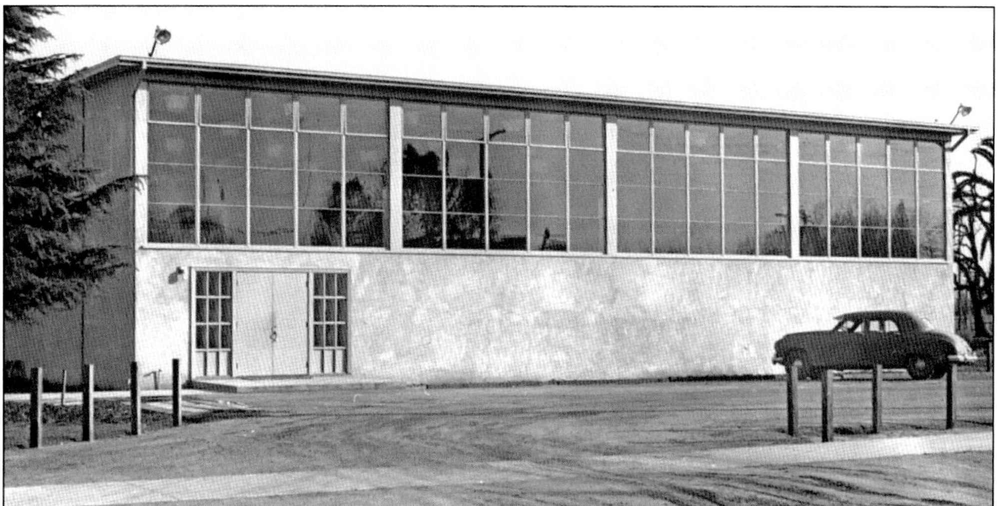

The Waterford Elementary School gym pictured shortly after its construction in 1951. It is still in use today. Note the now-vintage automobile parked at the west end of the gym's north side. (Waterford Historical Society.)

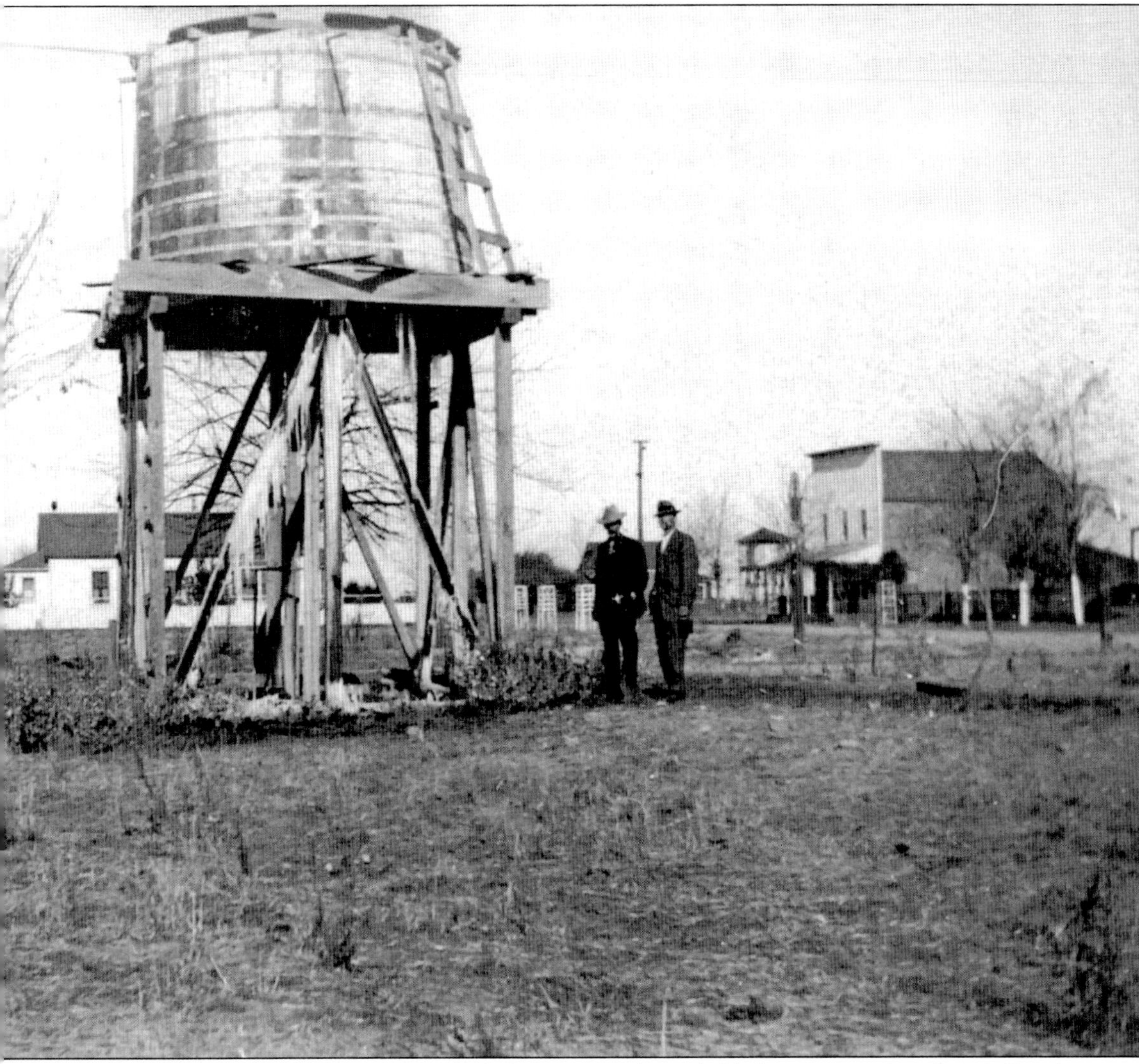

Two gentlemen check out icicles on a leaky water tank, probably between 1910 and 1918. Bentley Street is obscure behind the men, before the Wallis Building went up in the 1920s. The two-story Bertrandt Hotel at 312 E Street is seen at right. The hotel was first known as the Hilderbrand Hotel after S.K. Hilderbrand, a veteran of the Modoc Indian War, built it in 1891. In 1897, Joseph Bertrandt used it to house workers building the La Grange Dam. His daughter, Alice Bertha Bertrandt Maitland, was born on September 14, 1892, and lived many years in the hotel. Burr and Ethel Sinclear owned it from 1942 to 1977. Time and neglect led to its removal in the early 1980s. The hotel sat on the vacant lot between the Waterford Police Station and Pizza Plus. (Valerie Turpen.)

Eight

Community Life 1900 to 1940s

Before 1891, Waterford's center was at Yosemite Boulevard and Tim Bell Road. By 1870, approximately 40 people called Waterford home, and the town grew to 63 by 1880. The entire town shifted, however, when the Southern Pacific Railroad finished its Stockton-Visalia line primarily for passenger service and for hauling grain to markets. "Old Town" was abandoned as a new business district was built near the tracks on Front Street (now F Street or the Oakdale-Waterford Highway.) New homes were constructed east of the tracks.

As the booze flowed, Waterford's reputation grew notorious. Norwegian immigrant Oline Roen observed: "There were many saloons in the early days, especially after 1900, when the entire town moved up the hill to be near the railroad. . . . I count, off hand, 11 saloons, although some claim there were 13. Anyway, the little town was notorious for its saloons, drunken brawls, and dives." A God-fearing woman, Roen crusaded against the saloon saturation after a series of deadly shootings. Around 1904, someone mugged and killed Tom Lumpey, wrapped his body in a blanket, dragged it into the Curtzwiler Saloon, and burned the building in an attempt to hide the evidence. In 1907, at Eldred's Saloon on E Street behind the Roen family's D Street house, shots rang out. John Roen ran over only to witness bartender Dick Couzens, blood streaming down his face from bullet holes in his head, kissing his wife farewell. The effect of Roscoe Bradley's bullets on Joe Little was more immediate; both Couzens and Little died. Another Waterford saloon shooting left Henry Fine dead.

In response, Oline Roen helped form a chapter of the Women's Christian Temperance Union and sought the help of County Supervisor John McMann in regulating the saloons. One by one, the saloons were "weeded out," according to Roen, "many of them burned, always in the night, by jealous competitors."

Around 1913, Thomas K. Beard and his Beard Land Development subdivided parcels around Waterford for small farming operations. In 1920, smaller farms were growing Kadota figs and later peaches, grapes, nuts, and beans. Beard hired colonizer Levi Winklebleck to sell parcels and promote Waterford in Midwestern states. Waterford's population grew little between 1900 and 1920. But as the 1930s Dust Bowl refugees from Oklahoma, Arkansas, and Texas settled in California, Waterford's fields and farms drew unskilled laborers. By 1945, approximately 1,000 lived in Waterford.

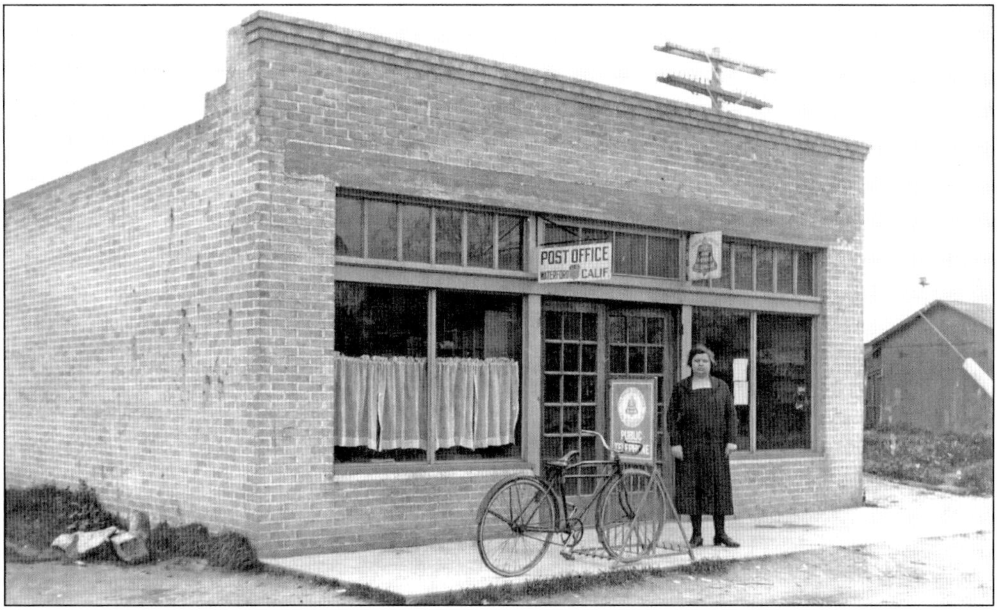

Phone service came to Waterford in 1904, and Jennie Kirk (here) was the switchboard operator and postmistress. The office was located on Bentley Street's south side east of the Bank of the West. George and Jennie Kirk were in charge of postal operations from 1922 to 1928. Others postmasters included John N. Prather, 1872–1873; Henry H. Howell, 1873–1877; Adrian Faure, 1877–1886; William K. Summers, 1886–1887; John P. Harbert, 1887–1893; Charles Horsley, 1887–1893; John Hennemuth, 1897–1913; Joseph J. Knowlton, 1913–1915; Leland R. Hayter, 1915–1918; Manila Walther, 1918–1920; Edward Arbios, 1920–1922; Jennie Sanford Root, 1936–1945; Schuyler Fager, 1945–1967; Clark Billups, 1967–1971; and Will Wasson, 1971–1992. (Waterford Historical Society.)

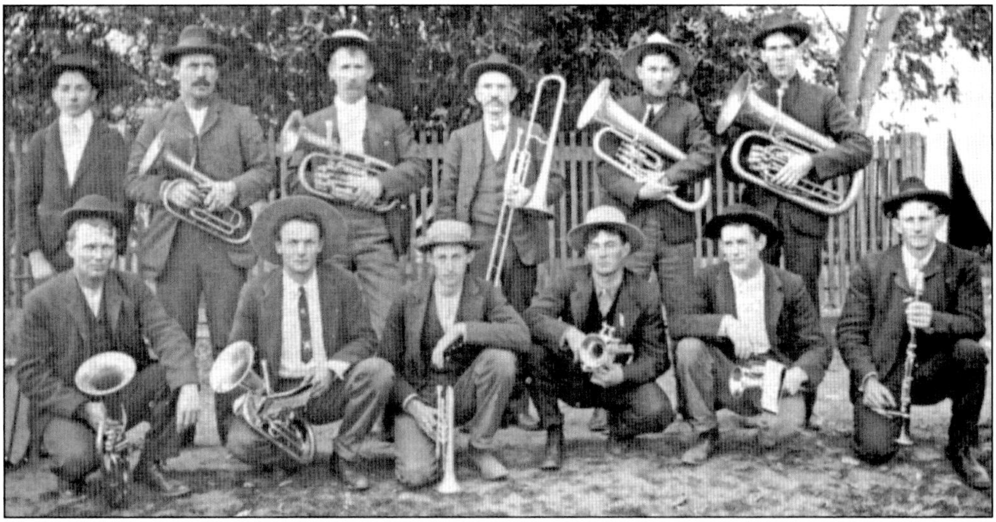

Waterford had a men's band that played for the community's benefit around 1915. Specific identifications are unknown but the names are likely among a roster of band members: leader C.C. Horsley, W.T. Pinkston, H.L. Dallas, Ernest Welch, Roy Fox, W.A. Hayter, Clarence Hughes, Al Murdock, Martin Hagen, James R. Browder, William Darby, Fred Voight, Charles A. Walther, Leland Hayter, Dolph L. Browder, Royal O. Ballard, Hans Erickson, and A.D. Cowden. (*Waterford Centennial: 1857–1957.*)

Albert Sigwardt Roen was a small lad when a traveling photographer came through Waterford around 1904. Albert was encouraged to pose for this adorable photograph with the photographer's dog in his lap, but he still looks a bit apprehensive. Born in 1900 to John and Oline Roen, Albert became a cattle rancher and helped organize the La Grange Rodeo. The father of John Roen, Albert died in 1959. (Betty Roen.)

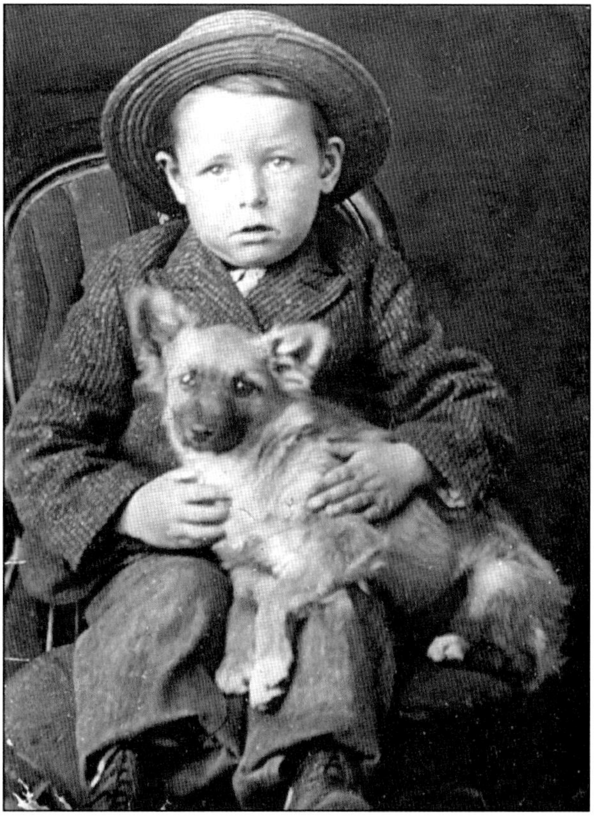

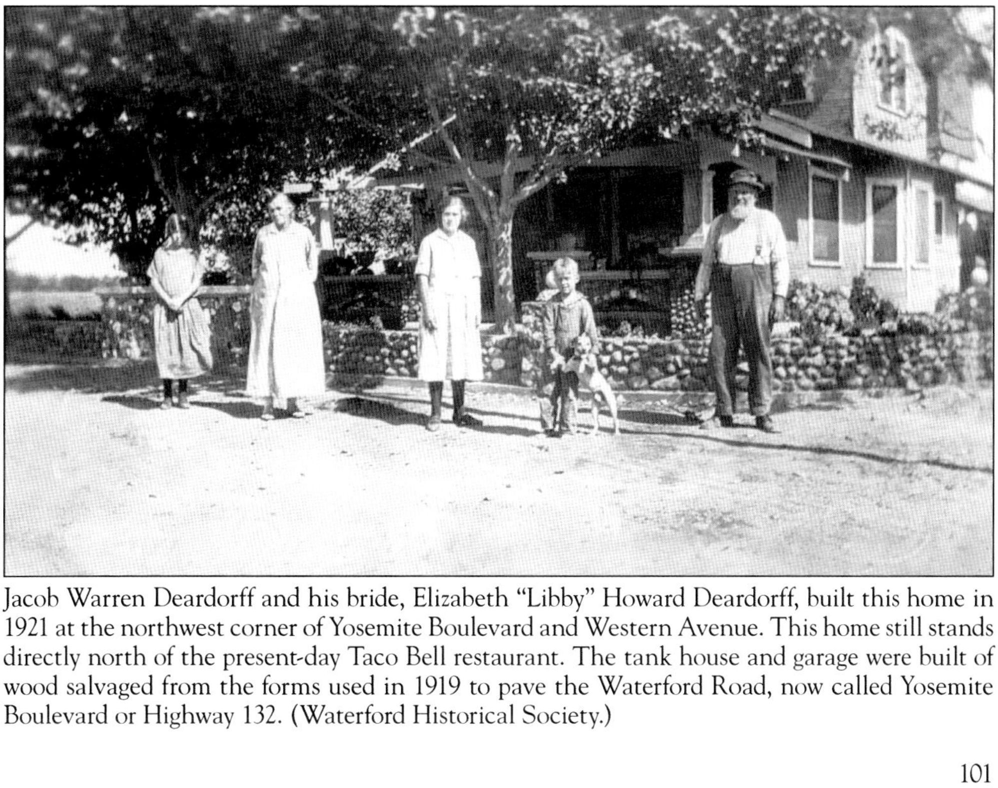

Jacob Warren Deardorff and his bride, Elizabeth "Libby" Howard Deardorff, built this home in 1921 at the northwest corner of Yosemite Boulevard and Western Avenue. This home still stands directly north of the present-day Taco Bell restaurant. The tank house and garage were built of wood salvaged from the forms used in 1919 to pave the Waterford Road, now called Yosemite Boulevard or Highway 132. (Waterford Historical Society.)

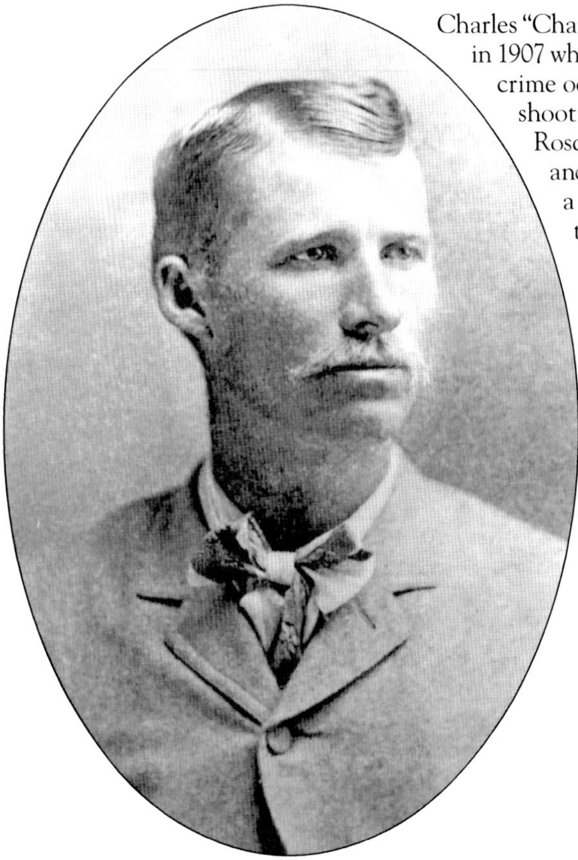

Charles "Charlie" Walther was constable in Waterford in 1907 when things got out of hand and a celebrated crime occurred at one of Waterford's saloons. A shooting occurred in Eldred's Saloon, where Roscoe Bradley shot and killed Dick Couzens and Joe Little. Walther later concentrated on a business venture—owning and operating the Summers Hotel (later renamed the Waterford Hotel and appearing on the front cover). An advertisement placed by him in 1915 is seen on page 59. Walther lived in the hotel with his family and sold it in 1918 and moved out. (Valerie Turpen.)

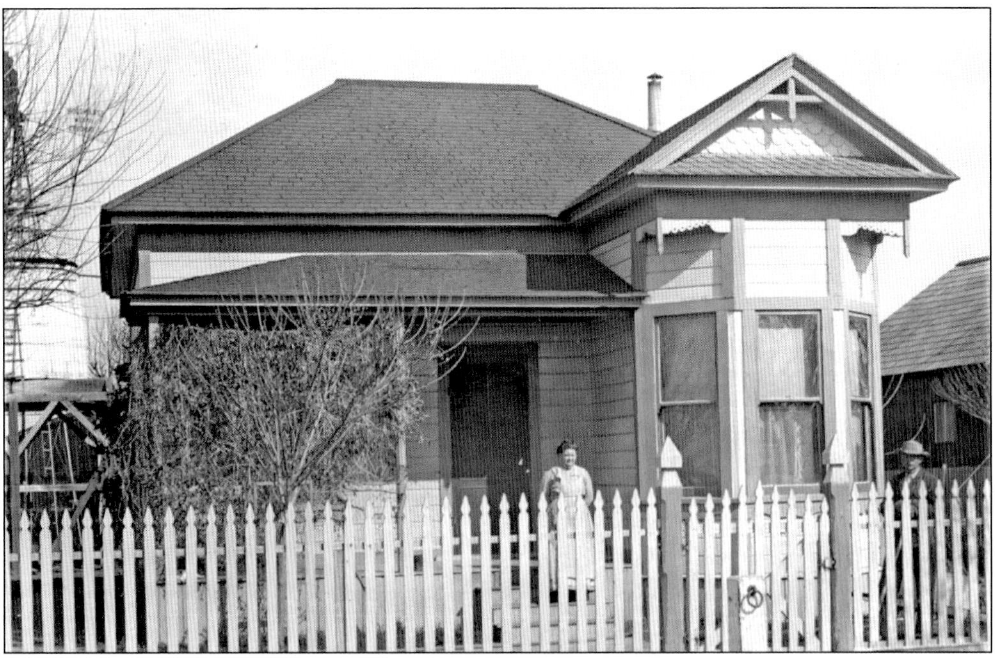

This D Street home is typical of its era and is still standing. (Waterford Historical Society.)

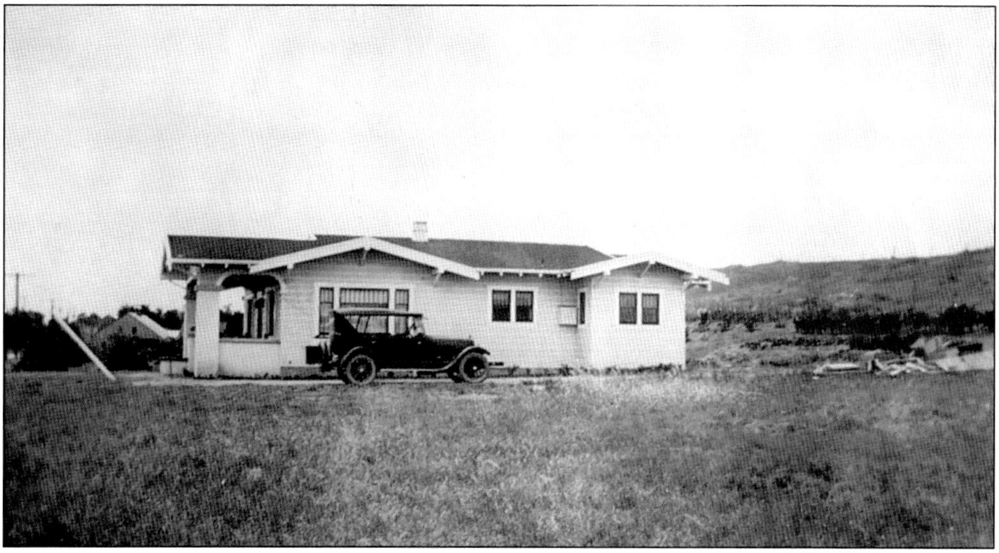

This was the home of Lee and Alma Prouty, located at 13255 Yosemite Boulevard. Lee was the son of early-day blacksmith Joseph Prouty. This 1922 view shows the bluff to the north as well as his father's blacksmith shop west of the house. Lee Prouty was born on February 23, 1887, and died on May 24, 1972. (Betty Roen.)

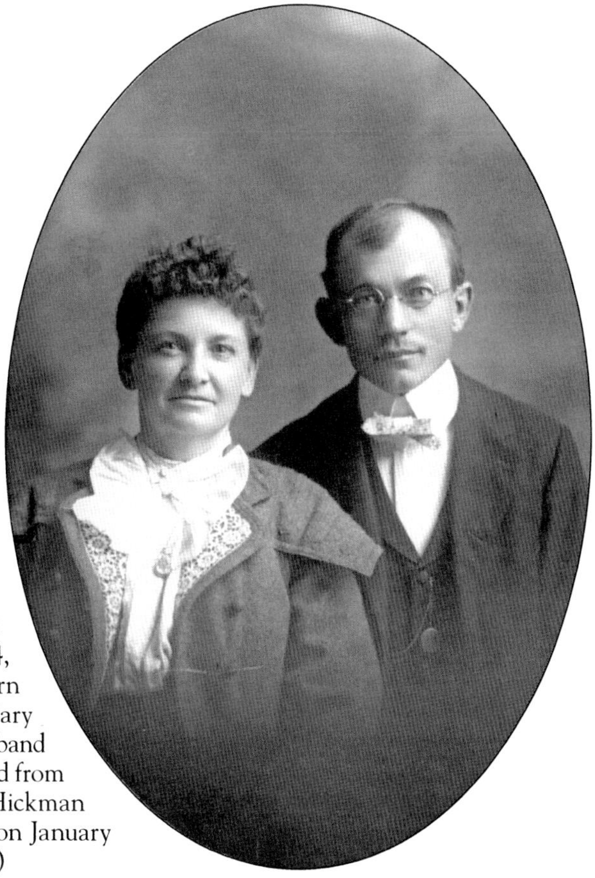

Early-day Waterford residents Clara and Fred W. Voight lived on D Street. Fred was born on June 10, 1876, in Germany and came to the United States in 1884, when he was 8. During the Spanish-American War, Fred served as a member of the 6th Infantry, Company D of Modesto, which never left California. Fred was lured to Alaska with the family of Charles Walther during the Klondike Stampede gold rush in Alaska of 1897 and 1898. Fred made a living with carpentry and janitorial skills. On August 22, 1904, he married Clara Turpen, who was born in Empire in 1870 to Benjamin and Mary Turpen. Clara had divorced her first husband before she met Fred. Clara later suffered from diabetes and went blind. She died in Hickman on March 19, 1935. Fred Voight died on January 3, 1960, in Hickman. (Valerie Turpen.)

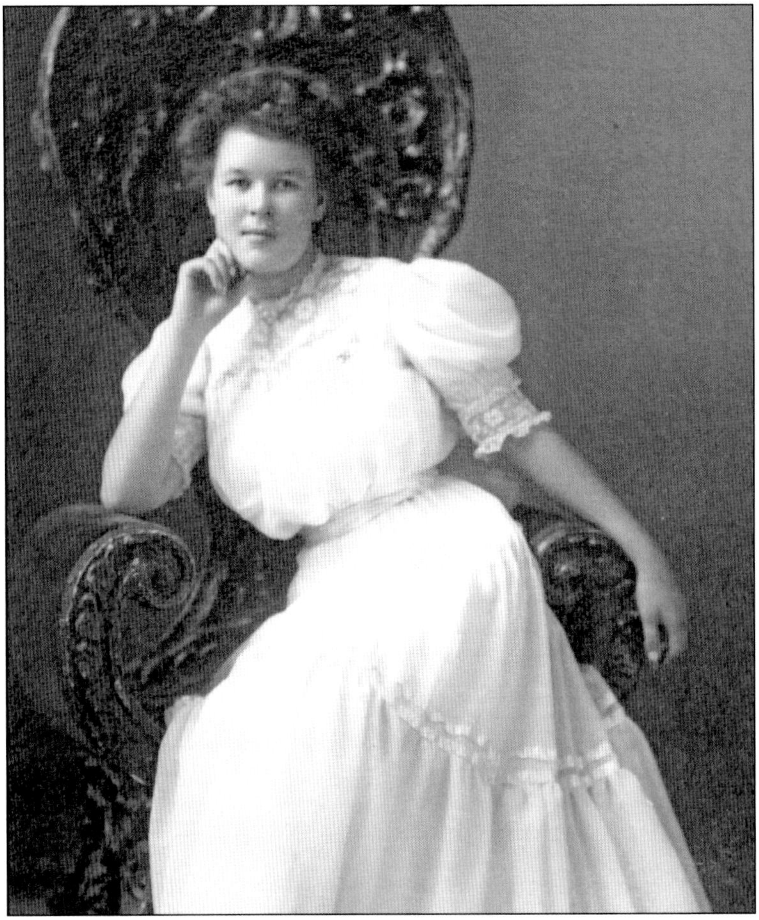

Olga Gustava Roen, the pretty daughter born to John and Oline Roen on June 15, 1888, brought refinement and culture to Waterford. After attending music school in San Jose, Olga traveled by horse and buggy from home to home in Waterford to give piano lessons to youngsters. She developed tuberculosis and died on March 15, 1915, at age 26. (LaVerne Johnson.)

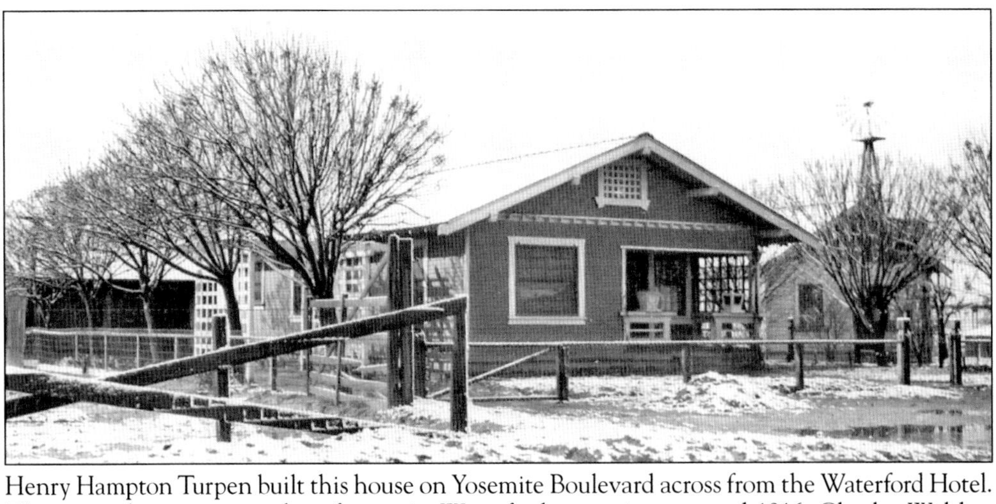

Henry Hampton Turpen built this house on Yosemite Boulevard across from the Waterford Hotel. This was taken on a rare day of snow in Waterford some time around 1916. Charles Walther deeded the property to Henry Hampton on November 1, 1915, after he married Ruth Walther. (Valerie Turpen.)

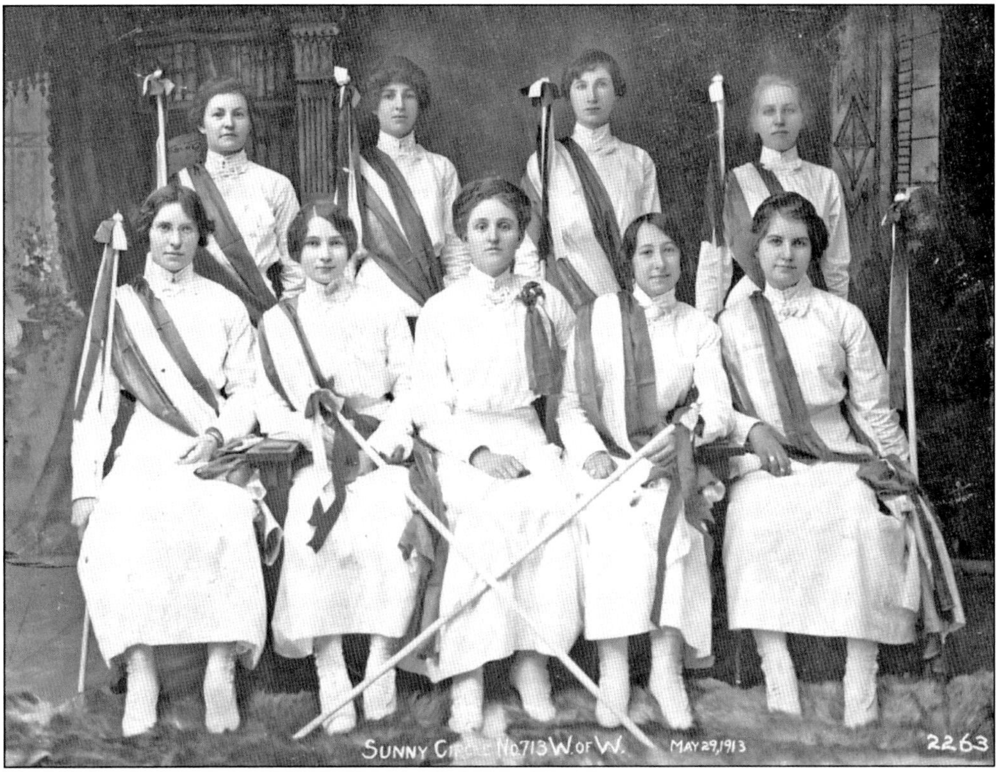

Civic groups in Waterford included the Sunny Circle No. 713 of the Women of Woodcraft. From left to right, pictured here on May 29, 1913, are drill-team members (first row) Edith Horsley Bentley, Irma Collins Gurley, Lottie Anderson Browder, Georgia Knowlton, and Manila Walther Gatzman; (second row) Lena Browder, Marguerite Dallas Hayter, Ruth Walther Turpen, and Alma Johnson Prouty. (Valerie Turpen.)

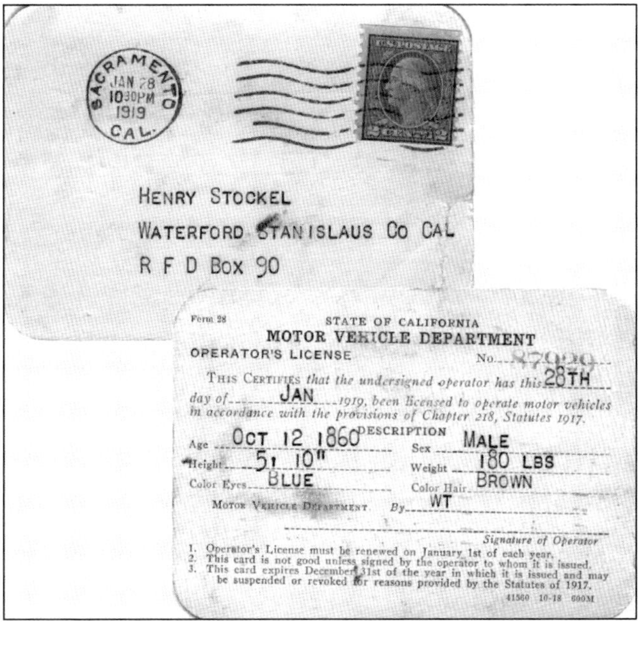

SACRAMENTO JAN 28 10:30 PM 1919 CAL.

HENRY STOCKEL
WATERFORD STANISLAUS CO CAL
R F D Box 90

Form 28

STATE OF CALIFORNIA
MOTOR VEHICLE DEPARTMENT
OPERATOR'S LICENSE No.

THIS CERTIFIES *that the undersigned operator has this* 28TH *day of* JAN *1919, been licensed to operate motor vehicles in accordance with the provisions of Chapter 218, Statutes 1917.*

DESCRIPTION

Age OCT 12 1860 Sex MALE
Height 5' 10" Weight 180 LBS
Color Eyes BLUE Color Hair BROWN

MOTOR VEHICLE DEPARTMENT *By* WT

Signature of Operator

1. Operator's License must be renewed on January 1st of each year.
2. This card is not good unless signed by the operator to whom it is issued.
3. This card expires December 31st of the year in which it is issued and may be suspended or revoked for reasons provided by the Statutes of 1917.

41560 10-18 600M

Henry Stockel of Waterford, born in 1860, was among the first 90,000 California drivers who received driver's licenses in the first years as motor vehicles proliferated. The 1919 license was unsophisticated in comparison to today's. (Waterford Historical Society.)

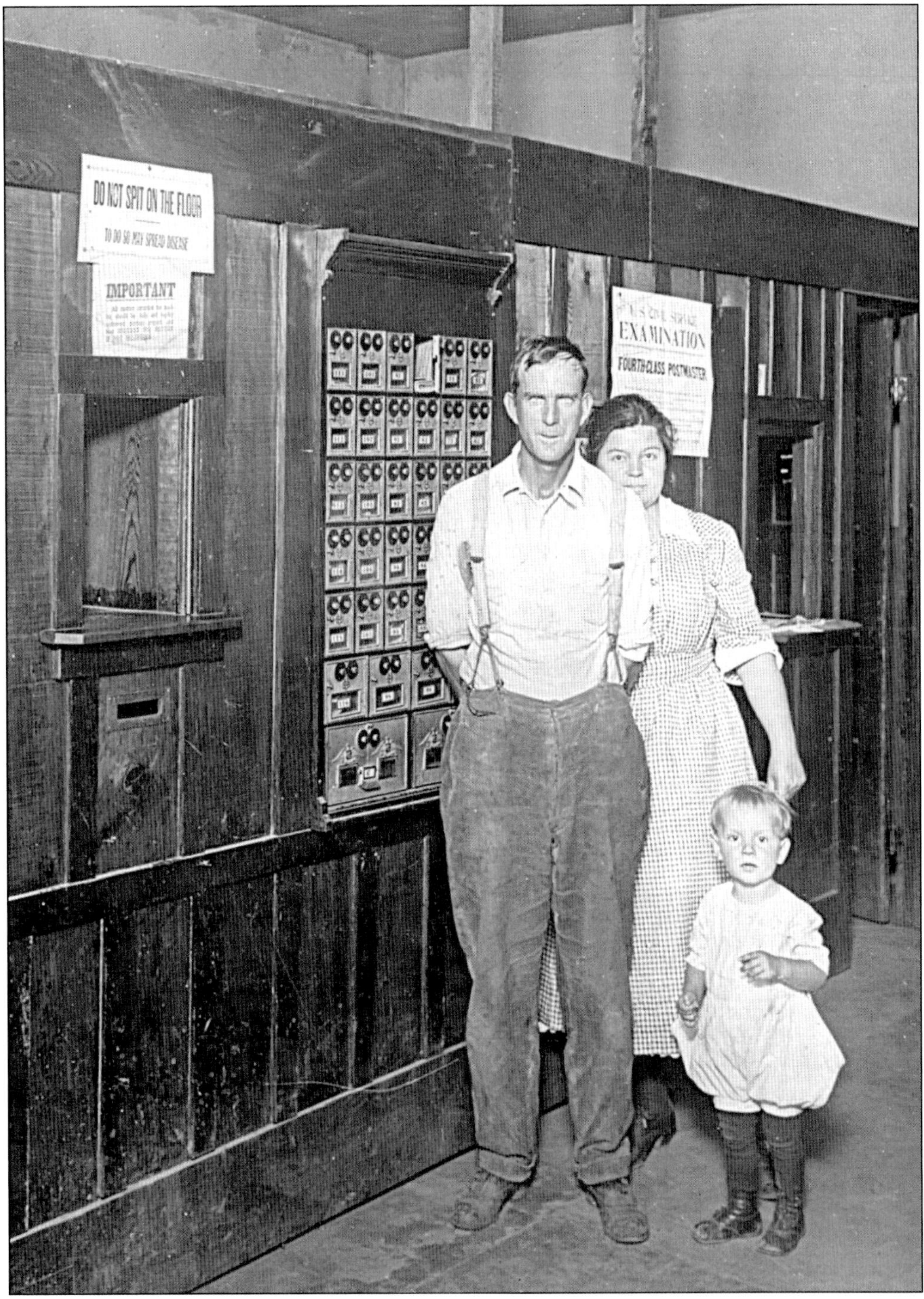

George and Jennie Kirk tag teamed as postmaster in the 1920s. They are pictured around 1925 standing inside the post office with son Mancell Kirk. Many went barefoot in those days, thus the wall poster advises patrons: "Do not spit on the floor . . . to do so may spread disease." Mancell Kirk later served on the Waterford Community Services District. (Kim Petroni.)

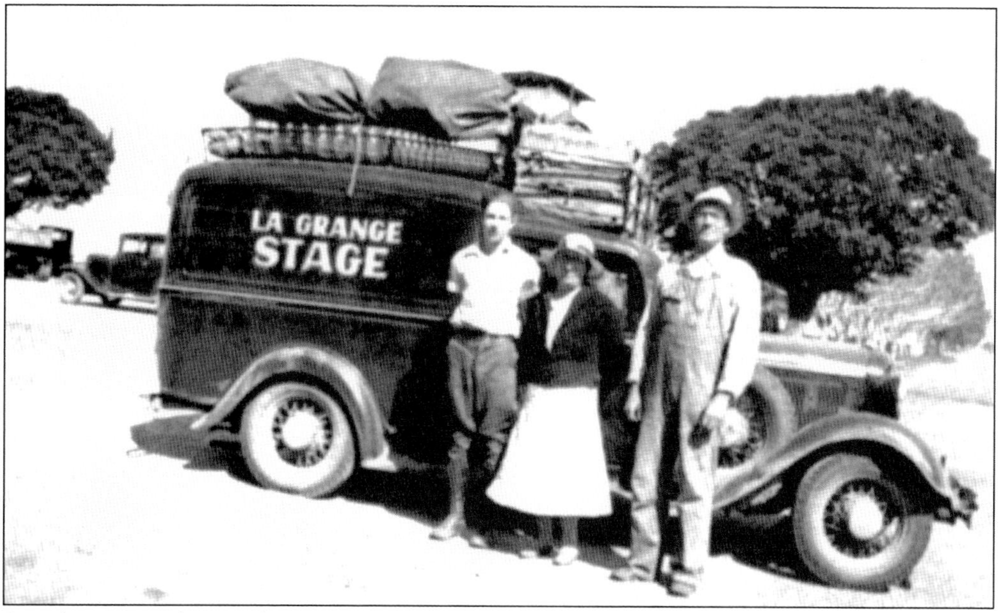

Seen here around 1923, the Overstreets operated the La Grange Stage Company after securing a $78-per-month contract to deliver mail to Waterford, La Grange, and Empire in 1929. Chantham Overstreet (right), pictured with son Leo and wife Levina, bought the stage business in 1931 from a "Dad" Bartlett for $300 and hauled supplies to Carpenter's Garage in Waterford, the Hammond and Bates store in La Grange, and to the La Grange dredge-mining headquarters. (Leo Overstreet.)

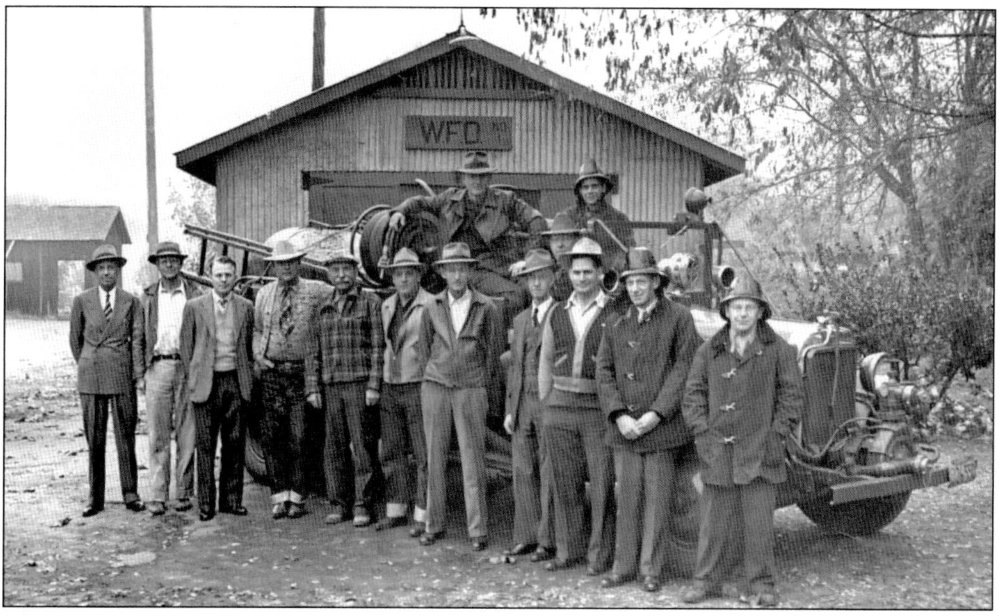

The Waterford Fire Department posed for this photograph with their 1929 Dodge fire pumper in 1930. From left to right, seen here are (first row) fire commissioner Lee Prouty, ex-fire chief Bill Lehmkuhl, fireman Leo Holzer, fire commissioners Albert Roen and Charlie Nielsen, firemen Robert "Bob" Carpenter, Lucien Bertrandt, Bill Reed, Levi "Tex" Brewer, and Ora Breshears, and fire chief Shorty Rager; (second row) Hans Nielsen, Hardy Monk, and "Punk" Carpenter. (Waterford Historical Society.)

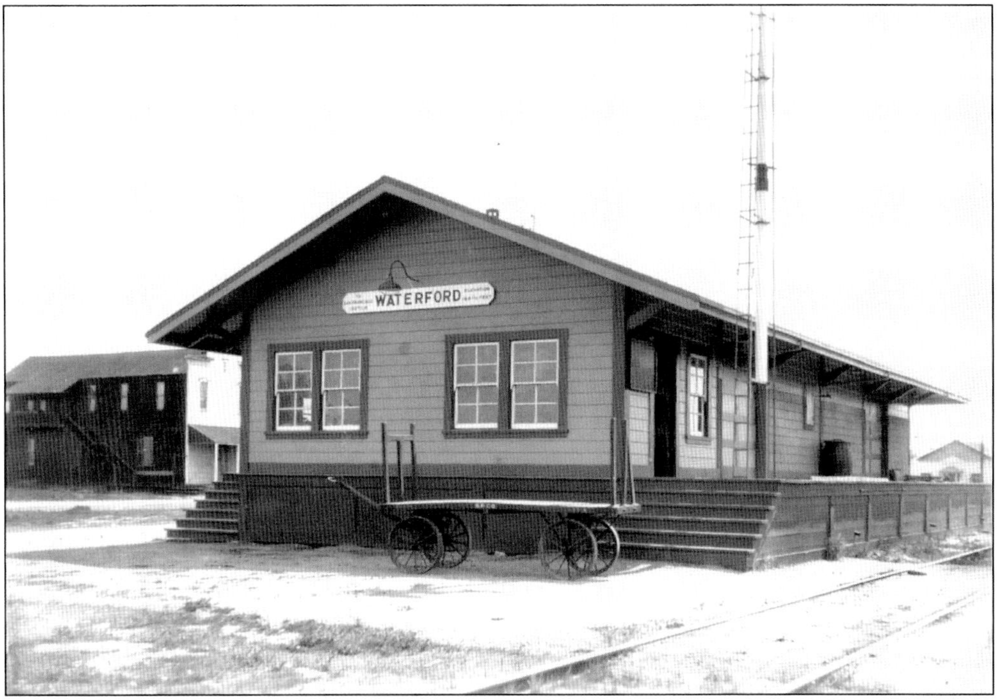

The second Southern Pacific Railroad depot was constructed in 1922, after the first depot burned in 1921. The depot was located just to the north of the present-day Waterford Post Office. It was purchased by Rob Bearden and moved to Big Bear Park in the 1980s to become the clubhouse. When the park was wiped away for Riverpointe subdivision, the depot was moved to an empty lot on Yosemite Boulevard east of Tim Bell Road, where it sits today. (Waterford Historical Society.)

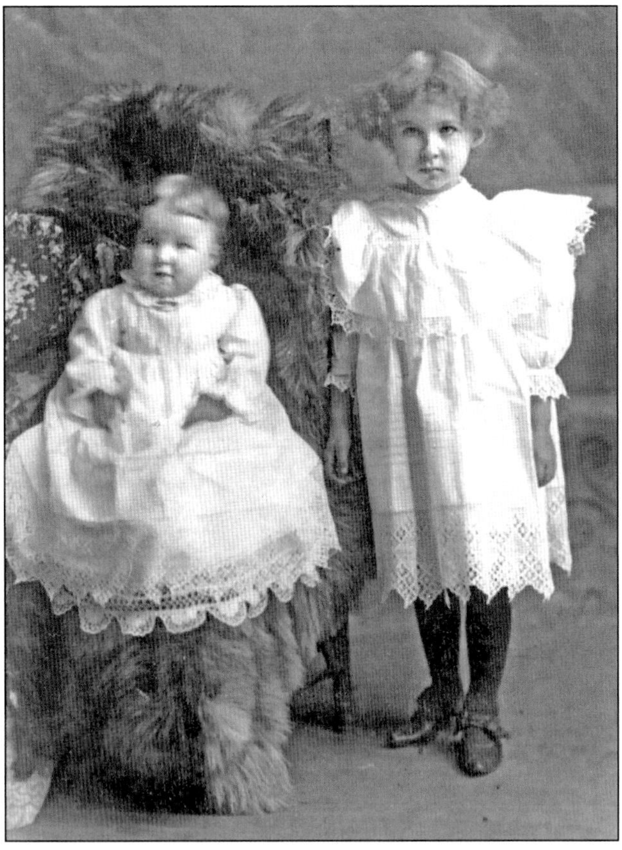

Manila Walther (right) and sister Ruth were the daughters of Charles and Sophia Walther. Manila grew up to become the first woman to handle Waterford's mail. The 10th postmaster, she served from 1918 to 1920. (Valerie Turpen.)

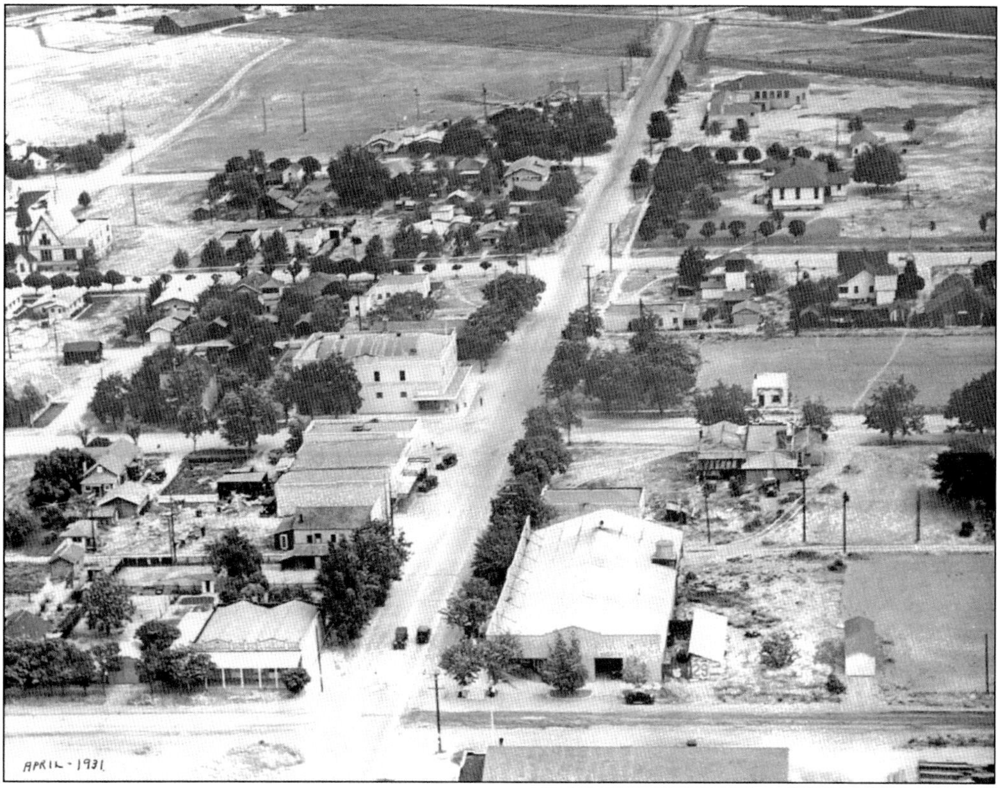

Waterford was a small community when this aerial photograph was taken in April 1931. The Ford garage dominates the foreground. The two-story Gordon Building is on Bentley Street at the center of town. Community Baptist Church is at far left, with Main Street ending just past C Street. A dirt country road in those days, Tim Bell Road is at upper right. (Waterford Historical Society.)

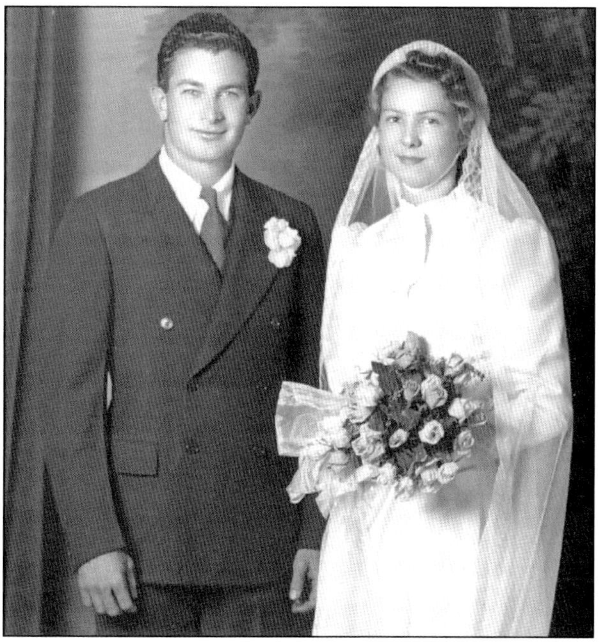

Neil Weichert of Waterford married Dorothy Hawkins, a Roberts Ferry native, on August 5, 1939. Five years after their wedding, Neil went to war, working as a clerk in Manila, the Philippines, at the headquarters of Gen. Douglas MacArthur. Weichert taught school for 43 years and was a coach and counselor at Oakdale High School for 35 years. Dorothy Weichert was a teacher's aide and a substitute teacher. The couple celebrated their 71st wedding anniversary in 2010 just prior to her death. (Neil Weichert.)

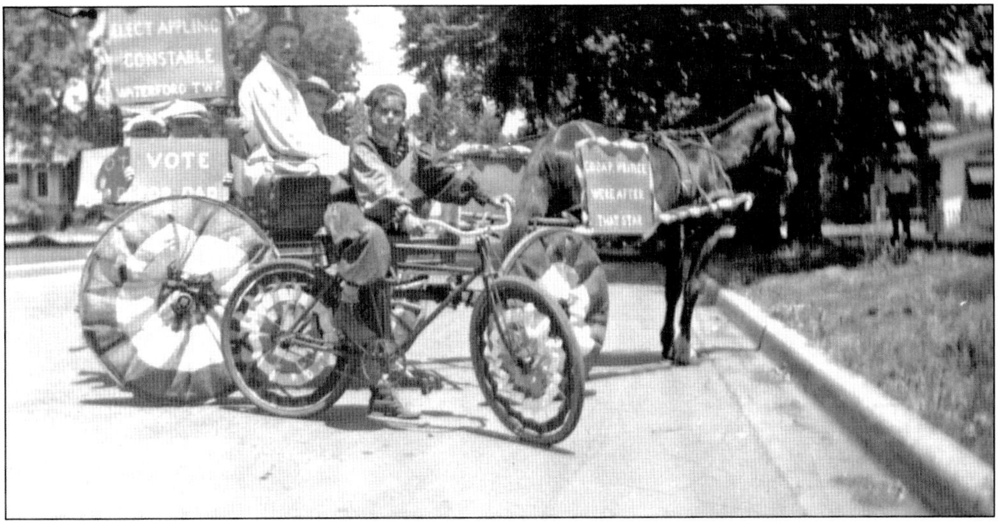

Constable candidate Raymond Appling entered the 1934 Fourth of July Parade in Waterford with his children. Appling sits here in an antique buggy decorated with red, white, and blue crepe and bunting while children Warren and John ride along on bicycles also decorated. A sign on the horse reads, "Giddap, Prince, we're after that star." The TWP on the sign behind Appling may stand for Township. (Sandra Burley.)

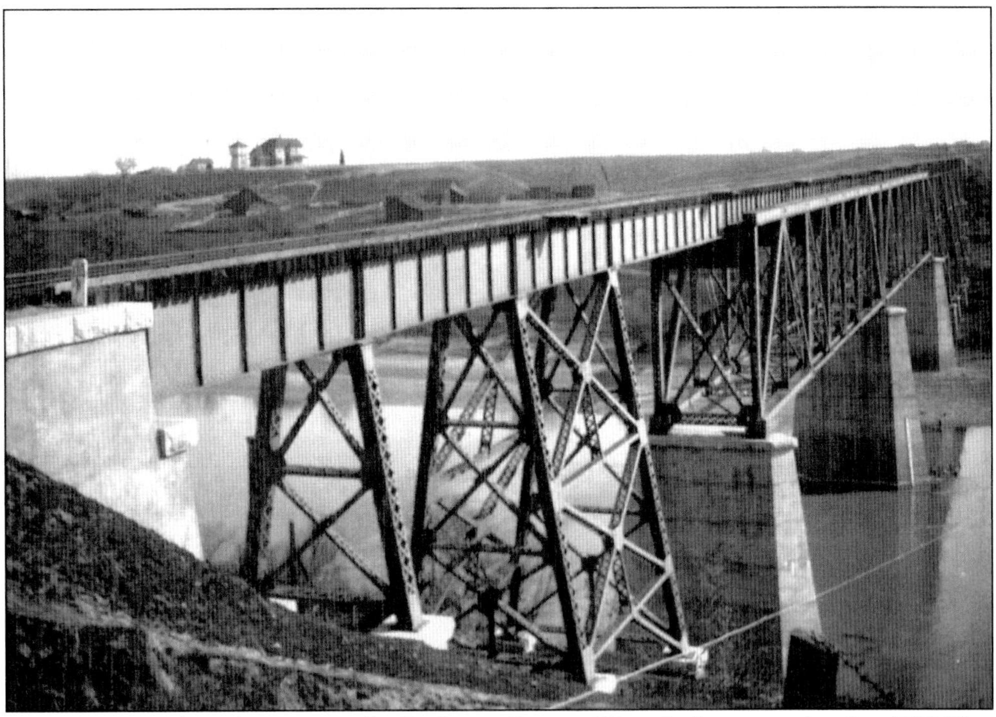

This iron railroad trestle spanning the Tuolumne River at Waterford was completed in 1907. This line connected Waterford to Hickman and Montpelier beyond. A train last used this bridge on January 28, 1977. The Appling house is seen on the Hickman side. (Candy Schmidt.)

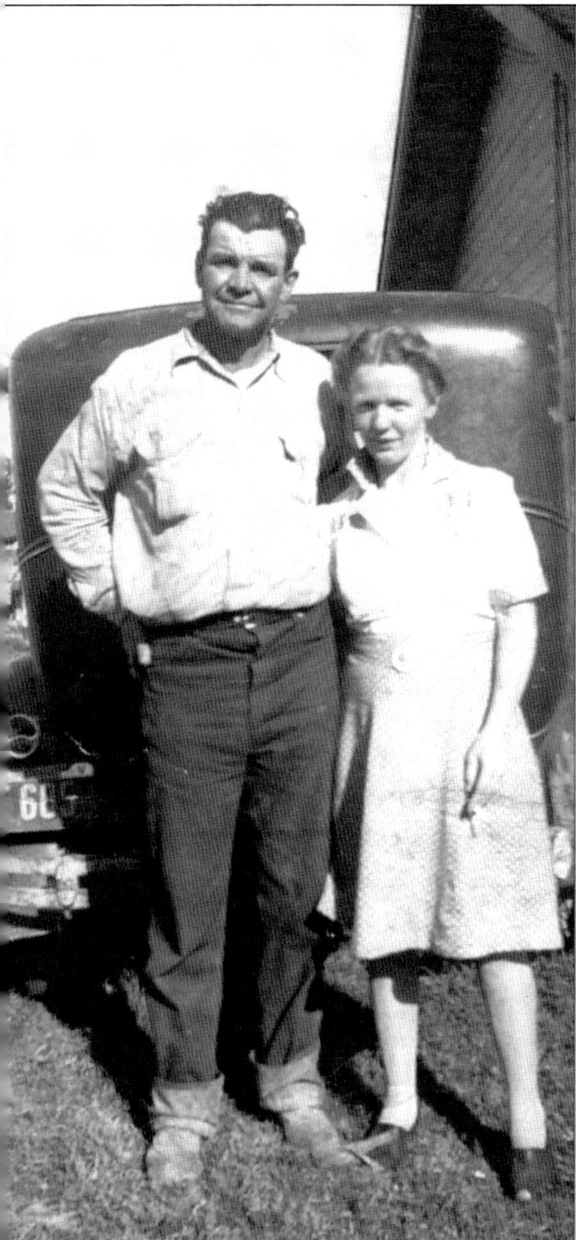
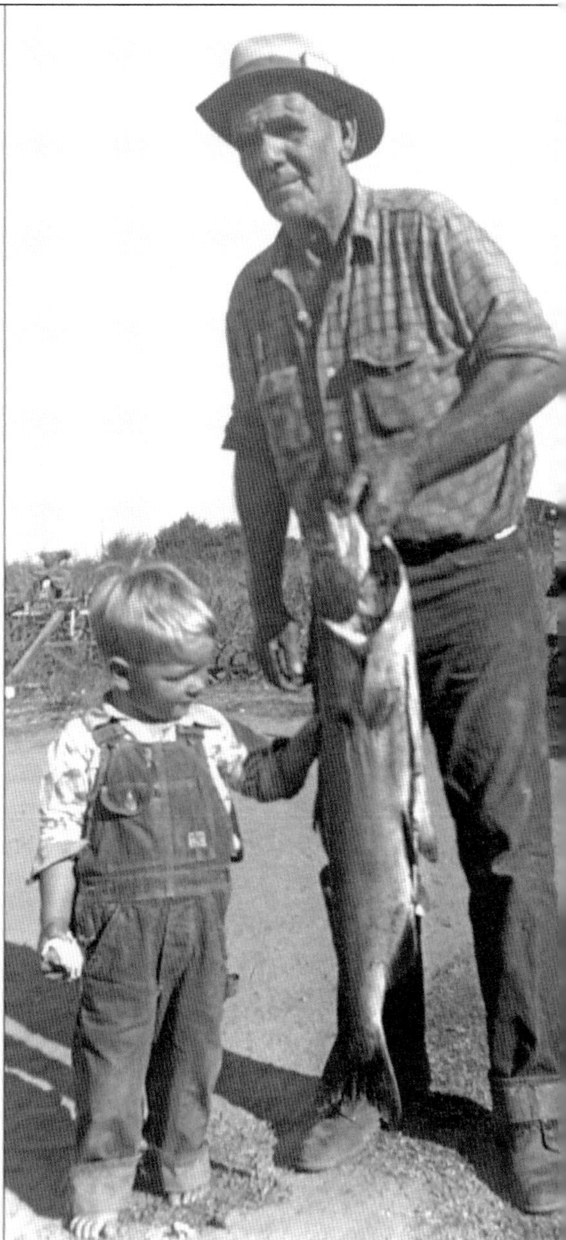

The Casey family has been part of Waterford for over six decades. At left, standing in front of their 1930 Model A, Dan and Ilean Casey pursued California as the golden dream. After marrying in Modesto, they came to Waterford in 1946 to farm 26 acres near the Tuolumne River east of town. Dan was a native of Missouri. Ilean came to California as a girl in the early 1920s. Her family came from Oklahoma part of the way in a covered wagon. At right, their barefooted son, Pat Casey, is taken by the large salmon caught by grandfather Scott Miller in the river near the Casey farm just outside of Waterford in the 1940s. (Joe Casey.)

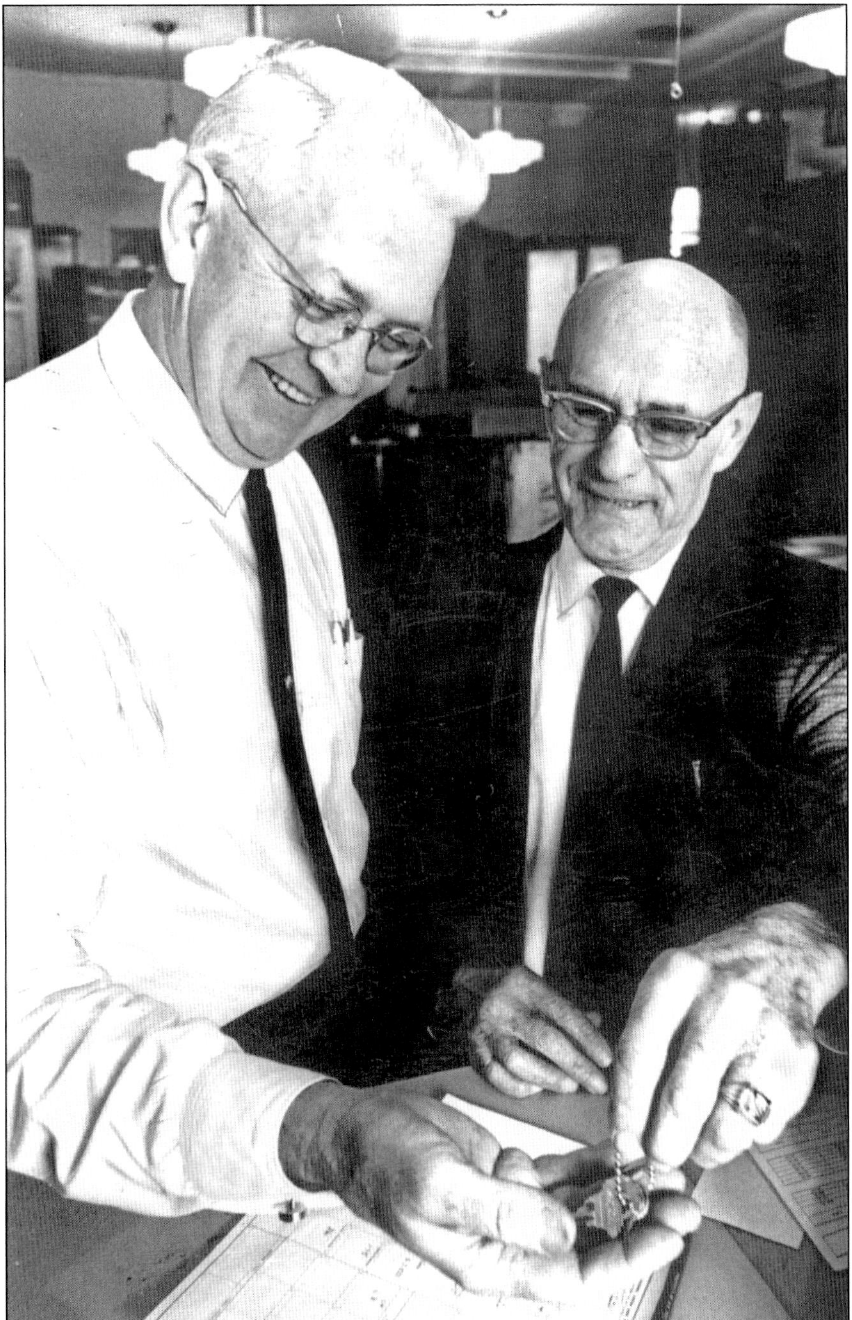

L. Clark Billups (left) was handed the keys to the Waterford Post Office by retiring postmaster Schuyler Fager in 1967. Billups was also the publisher of the *Waterford News*. At the time, the post office was located on the east side of E Street south of Bentley Street. On January 26, 1969, a new post office was dedicated at the southwest corner of E Street and Welch Street. It was later abandoned for the current post office and razed. Billups, who died in 1971, served as fire chief. (Mildred Dennis.)

Nine

Community Life
1950 to Present

Waterford grew from a town of 1,775 residents in 1950 to a city of about 2,800 residents by the late 1980s. Today, it's home to about 9,000 residents but remains a town driven by agriculture. After World War II, educator Richard Moon led a drive to incorporate Waterford as a city. Moon looked at the success of Escalon, a San Joaquin County town of roughly the same size, which had incorporated because it desired its own police force. Merchants, however, saw little merit and fought the idea, since sheriff's deputies maintained law and order. The idea would rest until October 1969, when Waterford residents voted 302 to 270 to incorporate as the eighth city in Stanislaus County. Thelma Woodbridge was instrumental in obtaining signatures on petitions for a vote on incorporation. The city's first police chief came in 1981, when Walton Richison of Brea was hired for $660 per month.

In the 1950s, Waterford was growing an exceptional baseball player in Joe Rudi, who would aid the Oakland A's in winning the World Series in 1972, 1973, and 1974. Rudi, who attended Waterford Elementary School from 1951 to 1960, gained national fame with his memorable catch against the wall in the ninth inning of Game 2 of the 1972 series against the Cincinnati Reds.

Joe Rudi was possibly skipping down the sidewalk as a preschooler when U.S. Senate candidate Richard Nixon quietly slipped into town for votes in 1950. Cecil Fager recalled the day Congressman Nixon popped into the barbershop for campaign handshakes.

In October 1957, the community hosted a large shindig to celebrate its history. The Waterford Centennial event included a parade, a drama, a special commemorative booklet, beard growing contests, and other events. The event prompted the town to host fairly regular Western Heritage Day celebrations.

Community pride swelled in the 1960s when Nora Ballard's small and cramped library building was replaced by a cement-block building. Max Foster of Foster Farms donated the lot on E Street. Community leader Haswell Leask and Supervisor Robert Fahey helped dedicate the facility on October 16, 1965. Traffic flow between Waterford/Hickman and Turlock improved in 1964, when the county built a new concrete bridge over the Tuolumne River. Today, Waterford has retained its unique small town flavor and agricultural roots.

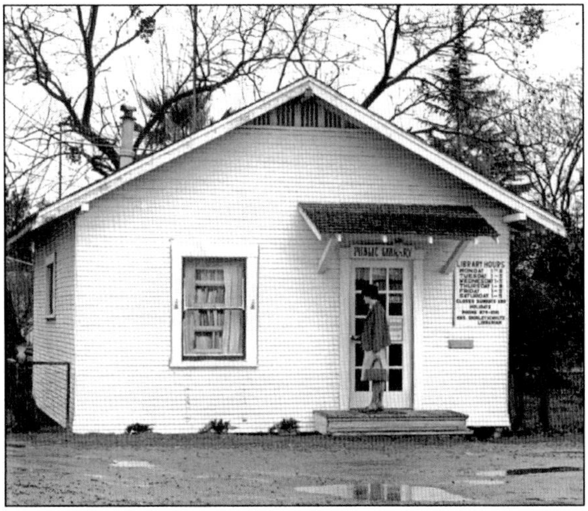

In January 1965, Shirley Schultz enters the cramped 500-square-foot building that served as the Waterford Library from 1924 to 1965. The old library, built by Royal "Roy" Ballard for his librarian wife Nora Ballard, was located at 12817 Beard Road. Neither the building nor road exists today; it was north of Yosemite Boulevard between E and F Streets. This library was replaced in 1965 by a block building on E Street, which is still the current library site. Schultz was librarian from 1956 to 1982, then operated Shirley's Fabrics in Waterford. (Shirley Schultz.)

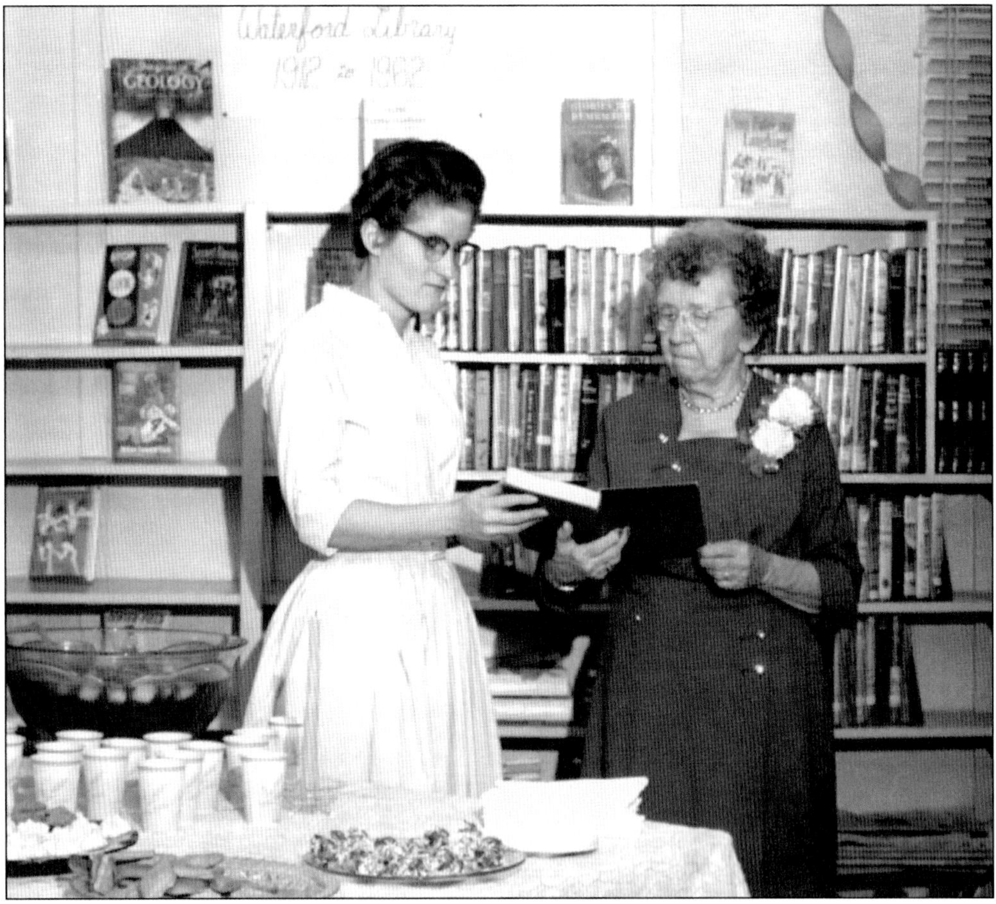

Nora Roberts Ballard (right), with Shirley Schultz, attended the 50th anniversary celebration of the Waterford Library in 1962. Ballard came to Waterford in 1911 and married Royal Ballard, a harness-maker and shoemaker. She started the first library in Waterford in the basement of the Baptist church in 1912 with 12 of her own books. She would drive her buggy to Modesto to borrow books from the county library for Waterford readers. She died in 1964. (Nora Ballard Library.)

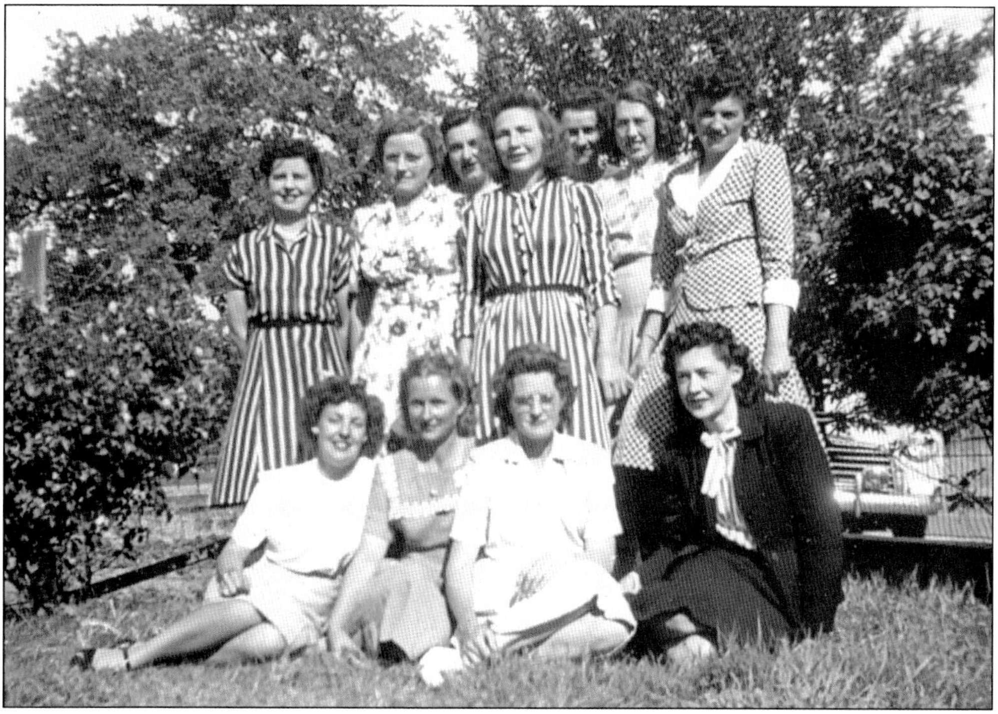

The D.I. Club, formed in 1946, was comprised of women from Waterford, Roberts Ferry and La Grange. From left to right, gathered here some time in the latter 1940s are (first row) Maxine Vasche Emig, Reca Painter, Helen Pippen, and Berniece Crabtree; (second row) Helen Welch, Nora Roen, Shirley Ingalls, Evelyn Welch, Mazie Erickson, Lois Rumsey, and Marie Roen. The women darned socks, hosted dances, and raised money for charitable events. (Betty Roen.)

The Waterford Grange Hall, which stands at the corner of Bentley Street and Yosemite Boulevard in Waterford, has been a landmark since 1938. The Grange first met here on April 12, 1938. After the Waterford Grange disbanded, the building became the city's museum. In front of the building is one of three entry signs erected by the Waterford Chamber of Commerce in 1960. (Jeff Benziger.)

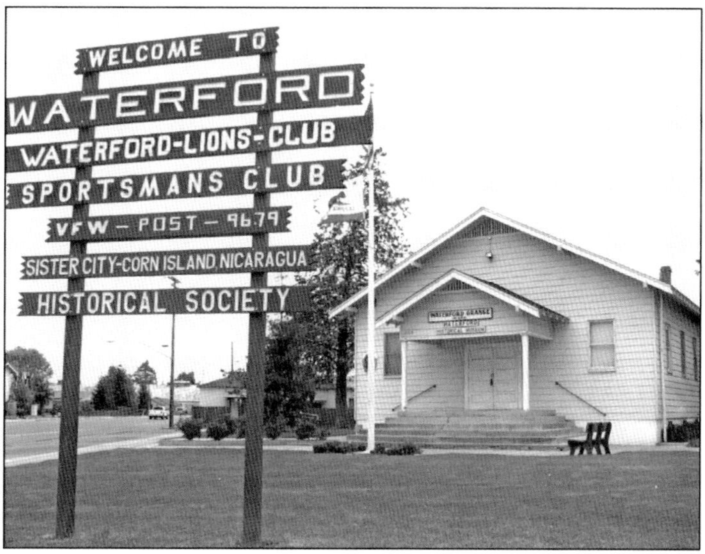

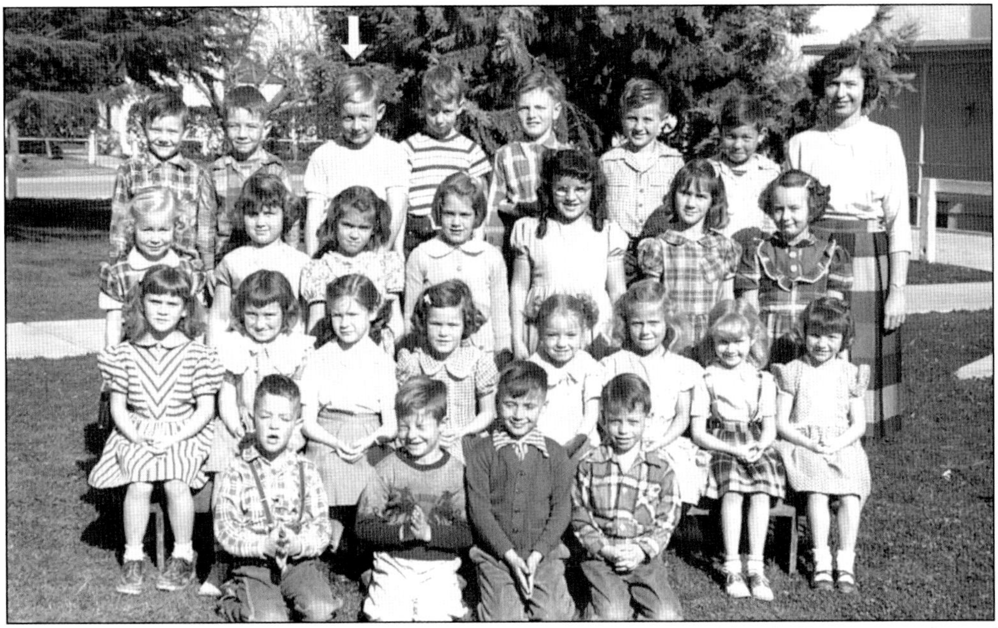

Joe Oden Rudi, one of the most successful left fielders in professional baseball, was a product of Waterford. Born to Oden and Bessie Rudi on September 7, 1946, Joe was raised in Waterford and is seen above in Lorraine Cederlind's class photograph. Joe, third from left at top, attended Waterford Elementary School starting in 1951 and graduated eighth grade in 1960. He spent two years at Oakdale High School before transferring to Downey High in Modesto. He played for Kansas City before contracting with the Oakland A's in 1968. He helped the team win the World Series in 1972, 1973, and 1974. Rudi was known for a memorable catch against the wall in the ninth inning of the final game. Joe's grandfather came to Waterford in 1905. Rudi's dad and uncle operated a meat market in Waterford in the 1920s and 1930s. (Both, Waterford Historical Society.)

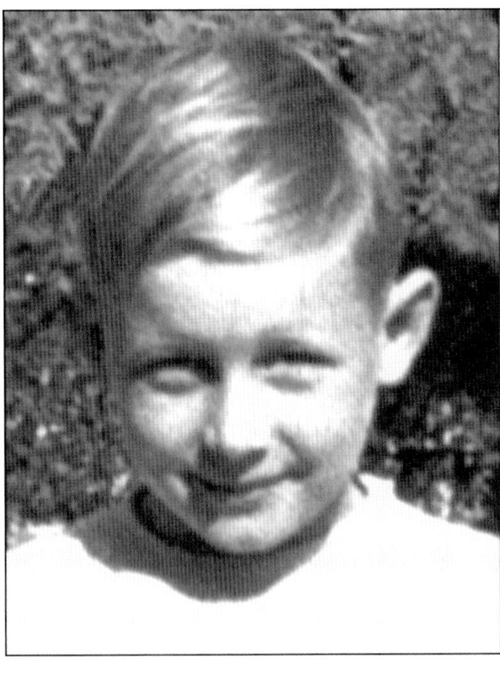

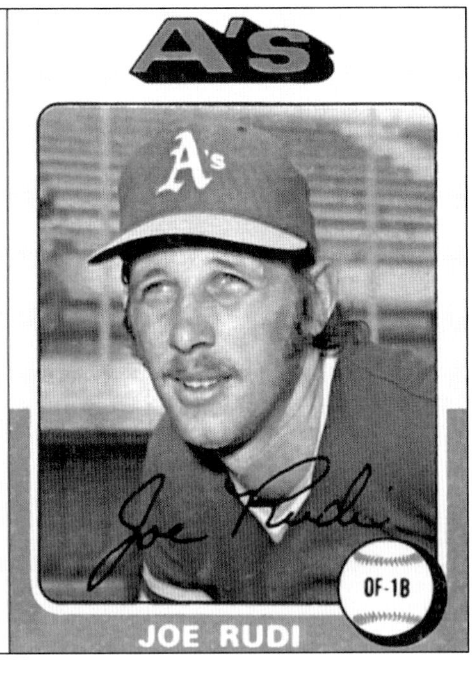

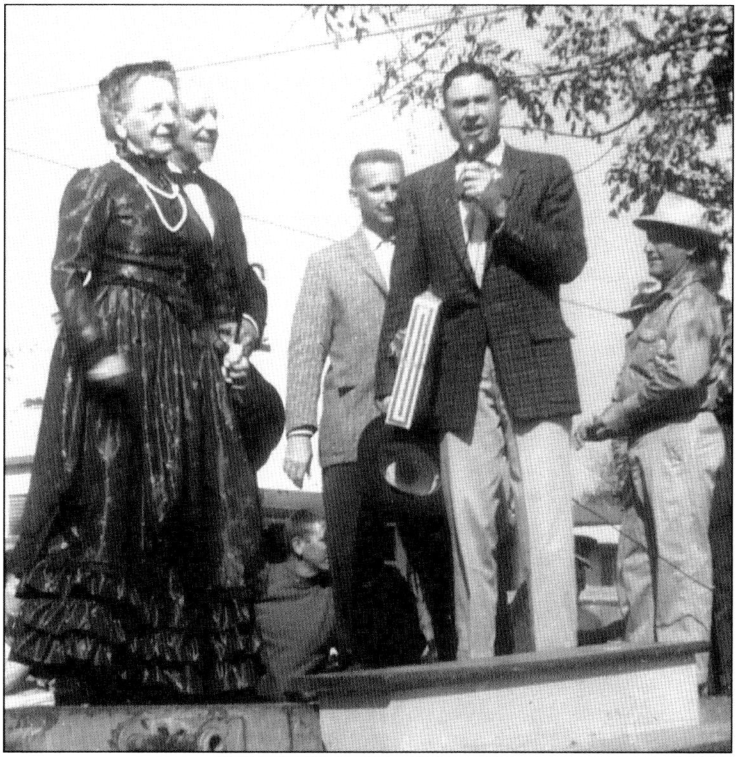

Congressman John J. McFall presented honors to Alma Prouty as Waterford Centennial Queen during the 1957 celebration. Husband Lee Prouty, son of pioneer blacksmith Joseph Prouty, is to her left. Only women who had lived in Waterford for at least 50 consecutive years were eligible for the honor. Behind McFall is emcee Maxon Sayre, known for his smooth radio voice. The stage was in a park where the Bank of the West sits today. (Waterford Historical Society.)

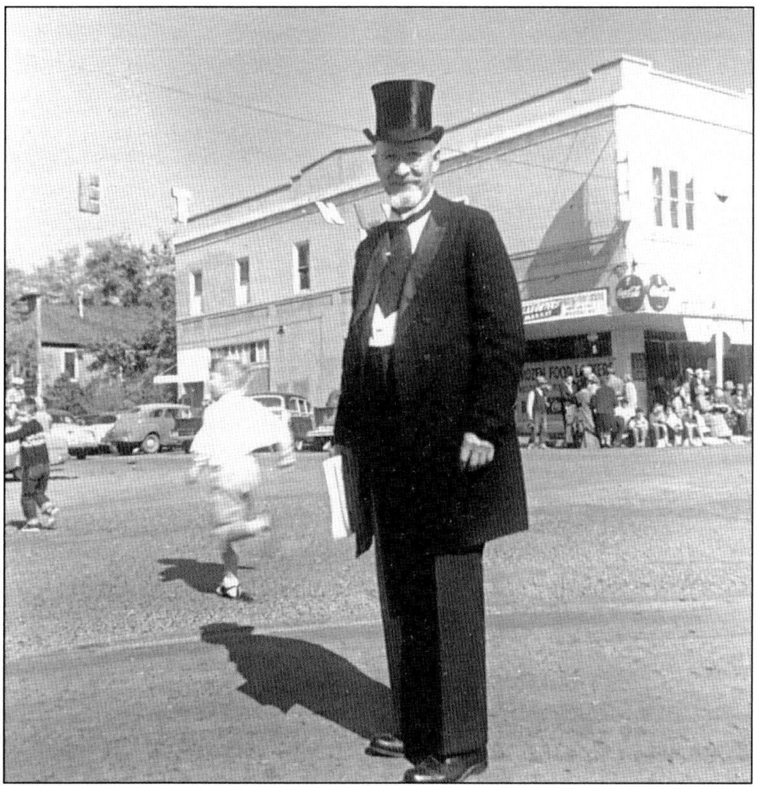

Former constable Ray Appling stands in a black frock coat and pants during the 1957 Waterford Centennial. Born in 1889, Appling became constable in the 1930s and died in 1963. In the background is the Gordon Building with Slaughter's Market on the first floor and Marco Theatre on the second. The two-story Maitland Hotel, visible behind the Gordon Building, was razed in the 1980s. (Waterford Historical Society.)

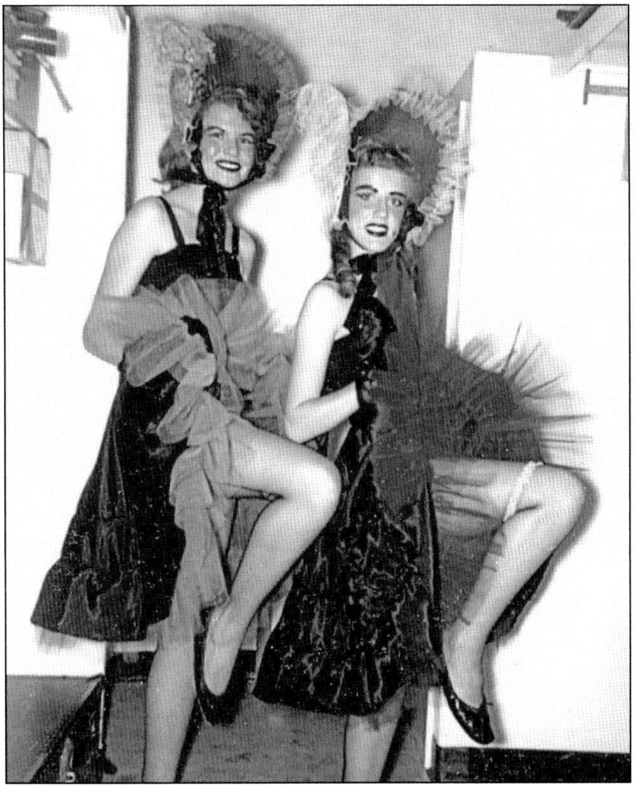

Kay Elkins (left) and Barbara King (right) raise saloon girl skirts to show some leg in preparation for the "Goldrush Cavalcade" drama at the 1957 Centennial. A group of local girls and women portrayed saloon dancers from Waterford's first drinking hole, Elder's Saloon, inside the Waterford School gym. (Waterford Historical Society.)

Getting into Waterford Centennial spirit were these four men who had this unique parade entry. Pictured in Pierce Miller's barn west of Waterford alongside his antique hearse were Bob Riddle on the buckboard and, from left to right, Miller, Snively Riddle, and Roland "Whitey" Whitehead holding an amusing sign. (Waterford Historical Society.)

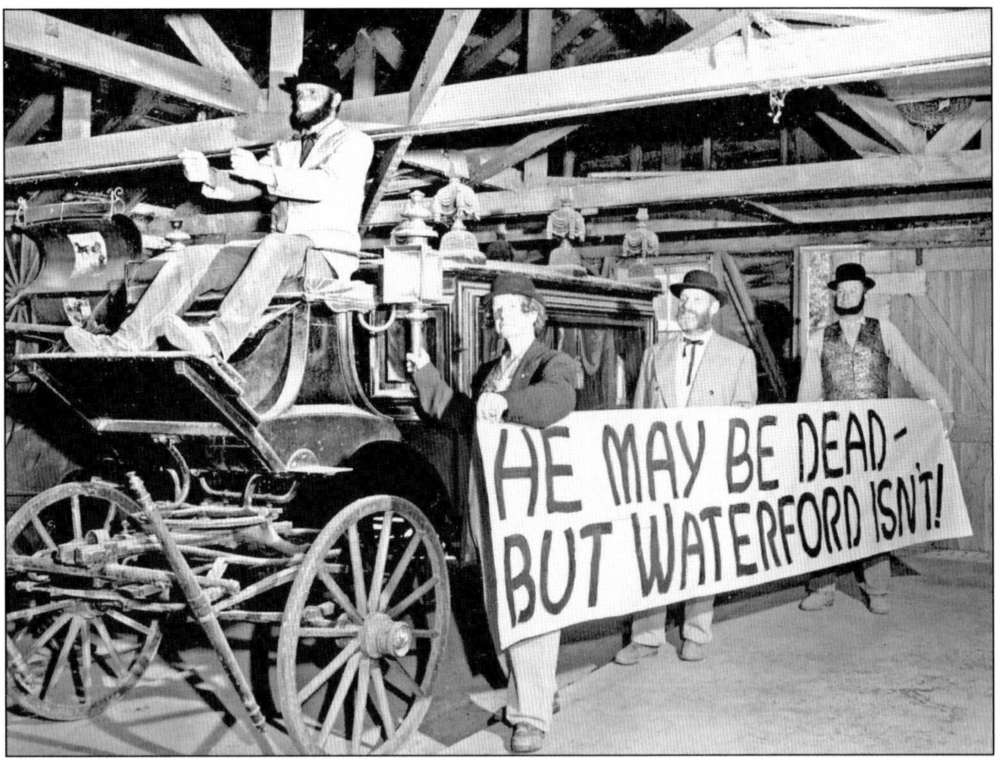

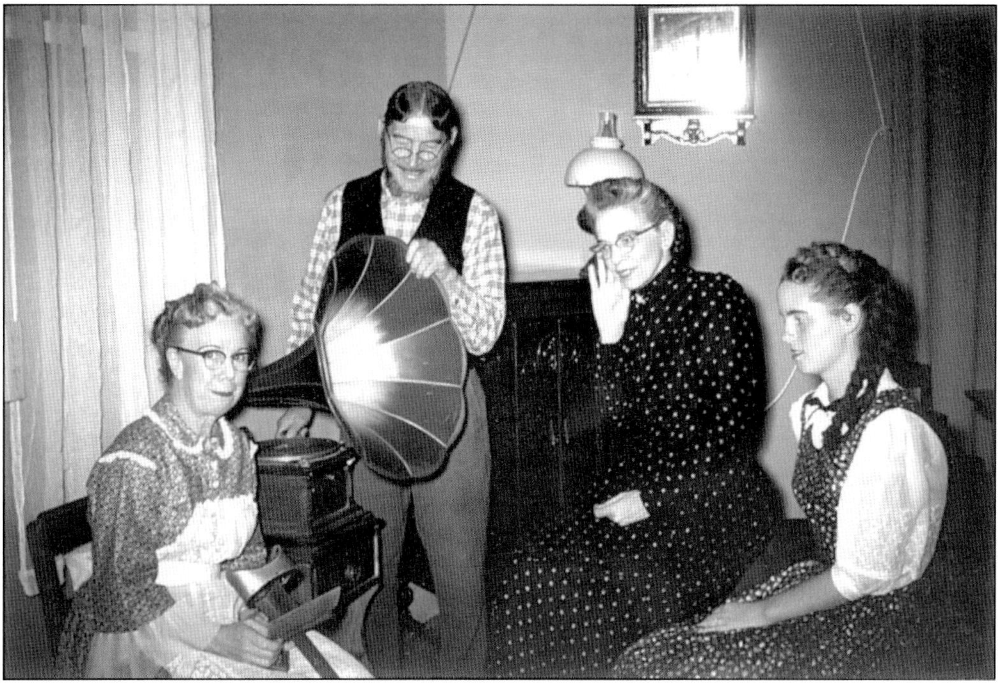

From left to right, Florence Brush, Earle Zimmer, Celeste Herbert, and Peggy Newbill were part of the "Gold Rush Cavalcade," a drama performed at the Waterford Centennial on October 18–19, 1957. The show recreated the origins of Waterford from the first pioneers who left Berryville, Arkansas, in the 1850s. (Waterford Historical Society.)

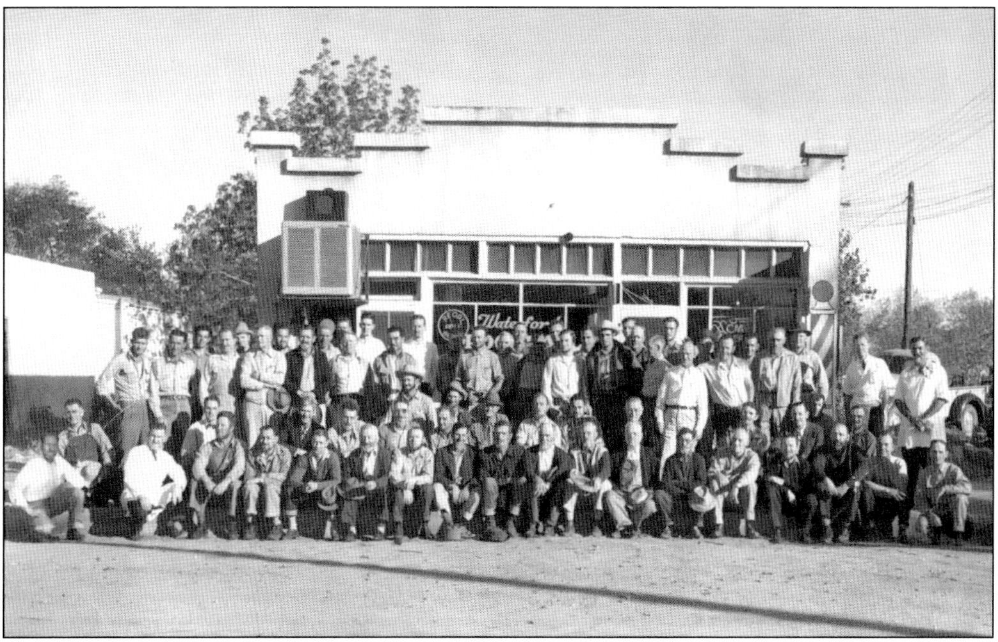

The men of Waterford had a contest to grow beards for the 1957 Centennial celebration. Here the men are gathered in front of Ed Ludlow's pool hall and barbershop at 12634 Bentley Street. (Waterford Historical Society.)

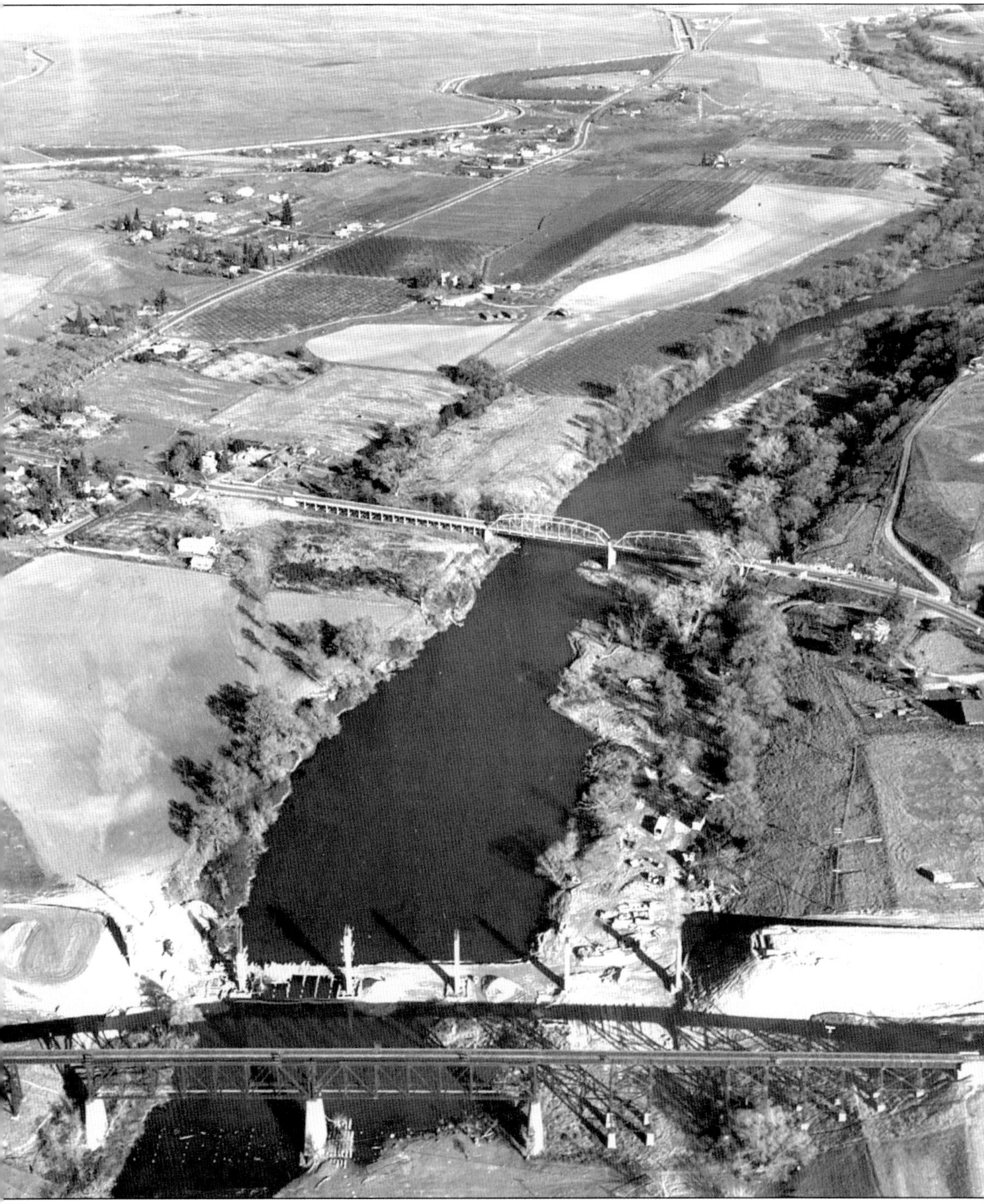

Stanislaus County constructed a cement bridge over the Tuolumne River between Waterford and Hickman in 1964 to replace the old iron bridge upstream. The old iron railroad trestle is seen at bottom. From this aerial photograph, the progress of the new bridge is visible. In order to build the tall cement columns, workers had to create dry land in the riverbed by diverting the river flow. (Waterford Historical Society.)

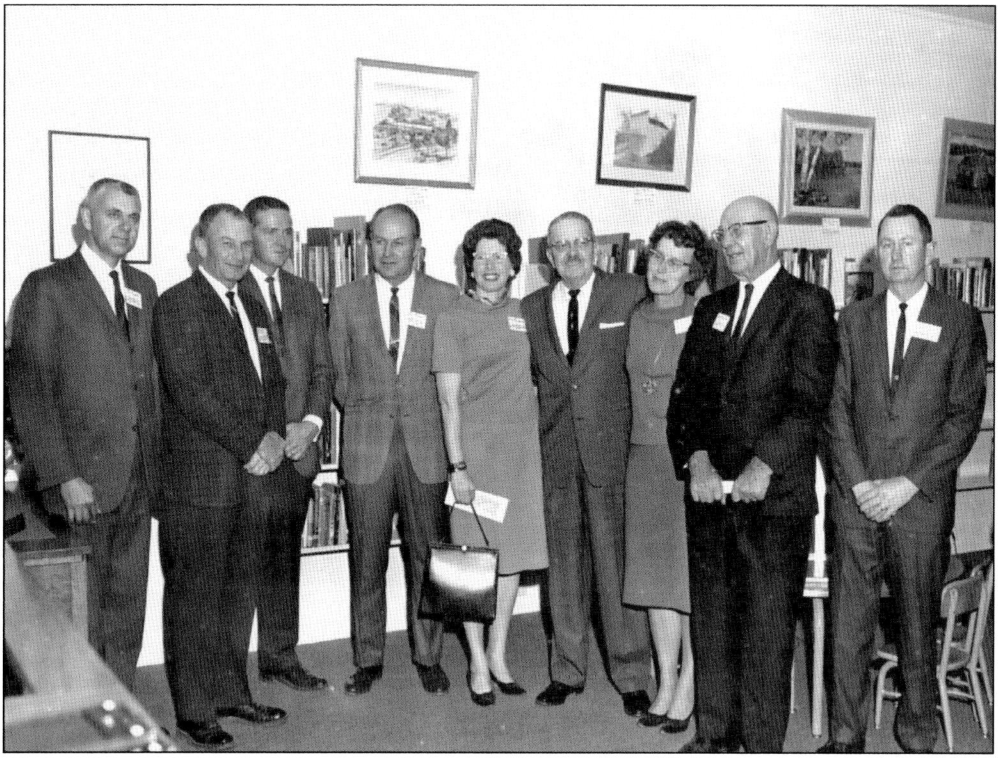

Gathered on October 16, 1965, to dedicate the Nora Ballard Library were, from left to right, Waterford Community Library Funds, Inc., members Richard Grenell, Neil Weichert, Tom Sawyer, Richard Moon, Mildred Lundberg, builder Harry Wallers, Carol Tyson, Haswell Leask, and Cecil Hensley. (Shirley Schultz.)

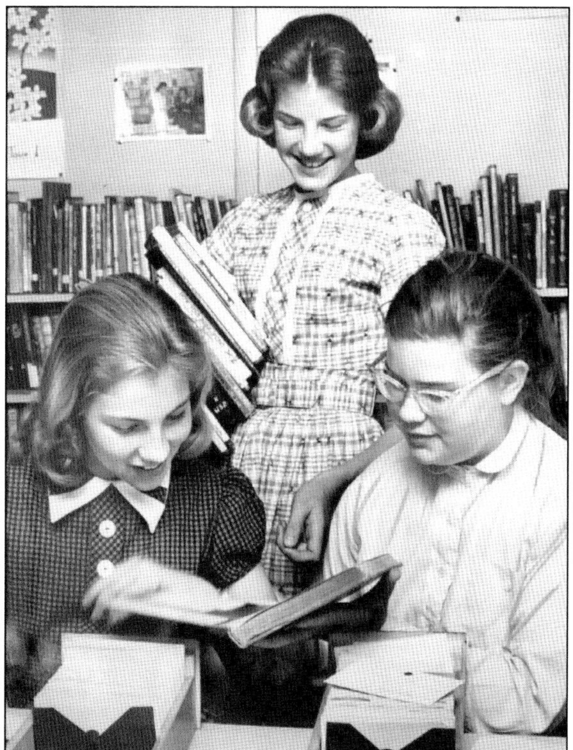

Students volunteered in the Waterford Library in 1962. Pictured here are Penny Newey (left), Barbara Stevens (right), and Suzanne Lundberg (standing). Barbara started the volunteer program in 1961. (Shirley Schultz.)

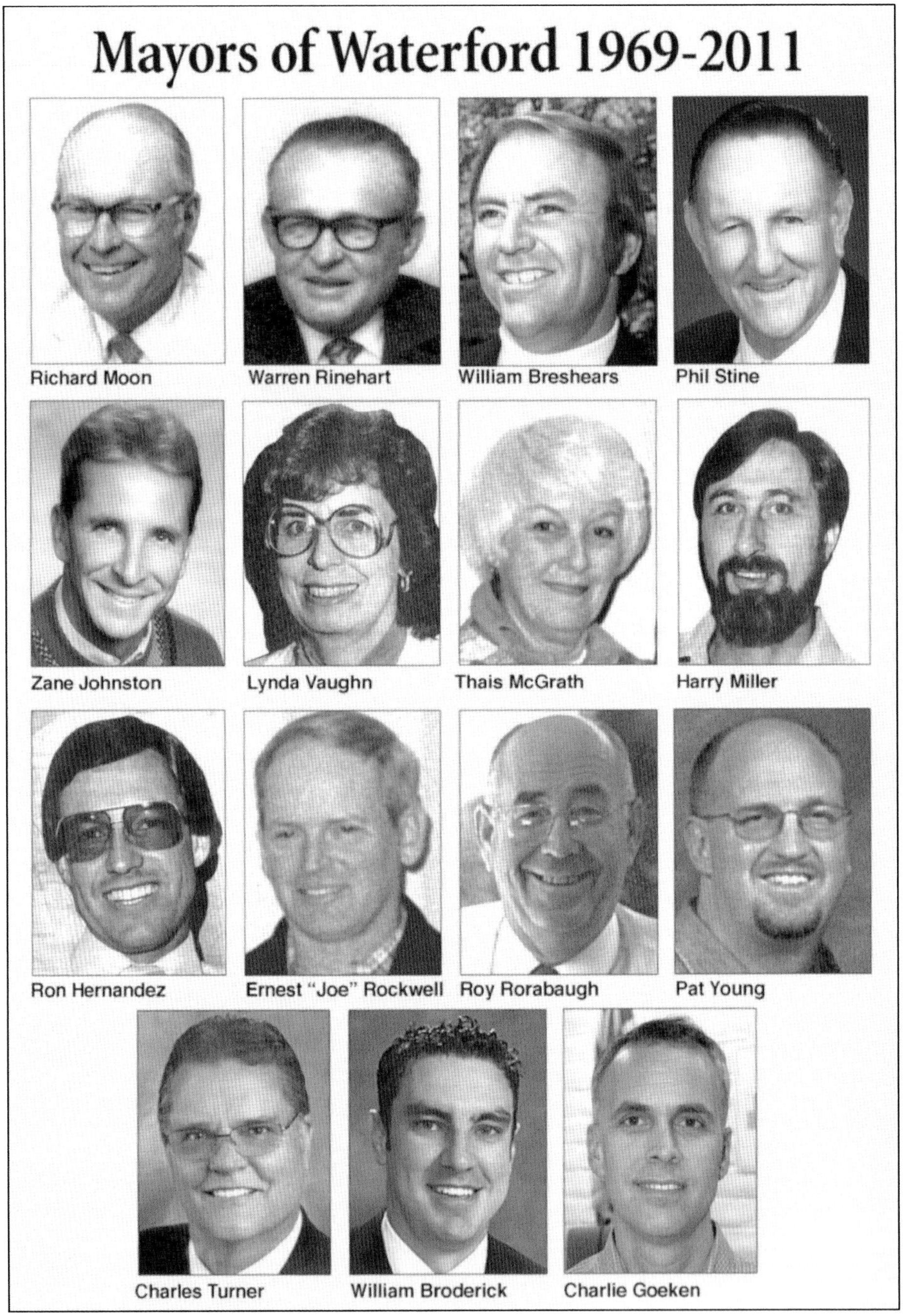

Since its incorporation in 1969, Waterford has been served by these mayors. The mayors and their terms of office are: Richard Moon, 1969–1972; Warren Rinehart, 1972–1973; William Breashears, 1973–1980; Phil Stine, 1980–1983; Zane Johnston, 1983–1985; Lynda Vaughn, 1985–1986; Thais McGrath, 1986; Harry Miller, 1986–1988; Ron Hernandez, 1988–1990; Ernest "Joe" Rockwell, 1990–1994; William "Roy" Rorabaugh, 1994–1995; Pat Young, 1995–1998; Charles Turner, 1998–2006; William Broderick-Villa, 2006–2008; and Charlie Goeken, 2008–. (Author's collection with courtesies to Hudson Photography.)

Serving on the first Waterford City Council in 1969 were, from left to right, Councilman Warren Rinehart, Vice Mayor Dan Jones, Mayor Richard Moon, Councilman Robert Carpenter Jr., and Councilman John J. Miller. Moon led for incorporation in the 1940s, but the idea was scoffed at by merchants, who saw no merit in the proposal. (Waterford Historical Society.)

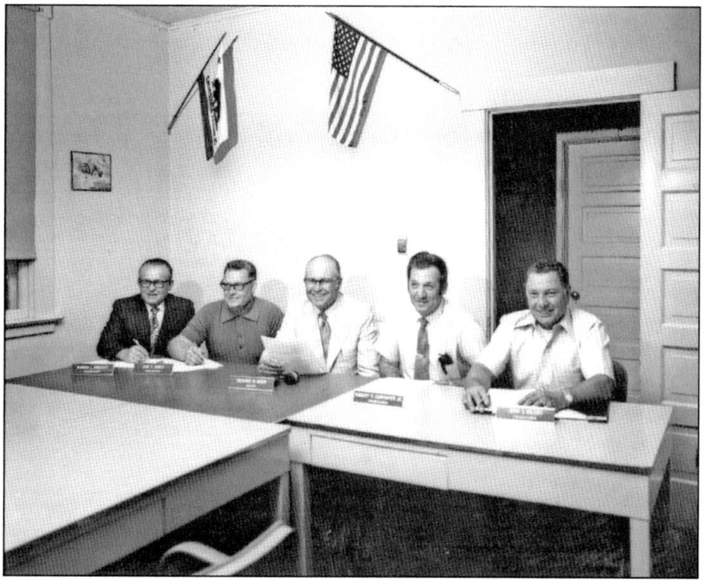

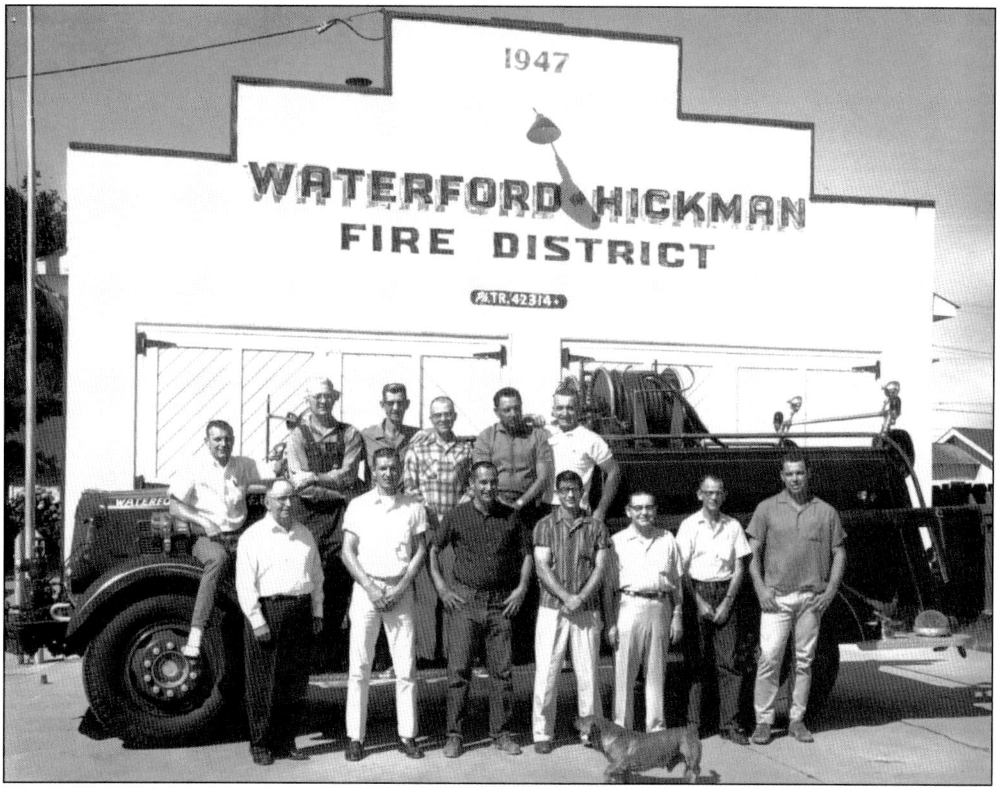

The Waterford-Hickman Fire Department built this station in 1947 on E Street between Main Street and Bentley Street. Seen from left to right in this August 2, 1964, photograph are (first row) Chief Walter Andrews, ? Fleming, Mac Carlton, Stan Armentrout, M.A. "Shorty" Rager, Bob Carpenter, and Bill Brewer; (second row) Assistant Chief Holly Breashers, driver Clark Billups, driver Bill Reed, First Assistant Chief Leo Holzer, John J. Miller, and ambulance driver Les Johnston. (Waterford Historical Society.)

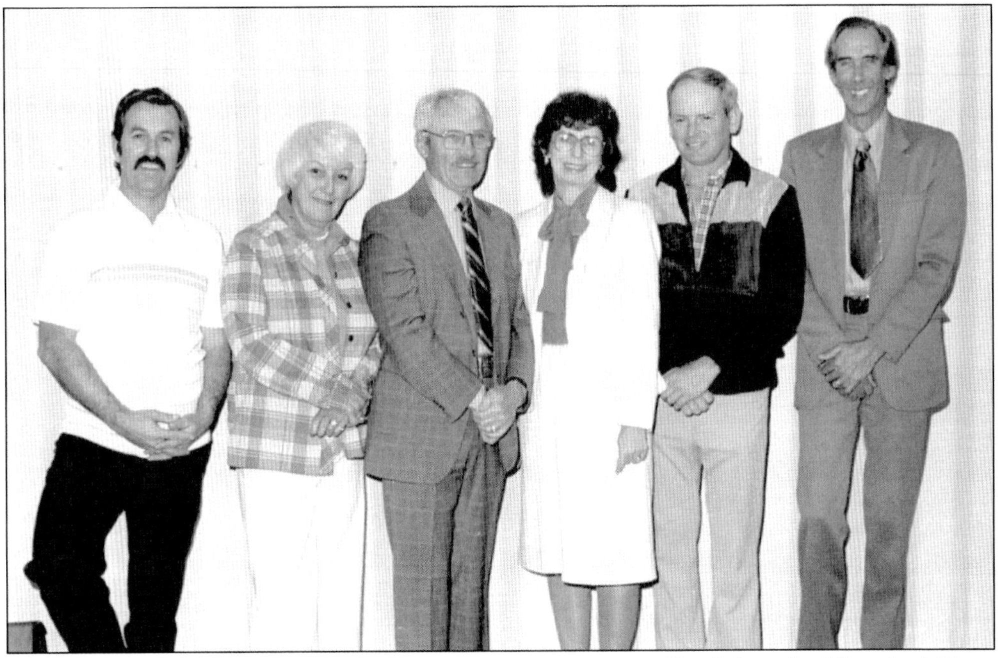

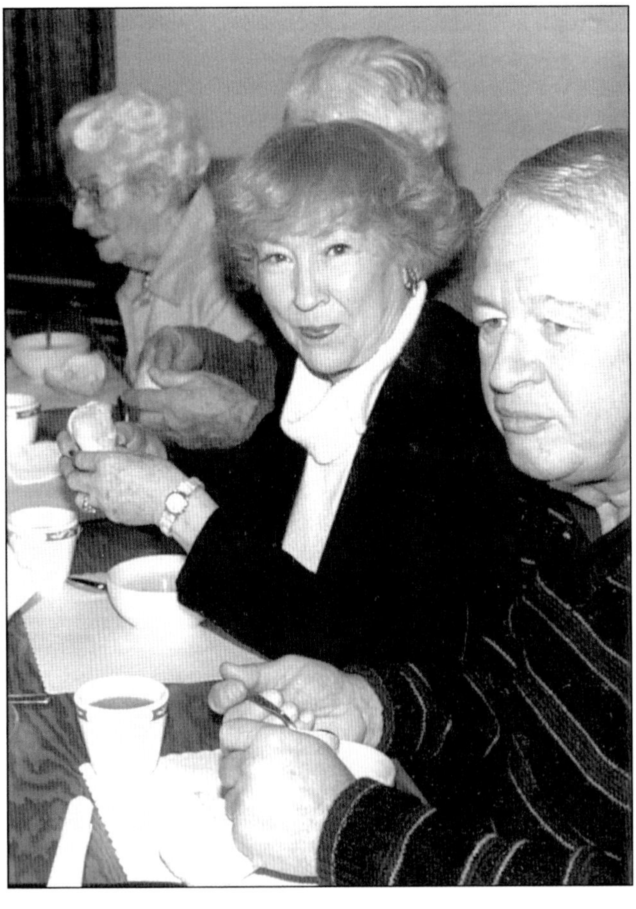

Candidates for Waterford City Council seats in November 1984 were, from left to right, Marvin Cole, Thais McGrath, Winfred Hinkle, Lynda Vaughn, Joe Rockwell, and Lee Shay. Vaughn, McGrath, and Rockwell all would later serve as mayor of Waterford. Vaughn was Waterford's first female mayor, and Thais McGrath was the second. (Author's collection.)

Edith Kirk Richards was a well-known city leader and Waterford activist. The beauty shop owner was Waterford's 1984 Person of the Year and served eight years on the Waterford City Council. Edith also founded the Miss Waterford pageant. At left are Velma and Mac MacMurray, and at right is Edith's second husband, Russ Richards. Edith died on February 9, 2011. (Donna Dugo.)

In 1994, the City of Waterford celebrated its 25th anniversary of incorporation. City Manager Les Crist commissioned a numbered and limited edition belt buckle cast. The first numbers went to members of the Waterford City Council. The rest were sold to the public. (Author's collection.)

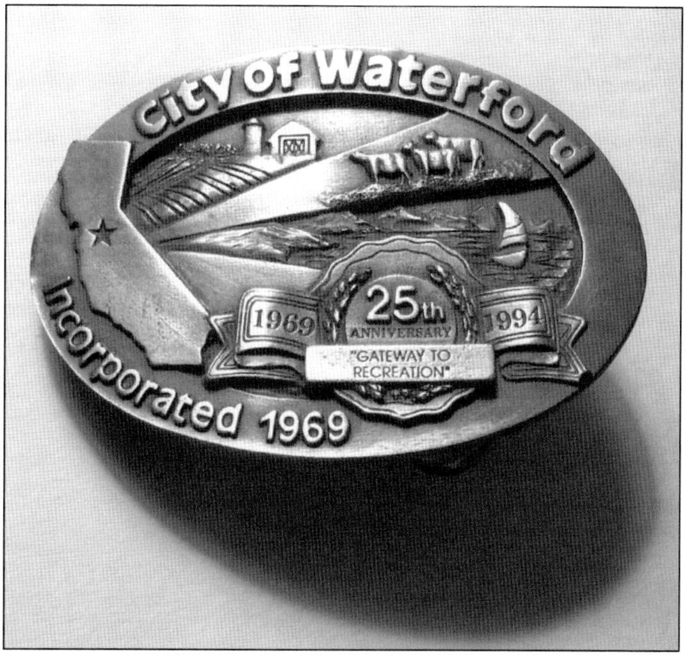

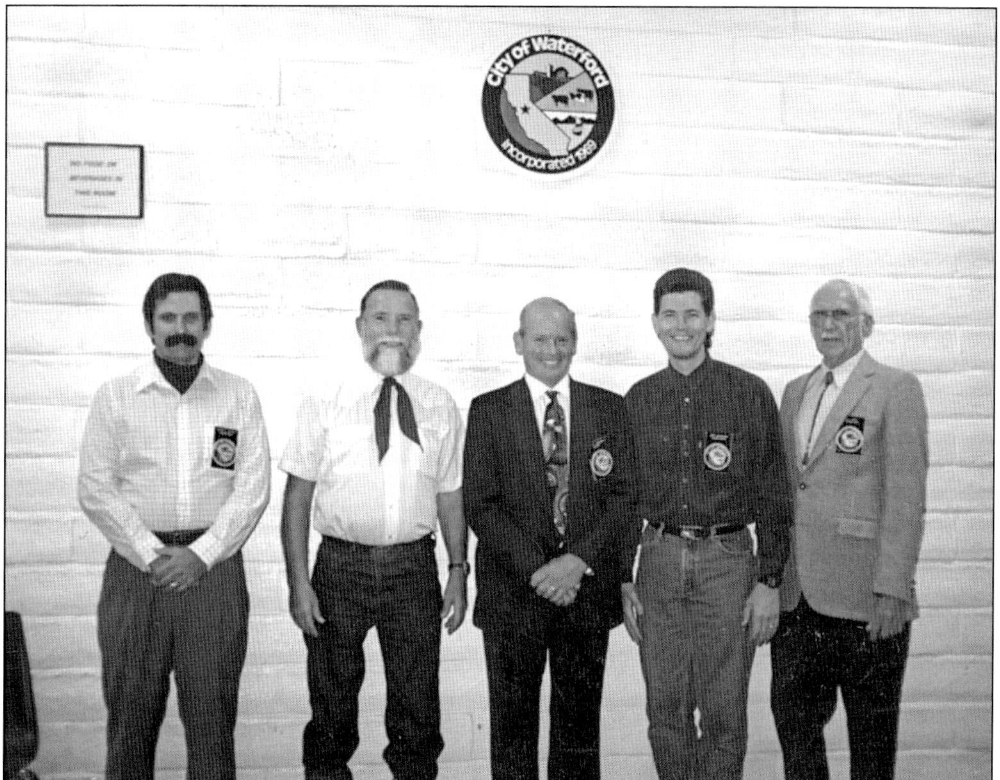

These men comprised the second Joe Rockwell–led city council from 1992 to 1994. At the city's 25th anniversary celebration are, from left to right, Councilmen Keith Winter and Wayne Long, Mayor Joe Rockwell, and Councilmen Jeff Benziger and E.L. Davis. (Author's collection.)

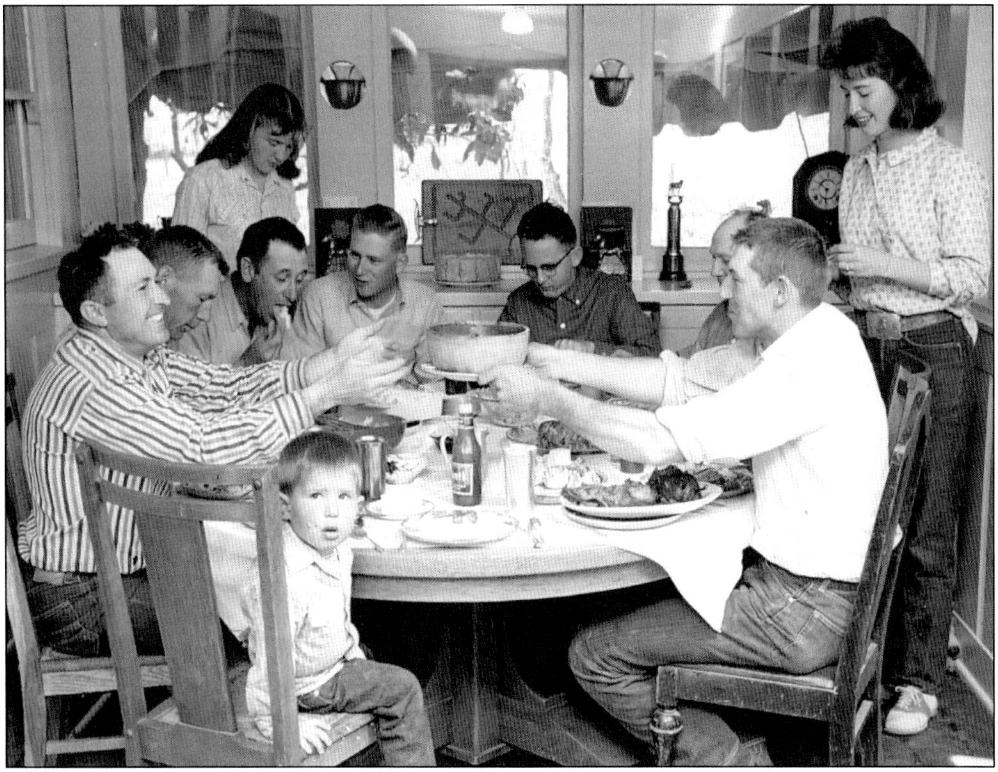

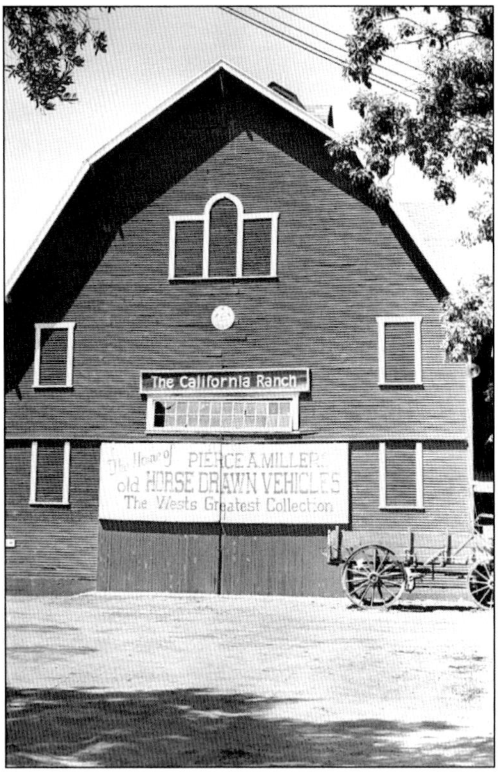

Breakfast started a busy day in 1960 on the Roen cattle ranch east of Waterford. Pictured clockwise starting in front are Eric Roen, Ron Painter, Ollie Funk, Alex Anderson, Candy Schmidt (standing), Billy Bonfantini, Jim Goodwin, Bill Bolter (partially obscured), John Roen, and Betty Roen (standing at right). Ranch-hand Bolter later made local news when he fell victim to foul play and disappeared mysteriously near the ranch on December 19, 1973. (Betty Roen.)

Miller's California Ranch was a tourist attraction a few miles west of Waterford from 1946 through the 1980s. This grand red Pennsylvania-style barn was built in 1911 or 1912 by Jay Hindman. Pierce A. Miller housed an amazing collection of horse-drawn wagons and farm implements here. A chicken restaurant in front of the barn operated until a fire destroyed it. Miller died in 1965. His widow, Mae Miller, taught school in Empire from 1943 to 1947. (Author's collection.)

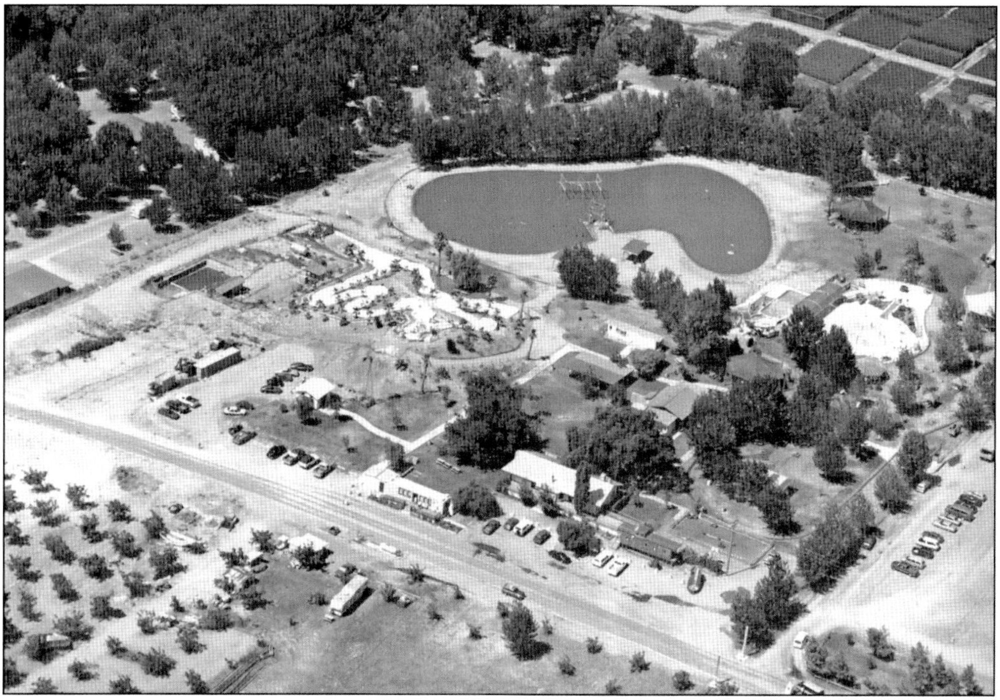

Waterford was "put on the map" with Big Bear Park (above and at right), which opened in June 1985 and ran until 2004. A large friendly waving bear chain-sawed out of a pine log, and standing 18 feet tall and weighing 14,000 pounds greeted visitors raring to have fun on waterslides, riding miniature train rides, swimming in the lagoon, or RV and tent camping. Rob Bearden created the park financed by his parents, Cullen and Dorothy Bearden. The park was situated south of Jimbo's Drive-In on Yosemite Boulevard. The park was sold for the development of the Riverpointe gated community. (Both, Rob Bearden.)

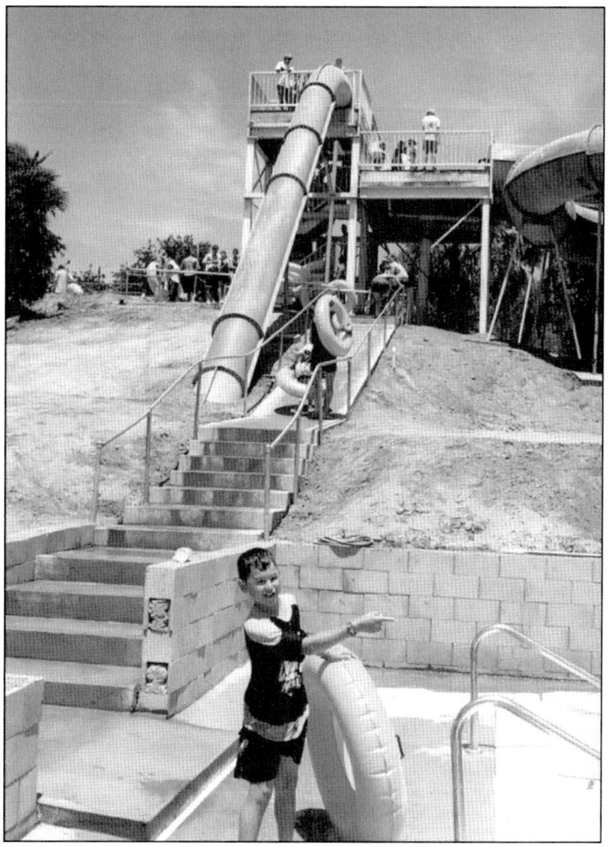